THE
HUMAN
BODY

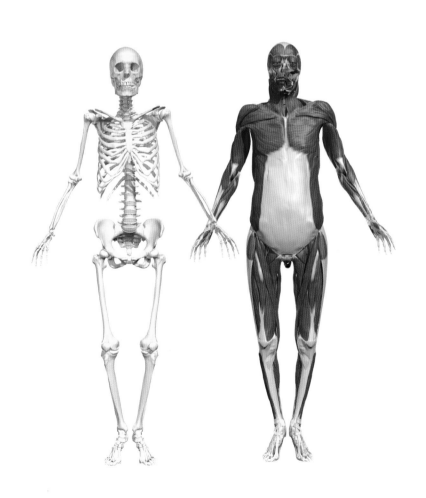

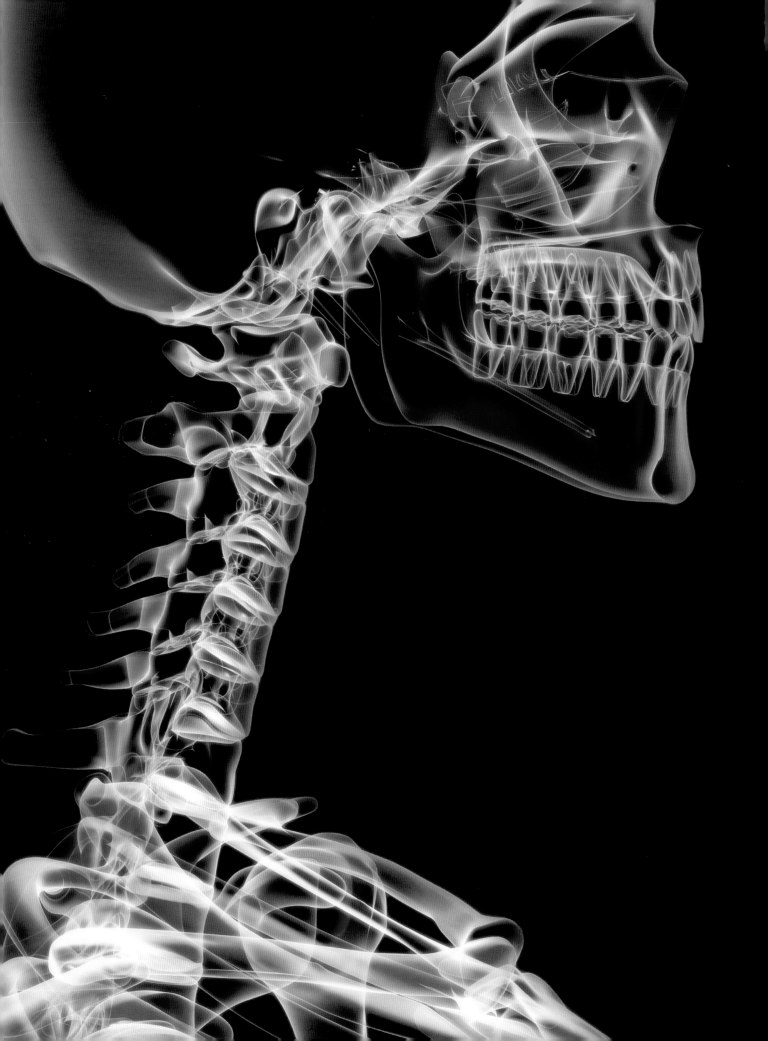

THE HUMAN BODY

A Visual Guide to Human Anatomy

Dr. SARAH BREWER

METRO BOOKS

New York

CONTENTS

14 THE CELL

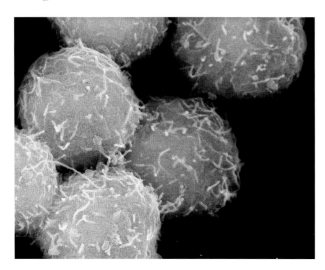

The body is made from millions of individual units called cells, which perform almost as many different functions. While each cell is different, the central nucleus of each one contains an identical set of genetic instructions.

26 INTEGUMENTARY SYSTEM

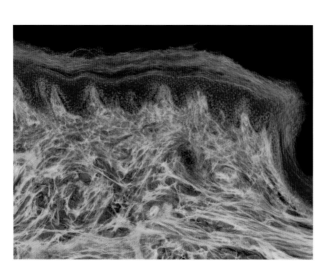

The body's main sources of protection against the environment are the skin, hair and nails. The skin is the largest organ in the body and provides a waterproof, protective outer layer for the whole body.

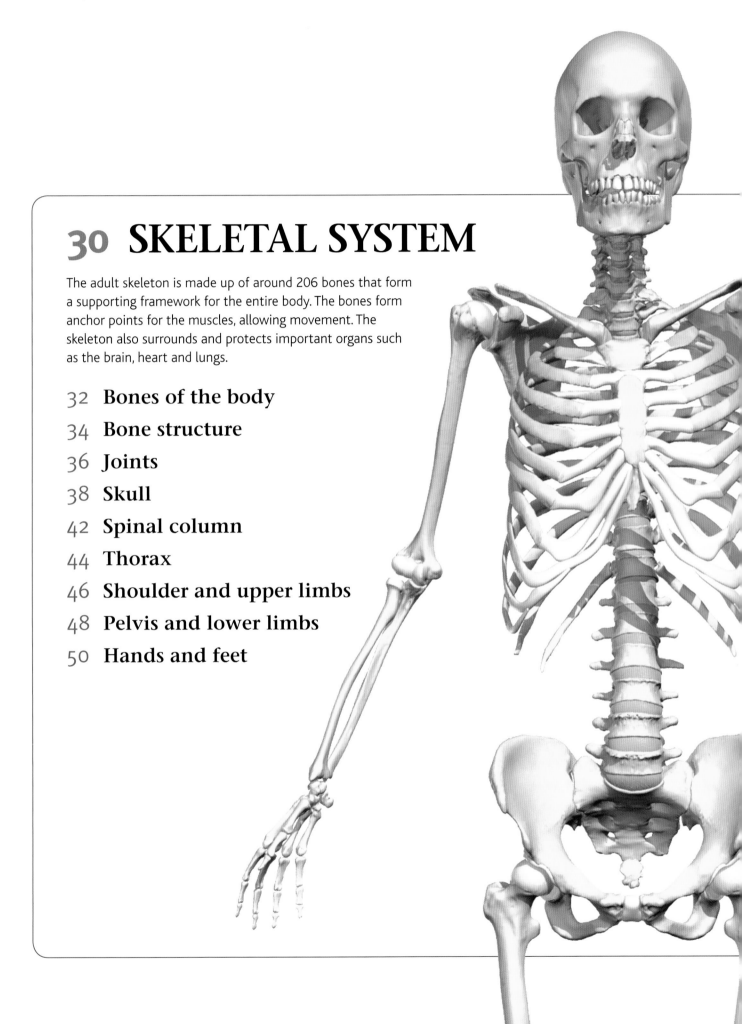

30 SKELETAL SYSTEM

The adult skeleton is made up of around 206 bones that form a supporting framework for the entire body. The bones form anchor points for the muscles, allowing movement. The skeleton also surrounds and protects important organs such as the brain, heart and lungs.

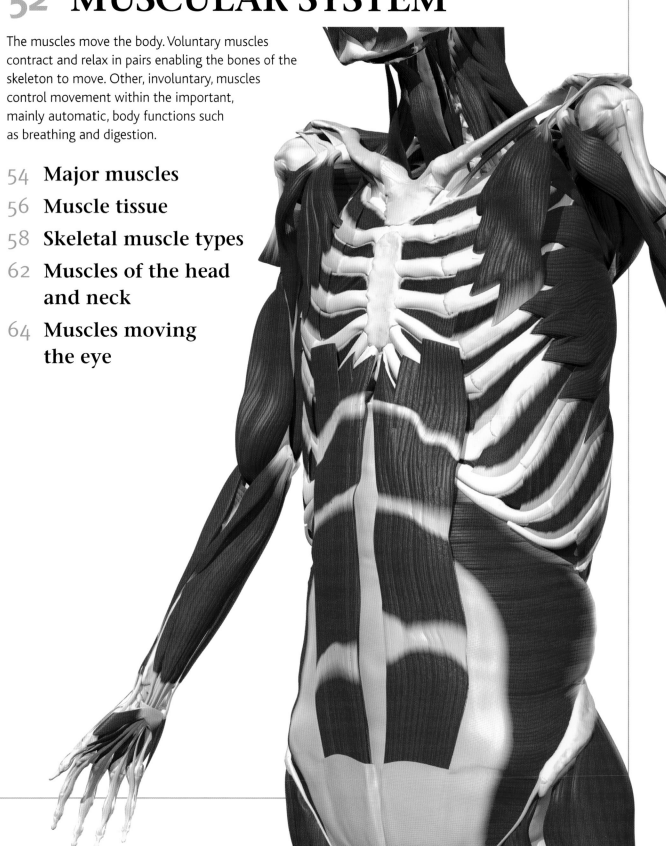

MUSCULAR SYSTEM

The muscles move the body. Voluntary muscles contract and relax in pairs enabling the bones of the skeleton to move. Other, involuntary, muscles control movement within the important, mainly automatic, body functions such as breathing and digestion.

66 NERVOUS SYSTEM

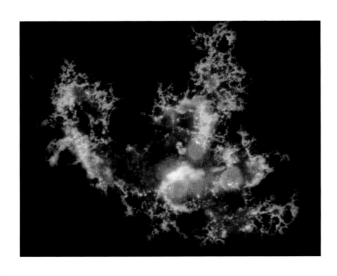

This comprises the brain and spinal cord (the central nervous system) and nerves (peripheral nervous system). The nerves carry messages from all over the body to the brain and spinal cord. The brain also controls the interaction between body systems, regulates consciousness and sleep, and is capable of original thought. The autonomic nervous system coordinates automatic body functions such as breathing. The special senses allow complex interactions with the environment.

110 RESPIRATORY SYSTEM

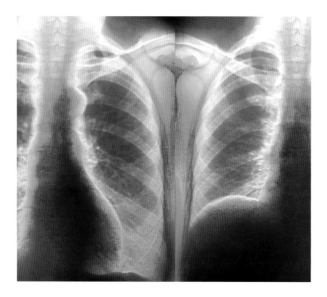

This system is made up of the air passages and lungs. It provides the body with oxygen, and removes carbon dioxide – the waste product of breathing – from the body. Air containing oxygen is drawn into the lungs via the nose and mouth and trachea. The thin walls of the air sacs in the lungs and their blood capillaries allow the oxygen into the blood and carbon dioxide gas to be removed from it.

118 CARDIOVASCULAR SYSTEM

Your cardiovascular system consists of the heart and three types of blood vessel – arteries, veins and capillaries. This system transports blood carrying oxygen, glucose and nutrients to the body tissues and removes waste products such as carbon dioxide and lactic acid from them. The heart is the central pump that 'pushes' the blood around the body. Arteries carry blood to the tissues and veins take the blood back to the heart. Exchange of gases takes place in the thin-walled capillaries.

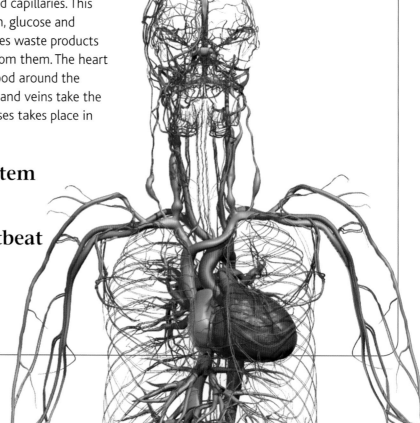

130 IMMUNE SYSTEM

This is the body's internal defence system. The body is teeming with a complex collection of immune cells that detect infection, fight disease and make antibodies to prevent reinfection. These cells are carried in both blood and a special fluid called lymph. The latter circulates through its own system of vessels and nodes that collect, filter and flush away waste materials via the hepatic system.

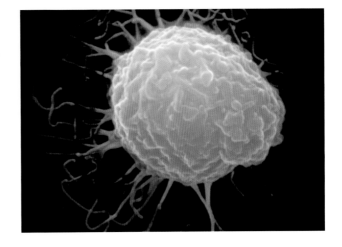

142 ENDOCRINE SYSTEM

A series of ductless glands and organs of the body secrete special chemical messengers called hormones into your bloodstream. Hormones coordinate and regulate short- and long-term body processes from metabolism and sexual reproduction to sleep. The overall production of hormones is controlled by the master gland – the pituitary – that sits just beneath the brain.

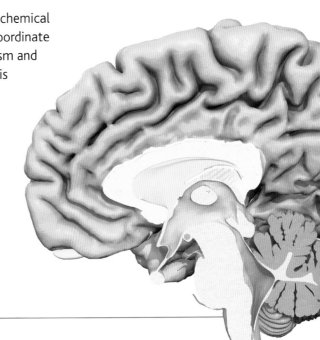

154 DIGESTIVE SYSTEM

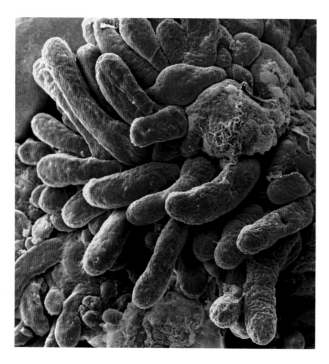

Your gastrointestinal tract forms a long tube that begins at your mouth and ends at your anal sphincter and acts as a food-processing system. It accepts complex food molecules at one end, and breaks them down (with the help of body chemicals such as hormones and enzymes) into simpler, more soluble components. These are either absorbed for use by the body or expelled as waste products.

168 HEPATIC SYSTEM

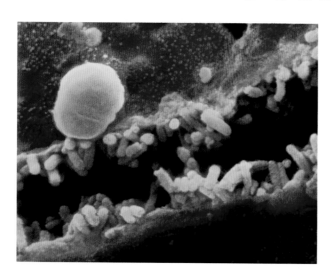

This system consists of the liver, gallbladder and pancreas, and functions alongside the digestive system. The organs of the hepatic system secrete enzymes and help break down fats. The liver, the largest of these organs, receives and processes products of digestion and deactivates poisons such as alcohol.

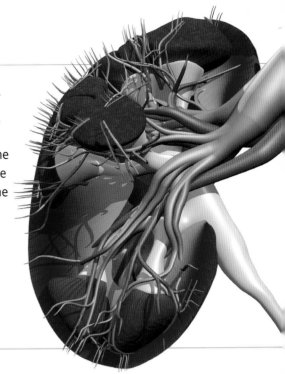

176 URINARY SYSTEM

This system filters the blood and removes excess fluid from the body in the form of urine. It consists of the kidneys, where the waste is filtered and the fluid concentrated, the bladder, which collects and stores the urine, and the ureter through which the fluid is excreted.

182 REPRODUCTIVE SYSTEM

This is the one body system that differs completely between male and female and does not function for a person's entire life span. The nucleus of the female egg and the male sperm also only carry half the chromosome count of other cells in the body – 23 single chromosomes instead of 23 pairs.

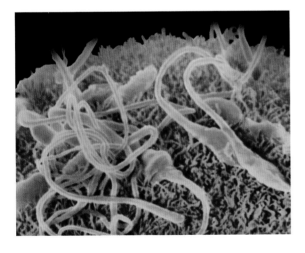

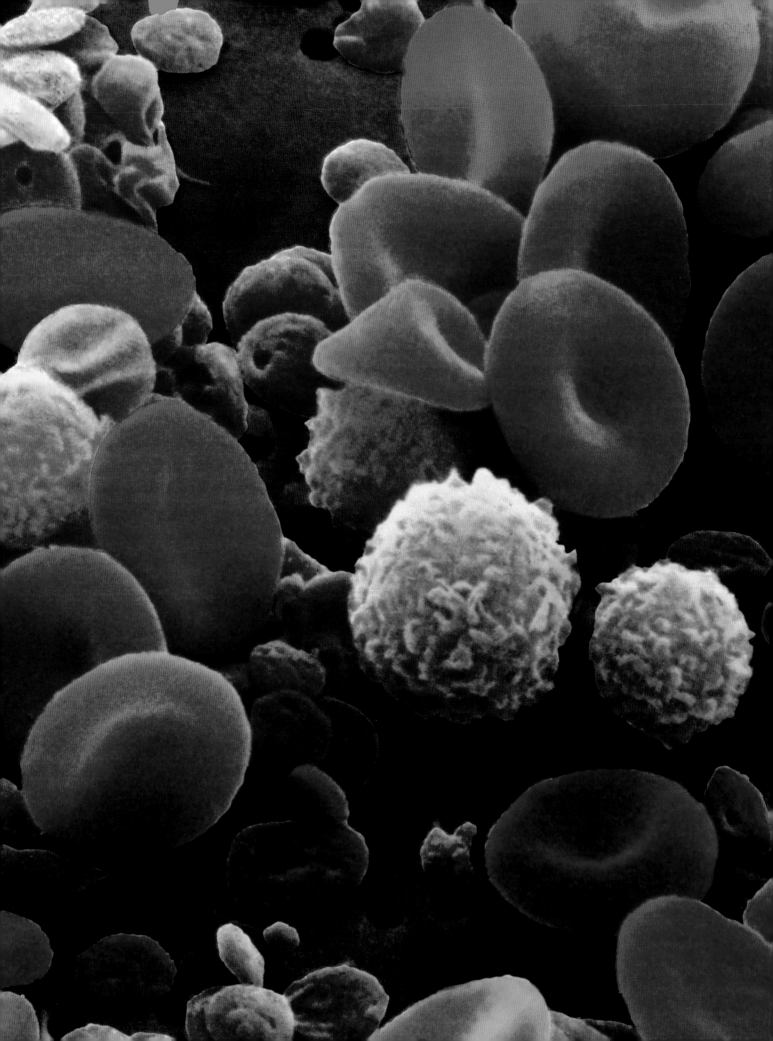

INTRODUCTION

The human body represents an incredible collaboration of cells, all working together to ensure the survival of the species. This strategy, whether the result of natural selection and evolution, or intelligent design, is so successful that the world's population currently stands at around 6.8 billion and rising. Despite this large number, no two of us are exactly alike (even identical twins show slight differences in behaviour or appearance that allow their parents to differentiate between them).

The human body is an intensively researched subject that still has many secrets to divulge. Techniques to visualize living cells are being perfected and new chemicals and receptors are being discovered on a daily basis. Each new finding acts as a stepping stone to the next discovery.

THE 'SECRET OF LIFE'

In 1953, James Watson and Francis Crick announced that they had found 'the secret of life' – the structure of deoxyribonucleic acid, or DNA. This double-helix, which can unzip to make exact copies of itself, forms the genetic blueprint that defines each of us as an individual. In other words, it is DNA that makes us what we are.

Exactly 50 years later, in 2003, the complete sequence of the human genome was published, pinpointing exactly where each of our 20,000–25,000 genes is positioned within our 46 chromosomes. From here, it was a short chronological step to the first individual having his or her entire DNA sequence, made up of around 3 billion base pairs of genetic code, deciphered and uploaded onto the Internet in 2007.

While researchers originally predicted that everyone's DNA would be 99.9 per cent identical, analysis of individual genomes now suggests that at least 44 per cent of our genes have variations. These variations dictate not only the colour of our eyes and skin, whether our hair is curly or straight, and the viscosity of our earwax, they also dictate how well our cells respond to different hormones, the diseases to which we are susceptible, and even how we respond to different medicines.

Yet, despite our dissimilarities, we are all built to the same basic template, with the same body systems, and our cells work in the same basic way.

APPROACHING ANATOMY

There are two ways in which to describe the anatomy of the human body. A regional approach looks at the different structures present in a particular region of the body, such as the hand, and dissects down through the different layers to explore what is present at each level. In contrast, the systemic approach looks at different body systems such as the skeletal system, nervous system and respiratory system and studies them one at a time. This approach shows how each bone relates to one another, for example, and how the brain and spinal cord relate to the peripheral nerves. This book takes a systematic approach as it allows a greater understanding of how the body works as a whole.

BODY SYSTEMS

The human body is made up of a number of different systems, each with their own separate function. The different systems link together and communicate through the circulatory and nervous systems. Together, all of these systems allow the body to move, explore and interact with its environment, and to perform vital survival tasks.

Left: A scanning electron micrograph of human blood, showing red blood cells, white blood cells and platelets.

THE
CELL

STUPENDOUS STEM CELLS

A coloured scanning electron micrograph of stem cells, unique because they have the potential to differentiate into any other cell in the body. The ones shown here will become blood cells.

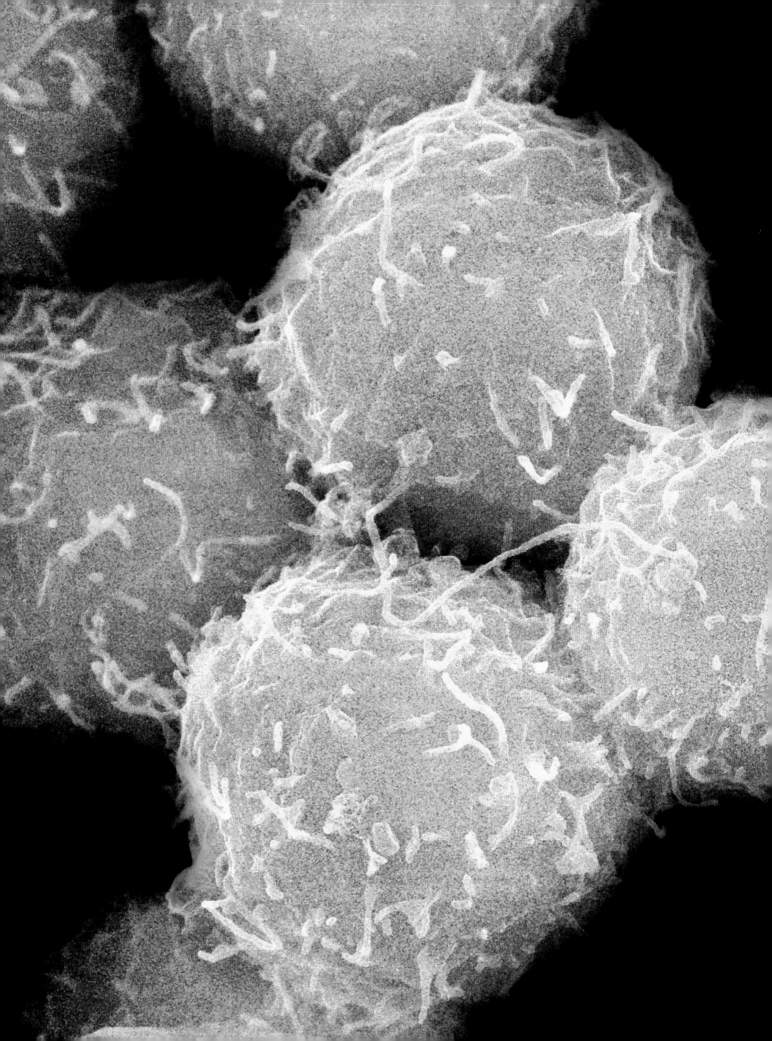

Cell metabolism

Although the human body is complex and diverse, it is made up from uniform structural units called cells. These units are the smallest building blocks of all animals and plants, and can only arise by division of pre-existing ones. Each tissue in the body serves a different function and appearance is variable, but all cells share basic structural similarities, enabling them to maintain life.

MICROFILAMENTS are fine thread-like fibres made from a protein called actin. These form part of the cell's internal skeleton, allowing the cell to change shape and to move by 'rolling' or 'crawling' along a surface

NUCLEAR ENVELOPE is the membrane that separates the nucleus from the rest of the cell. Chemicals can move to and from the nucleus to the cytoplasm via holes in the envelope known as nuclear pores

NUCLEUS is the largest organelle. It is the cell's control centre and contains the chromosomes. Most cells have only one nucleus; while a few specialized skeletal muscle cells have several nuclei and mature red blood cells and the clear cells found in the crystalline lens of the eye have none. The nucleus is separated from the rest of the cell by the nuclear envelope

CYTOPLASM is a transparent, gel-like region outside the nucleus, in which the organelles are suspended

MICROTUBULES are hollow tubes, made from a protein called tubulin, which form part of the cell's internal skeleton, maintaining its shape and assisting with cell division, movement of organelles within the cell and transport of vesicles

SMOOTH ENDOPLASMIC RETICULUM is an internal network of branching tubes involved in the production of fatty acids, steroids and the storage and release of calcium

RIBOSOMES are small units that assemble the amino acid chains that form proteins. Some ribosomes move freely within the cytoplasm, while others are attached to the rough endoplasmic reticulum, which funnels newly formed proteins to the Golgi apparatus

PLASMA MEMBRANE is the protective envelope that separates the inside of the cell from its surroundings. It contains specialized receptors that detect chemical messages, as well as pumps and pores that regulate the flow of substances into and out of the cell. The membrane also anchors the cells to the surrounding tissues and links adjacent cells at special junctions, to form tissues

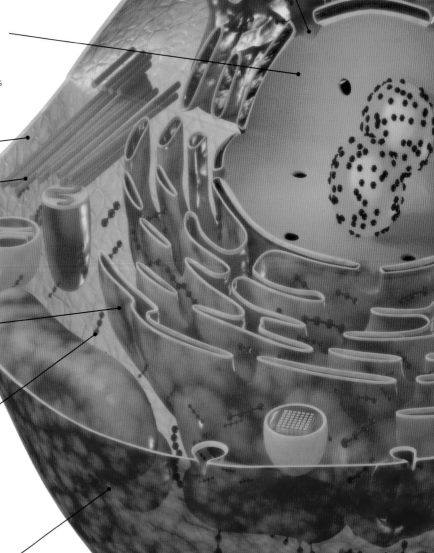

CENTRIOLES are small cylinders, at right angles to one another, made up of nine sets of fused microtubules. They are involved in cell division, and in the formation and elongation of the cell's microtubules

LYSOSOMES are small vesicles containing powerful acids and enzymes that break down worn-out organelles, and digest bacteria and foreign substances taken up by the cell

GOLGI APPARATUS is the cell's processing and transport area. It stores, sorts and modifies products made within the cell, and transports them to other organelles or to the cell surface in vesicles. Vesicles are membrane-enclosed sacs made when the cell pinches off bits of itself. Most cells need only one Golgi apparatus, but some have more

PEROXISOME are small vesicles that detoxify alcohol, hydrogen peroxide and other toxins that may be present within a cell

ROUGH ENDOPLASMIC RETICULUM is an internal network of flattened sacs, studded with ribosomes, which is involved in packaging proteins

Mitochondria

These are the batteries of a cell. They use oxygen, glucose and fatty acids to release energy plus waste carbon dioxide gas. There are as many as 1,000 mitochondria in energy-demanding cells. Mitochondria contain their own genetic material, and are believed to have evolved from symbiotic bacteria that combined with single-celled organisms at the dawn of life on earth.

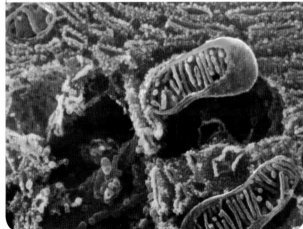

CELL STRUCTURE AND FUNCTION

While cells have different purposes, they all function in the same way. All cells:

- Exchange materials with their surroundings.
- Break down sugars or fatty acids to produce energy.
- Construct complex molecules from simpler building blocks.
- Detect and respond to environmental signals.
- Duplicate themselves.
- Contain your genetic blueprint – DNA – within the nucleus.

Your cells can survive only if they have enough energy to fuel their reactions, plus the requisite building blocks to be able to grow, repair themselves and divide. Although your cells can make some of the materials they need, others have to be delivered via the circulation and extracellular fluid.

Cells are microscopic – most are 0.002–0.12mm in diameter. A typical cell is surrounded by extracellular fluid, a watery salty medium. The outer cell covering (plasma membrane) separates the cell contents (the cytoplasm) from the extracellular fluid. The cytoplasm comprises a liquid (cytosol) containing an array of tiny structures called organelles, each of which has its own structure and function within the cell. The organelles are held in particular places within the ctyoplasm.

CELL ENERGY PRODUCTION

Like all living things, cells need energy to carry out their functions. Glucose and fatty acids (by-products of fat digestion) are used to produce energy in the cell. This energy is used firstly within the cell for repair and maintenance, and secondly to produce new cells by cell division. Energy is packaged in molecules called ATP (adenosine triphosphate) to be transported around the body.

Liver cells

Liver cells commonly have two nuclei (the large, round, light purple structures). They require a large amount of energy and therefore contain a large number of mitochondria (shown in pink). Rough endoplasmic reticulum (the brown lines) and glycogen granules (black dots) can also be seen.

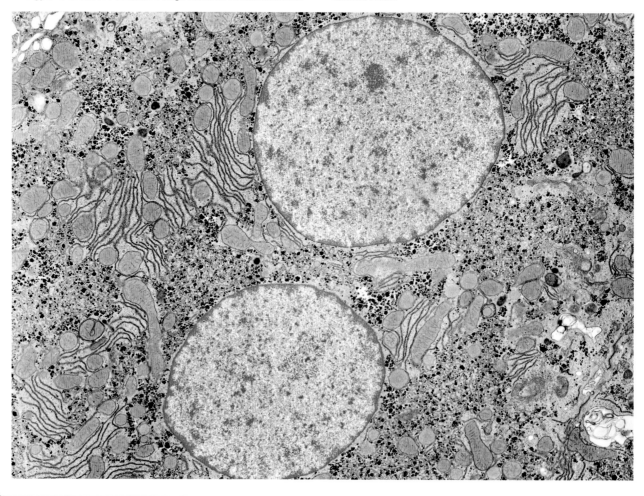

Cell facts

- The average cell is just 0.02mm (20 microns) across.
- The largest cell in the body is an egg cell (ovum), measuring 0.15mm (150 microns).
- The longest cells are the nerve cells supplying your legs – some measure as much as 1.2m (4ft) in length.
- Five million of your body cells die every second, but most are renewed.
- White blood cells are used in the fight against infection and may survive for only a few hours.
- Your gut lining cells last for three days or so.
- Red blood cells live for an average of 120 days.
- Your bone cells live for around 20 years.
- Your brain cells, which cannot regenerate, must last you a lifetime.

GLUCOSE DELIVERY

Glucose is carried into cells across the cell membrane via special transporting proteins. Striated muscle and fat cells need the presence of insulin (see page 153), a hormone made in the pancreas, to activate glucose transport into cells, while glucose enters other tissues, such as those in the liver, brain and kidneys, freely.

Once inside a cell, a glucose molecule has three possible fates:
- Some is broken down to be used as an immediate energy source (in all cells), see above right.
- Some (such as in liver and muscle cells) is converted into the starchy molecule glycogen; this will act as an emergency fuel store.
- Excess is converted into fatty acids for longer-term energy storage (in liver and fat cells).

ENERGY STORES

Glucose molecules are joined together in large highly branched molecules to form glycogen. Glucose molecules can be snipped off the ends of the chains when needed. The average adult has 70g (2.5oz) of glycogen stores in their liver, and 200g (7oz) of glycogen in their muscle cells. The breakdown of glycogen in the liver provides a constant supply of glucose to fuel brain activity during the period of overnight fasting that occurs while you sleep.

PRODUCING ENERGY FROM GLUCOSE

Your cells break down glucose by combining it with oxygen to form carbon dioxide, water and energy-rich molecules that drive other metabolic reactions. Some energy is also given out as heat. Cells liberate the energy from glucose in a controlled way, using a series of over 20 different chemical changes, each of which is regulated by a substance called an enzyme. Many of these enzymes need help in the form of vitamins, minerals and coenzymes to work properly.
- Organelles called mitochondria (singular: mitochondrion), oxidize glucose and fatty acids to produce energy for immediate use, see below.
- Excess glucose is converted into fatty acids for storage. This process occurs in the smooth endoplasmic reticulum (see page 16) of liver and fat cells, as well as in mammary gland cells during breastfeeding.

The breakdown (oxidation) of one molecule of glucose produces 31 molecules of the energy-rich substance ATP. The oxidation of a fatty acid can yield over 100 molecules of ATP, however, making it a far greater energy source.

FATTY ACIDS

These are another important form of cell fuel. Your adipose cells store fat in the form of triglycerides. These are made up of a molecule of glycerol to which three fatty-acid chains are attached to form a molecule shape that resembles a capital E.

When your cells need energy, but glucose levels are low, your pancreas stops making insulin, and instead makes a hormone called glucagon. Glucagon stimulates the breakdown of triglyceride stores to release free fatty acid chains for use as a fuel.

During exercise, your muscle and liver cells obtain most of their energy from the oxidation of free fatty acids.

PROTEIN BUILDING BLOCKS

Cells need protein for growth and repair of the body. The body produces over 30,000 different proteins, each made up of building blocks called amino acids.

The exact sequence of amino acids (the primary structure) within each protein is vital for its function and shape, and this sequence is dictated by the genetic code held in the DNA within a cell's nucleus (see page 20). The protein chains are formed in the cytoplasm with the aid of ribosomes.

DNA

The nucleus of each of your cells contains your full genetic blueprint, stored as 46 highly coiled molecules of DNA (deoxyribonucleic acid), known as chromosomes. Each molecule is made up of two chains of units, called nucleotides, which coil around each other to form a long, spiral-shaped, double helix.

NUCLEOTIDE STRUCTURE

Each nucleotide consists of a phosphate group, the sugar deoxyribose and one of four chemicals, called bases: adenine (A), thymine (T), cytosine (C) or guanine (G). These bases face inwards and pair up to form the rungs of the double-helix ladder. Importantly, A always pairs with T, and C always pairs with G.

The DNA provides the code needed for cells to make proteins, which are formed from a chain of amino acids. The code depends on the order in which the bases occur along one strand – known as the sense strand – of the DNA helix. Each run of three bases – called a triplet – provides the code for a particular amino acid. This code tells each cell the order in which to place amino acids in a protein chain.

GENES

The stretch of DNA that provides all the coding needed to make a single protein is known as a gene. Scientists from around the world have collaborated in the Human Genome Project to decode the sequence of genes that make up a human being. They have determined that we each own about 40,000 genes – a figure originally thought to be considerably higher.

The genes within every cell in a person are identical, but, depending on the type of cell, different genes are switched on and off, so the cell can make the particular proteins it requires. That is why liver cells, muscle cells, skin cells and fat cells are all so different from one another.

Each gene exists in many different forms within the population, according to the exact order of its A and T or C and G sub-units. You inherit 23 chromosomes from each parent. Although everyone inherits the same number and type of genes, the subtle differences within them make each person unique from the other 6.8 billion on this planet.

Some of the genes you inherit determine your visible features, such as your skin, hair and eye colour, while others determine how your metabolism functions and whether or not you are at risk of developing medical problems such as high blood pressure, diabetes or cancer.

Codes and codons

- The four mRNA bases (A, T, C and G) can be arranged to form 64 different combinations of three (4 x 4 x 4).
- Although there are 64 possible codons (a run of three bases in a mRNA strand that provides the code for a particular amino acid), only 21 amino acids are used to make human proteins.
- Some amino acids are specified by more than one codon (for example, GGU, GGC, GGA and GGG all specify the amino acid glycine).
- The codon AUG both acts as a 'start' signal, and specifies the amino acid methionine. All polypeptide chains therefore have methionine as their first amino acid, but this is usually removed during processing.
- Two codons (UAA, UAG) act as 'stop' signals. In addition, a third codon, UGA, acts as both a 'stop' signal and the code for the amino acid selenocysteine. Scientists have yet to work out how the ribosome knows which way to translate this codon.
- Most animals, plants and micro-organisms use this same universal genetic code. This suggests that life on earth evolved from a common ancestor, long after bacteria entered single celled organisms to become mitochondria (see page 17).

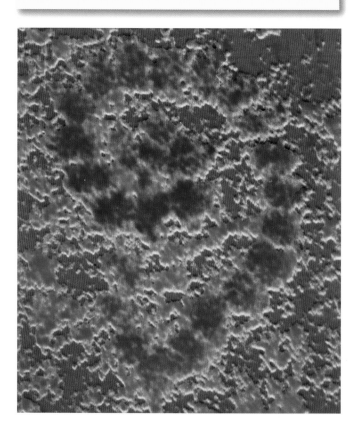

PROTEIN PRODUCTION

When a body cell needs a protein, the DNA double helix containing the appropriate gene temporarily unzips and makes a copy of itself, known as a template. The copy, known as messenger RNA, differs from DNA in that it forms just one strand of nucleotides (rather than two).

Newly formed messenger RNA leaves the nucleus for the cytoplasm, where it interacts with ribosomes, special cell sub-units that assemble the chains of amino acids that make proteins. Lengths of amino acids form simple chains known as polypeptides. These form linked or pleated shapes (the secondary structure). Longer chains of amino acids fold into complex three dimensional shapes (the tertiary structure). These shapes allow proteins to interact with one another physically as well as chemically and form the basis of cell recognition and immunity.

RIBOSOME CHAINS

The false colour transmission electron micrograph on page 20 shows a row of polyribosomes in a human brain cell, magnified 240,000 times. This is a ribosome "chain" (green) which is held together by a strand of mRNA during protein synthesis within the cell.

How protein forms

A section of the DNA double helix containing the appropriate gene temporarily unzips in the nucleus. It forms a copy of the sense strand within the gene made by using the anti-sense strand as a template. The copy, known as messenger RNA (mRNA), forms a single strand of nucleotides, containing the sugar ribose (instead of deoxyribose) and, in place of the base, thymine, uses a slightly different base called uracil (U).

Newly formed mRNA leaves the nucleus via the nuclear pores. Once in the cytoplasm, it interacts with ribosomes floating in the cytoplasm. Single amino acids are brought to the ribosomes by another type of ribonucleic acid called transfer RNA (tRNA). Like mRNA, this is copied from particular areas of the DNA molecule. Chains of amino acids make proteins, the assembly order is dictated by the sets of three bases – the triplets.

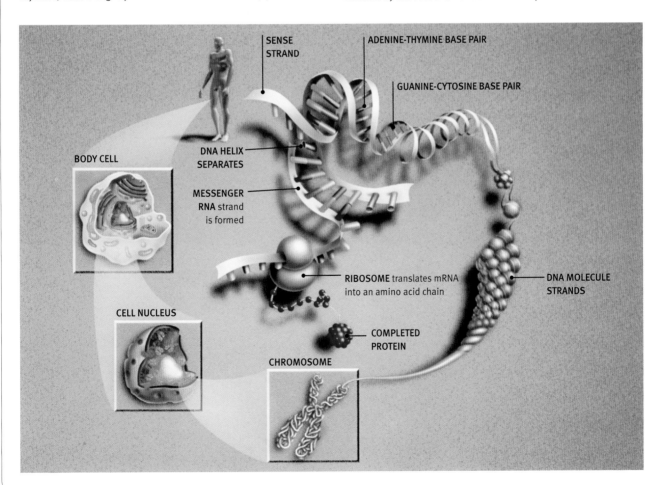

SENSE STRAND
ADENINE-THYMINE BASE PAIR
GUANINE-CYTOSINE BASE PAIR
DNA HELIX SEPARATES
BODY CELL
MESSENGER RNA strand is formed
RIBOSOME translates mRNA into an amino acid chain
DNA MOLECULE STRANDS
CELL NUCLEUS
COMPLETED PROTEIN
CHROMOSOME

Cell division

Your body started out as a single fertilized egg containing the full DNA. This cell divided to produce two cells, then four, then eight, sixteen and so on. Growth during embryonic and fetal life is rapid – in just nine months the fertilized egg, which is around the size of a full-stop, has multiplied enough to create a fully formed baby weighing 3kg (6.5lb) or more (see pages 196–203, on pregnancy and child growth). The process of cell division continues in adults, but the time between cell division varies from cell to cell, with rapidly growing cells dividing as often as once every 24 hours.

COPYING DNA

When a cell divides, each 'daughter' cell receives a full copy of the original DNA. Before a cell can divide, the DNA needs to be copied. First, the double-helix of each chromosome 'unzips'. The two sides, or strands, act as a template to which new nucleotides attach. An enzyme – DNA polymerase – ensures that each newly exposed nucleotide pairs with a new base – either adenine (A) and thymine (T), or cytosine (C) and guanine (G), see pages 20–21. The end result is two identical strands of DNA, each of which contains one strand of original DNA and one strand of newly synthesized DNA.

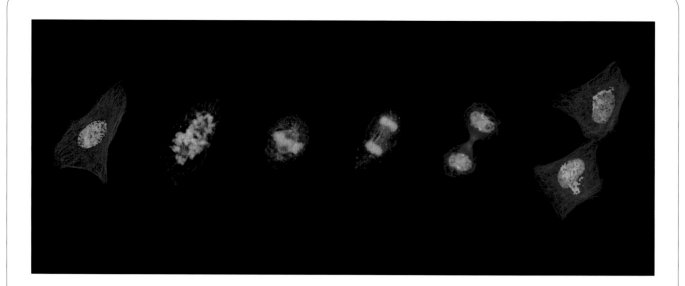

The process of division

Once the DNA is copied, a cell divides into two, and each daughter cell receives a full set of 46 chromosomes identical to those in the parent cell.

As the duplicated chromosomes condense, the nuclear membrane around the cell nucleus breaks down. The two centrioles within the cytoplasm produce spindle fibres that attach to the centromere of each duplicated chromosome.

The centrioles divide and one pair moves to each end of the cell, pulling the sister chromatids from each chromosome with them, before the cell cytoplasm divides.

Chromatin in the cell nucleus condenses to form duplicated chromosomes. The two centrioles are duplicated and move to opposite poles of the cell. Spindle fibres from the centrioles pull the duplicated chromosomes into a line at the cell's equator. The duplicated chromosomes split and the spindle fibres pull the sister chromatids apart. Contractile proteins cause the cell cytoplasm to pinch into two. The spindle fibres break down, the chromosomes unravel to form chromatin and the nuclear membrane re-forms. Two identical daughter cells result.

DNA copy machinery

- Each time a cell divides, the chromosomes shorten slightly – the end of each chromosome is never copied as it contains the copying 'machinery' – the telomere, which produces the enzyme telomerase.
- The telomere is made of repeating sequences of six bases: TTAGGG on one strand of DNA, bound to AATCCC on the other.
- Telomeres act like 'non-sense' strands that allow the DNA molecule to shorten without losing genes.

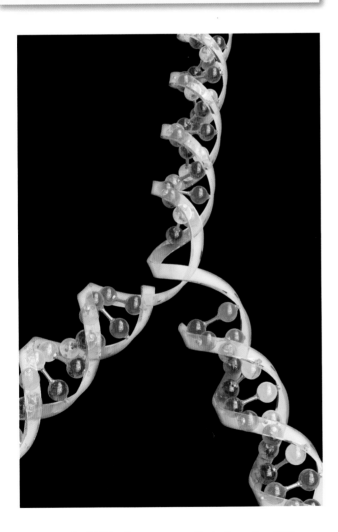

DNA REPLICATION begins as soon as the helix unzips. DNA polymerase works quickly, linking 50 nucleotides per second. It also proofreads the copies it makes, reversing direction if necessary to correct any errors

Chromosomes

The nucleus of every cell in the body contains 46 molecules of DNA, called chromosomes. There are 23 pairs. One of each pair was inherited from an individual's mother, the other from the father. Forty-four of these chromosomes contain genes that provide the code for proteins involved in the structure and function of every cell. The remaining pair of sex chromosomes contain information that determine an individual's male (Y) and female (X) characteristics.

The DNA molecules are loosely wound around special proteins (histones), which form a spaghetti-like complex called chromatin. Before a cell divides, each molecule of DNA is copied and condenses to form a duplicated chromosome. Each duplicated chromosome contains two identical strands of DNA, referred to as sister chromatids. The chromatids remain attached at a point called the centromere. The ends of the chromosomes contain repeating sections of DNA called telomeres, which never copy. After duplication, the DNA molecules condense again to form copies of the X-shaped structures known as duplicated chromosomes.

The image here is a karotype, or chromosome 'photograph', of a full set of chromosome pairs, arranged in a standard order. It shows a male as the last two chromosomes are an X and a Y. A female has two X chromosomes.

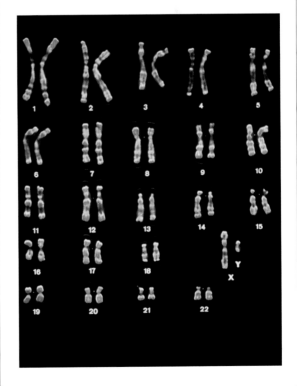

Formation of tissues and organs

We all start out as a single cell, a fertilized egg, that divides again and again to form, eventually, as many as 50 trillion cells.

During development, each of your cells becomes specialized to perform different functions, for example, movement (the muscle cells), structural support (bone cells), generation of an electric signal (nerve cells) or carrying oxygen (red blood cells). The process that transforms the original unspecialized cell into a specialized one (called differentiation) depends on which genes within each cell's DNA are switched 'on' and which are switched 'off'.

Altogether, more than 200 different types of cell exist within your body. However, the chemical signals that control why or how the different cells become programed to perform specific tasks, in a particular location, are still poorly understood.

TISSUES

As they differentiate and divide, cells move to new locations and join together with other specialized cells with similar properties to form tissue. The 200 different kinds of cells within the body fall into four main categories, and make up four types of tissue. Each of these types can be further divided into sub-types that perform specialized functions. Cells within most tissues divide regularly for growth, regeneration and repair. Some cells, such as mature brain cells, cannot regenerate.

CELL MEMBRANES

All the cells within a tissue stick together, and communicate via their cell membrane. These membranes contain a double layer of peg-shaped phospholipid molecules, the 'head' of which is attracted to water ('hydrophilic'), and the 'tail' repels water ('hydrophobic'). These properties allow the phospholipids to float around each other in a double layer that is more fluid than solid. Proteins with different functions attach to either side of the membrane, or pass through to form pores. Receptors on the cell surface detect hormone and immune chemicals that act as messengers, telling the cell, for example, to activate certain genes, to secrete a particular protein or to divide.

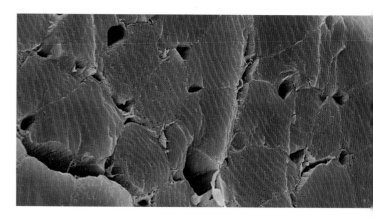

MUSCLE TISSUE This contains cells that are specialized to generate a mechanical force. There are three main types: skeletal, cardiac (heart) and smooth muscle cells. This image is of skeletal muscle fibres.

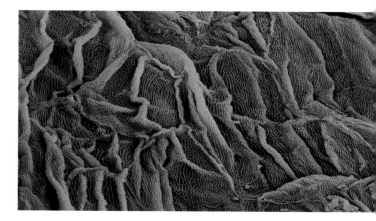

EPITHELIAL TISSUE This lines body surfaces and cavities. The cells that make up the tissue are specialized to secrete and absorb particular chemicals. There are three main types: flattened squamous cells, square cuboidal cells and columnar cells. Each type can form sheets that are only one cell thick (simple) or several cells thick (stratified). This tissue lines the oesophagus (gullet).

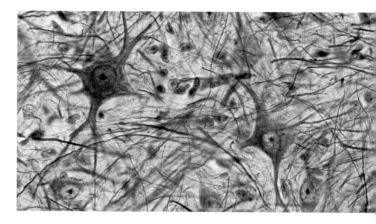

NERVE CELLS Also known as neurons, these are specialized to generate and conduct an electric charge. There are four main types of neuron: brain cells; sensory neurons that carry impulses to the brain; motor neurons that carry instructions from the brain; and interneurons that connect sensory and motor neurons together. This image depicts a mixture of brain cells.

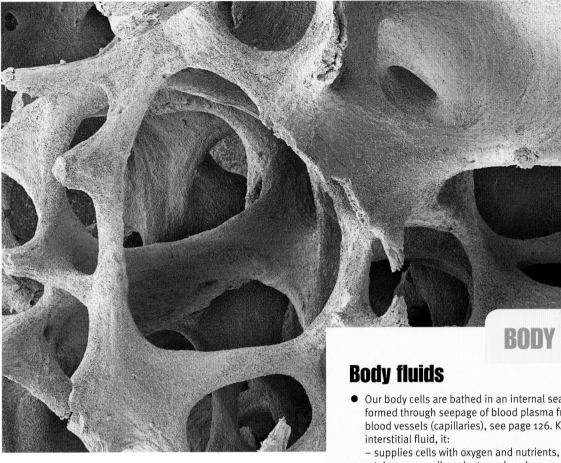

BONE TISSUE Connective tissue forms the cells that make up bone tissue. There are two types of bone tissue: compact (cortical) and cancellous (spongy). Cortical bone usually makes up the exterior of bone, while cancellous bone, shown here, is found on the inside. Cancellous bone is characterized by its honeycomb appearance, and is made up of a network of special rod-shaped structures that give bone its strength. Bone marrow, a blood-forming substance (see page 34) is made in the spaces. Stem cells are found in bone marrow.

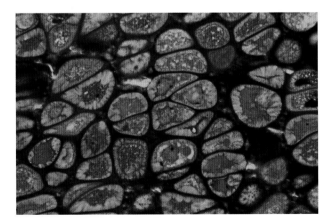

CONNECTIVE TISSUE This is made up of cells that are specialized to support body structures. There are many different kinds of connective tissue cells, for example, cartilage cells, bone cells, blood cells and fat storage (adipose) cells. This image shows a section through cartilage cells.

BODY FACT

Body fluids

- Our body cells are bathed in an internal sea of fluid formed through seepage of blood plasma from tiny blood vessels (capillaries), see page 126. Known as interstitial fluid, it:
  – supplies cells with oxygen and nutrients,
  – takes away cell products such as hormones and growth factors,
  – flushes away cell wastes such as carbon dioxide,
  – helps to maintain a constant cell environment.
- The amount of interstitial fluid bathing your cells amounts to 11 or so litres (18 pints).
- Interstitial fluid plus the 3 litres (5 pints) of plasma – the fluid part of the blood – are together referred to as the body's extracellular fluid.
- The amount of fluid found inside your cells (intracellular fluid) is a staggering 28 or so litres (47 pints).

ORGANS

Different tissues in the body come together to form your organs, which make up the key parts of your different body systems. Every organ in the body contains two or more of the four different kinds of tissue. These tissues are arranged to form sheets, tubes and layers that make up the different parts of each organ.

Each of your organs, such as the skin, lungs, kidneys, eyes, stomach, liver, heart and brain, carries out a specific function that is vital for your body's survival. Every one forms part of a larger system that may contain more than one organ – for example, the lungs are part of the respiratory system (see page 110), the heart is part of the cardiovascular system (see page 118) and the brain is part of the nervous system (see page 66).

INTEGUMENTARY
SYSTEM

SEPARATE SKIN LAYERS
This coloured light micrograph shows three layers of skin. The top (bands of purple and blue) is made up of flattened, dead skin cells. The middle (solid dark blue) is the living epidermal layer that creates new cells. The bottom (pale blue) is made up of nourishing fatty and connective tissue.

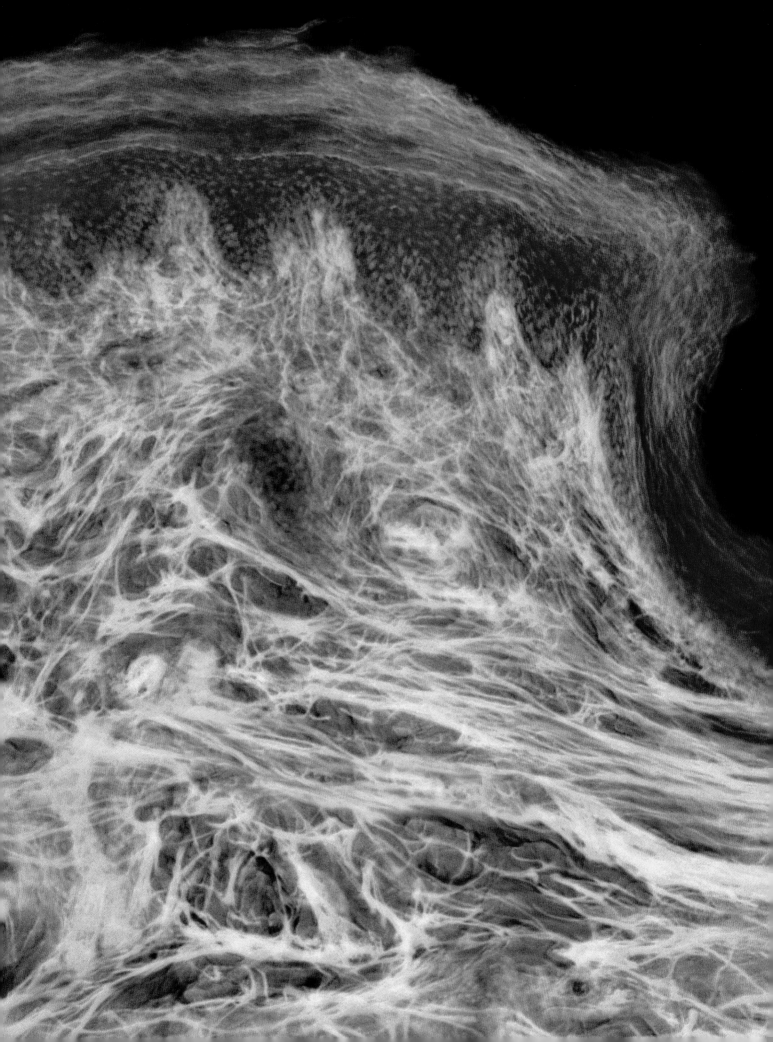

Skin, hair and nails

Your skin has two main layers – an outer epidermis and an inner dermis – each of which is several cell thicknesses deep. Beneath the epidermis and dermis is a layer of body fat, the subcutaneous layer. Nerve endings in the dermis detect pain, pressure and temperature.

DERMIS

The dermis is usually thicker than the epidermis and contains only living cells. It consists of dense connective tissue containing collagen and elastin fibres that give your skin tone and strength.

The inner dermis contains a network of small blood vessels, sweat glands, hair follicles, sebaceous glands and nerve endings.

EPIDERMIS

The outer skin layer is constantly renewed. The lowest level of the epidermis, the basal layer, consists of a single row of cells that continually divides and pushes new cells up towards the body surface. As the cells move upwards, each gradually loses its nucleus, and becomes filled with a tough protein called keratin. The cells become flattened and hardened and die to produce an outer, cornified protective layer. These surface cells, known as keratinocytes, are continually worn away and replaced. Interspersed among the basal cells are the melanocytes. They produce melanin that gives skin its colour.

MELANOCYTE-CONTAINING TISSUE

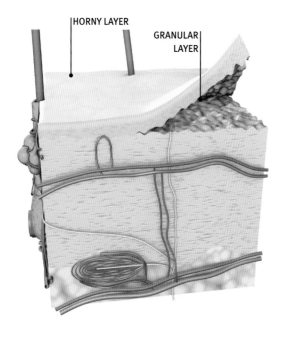

HORNY LAYER

GRANULAR LAYER

BODY FACT

Super skin

● Skin forms the largest organ in the body, and has a surface area of up to 2 square metres (22 square feet).
● The average skin thickness is 2mm (0.08in).

HAIR

Hair is a protein filament produced within follicles deep in the dermis; it provides you with warmth and reduces heat loss from your body. Each hair follicle contains a hair root that has its own network of tiny blood vessels and nerves.

A sebaceous gland is attached to each follicle and helps to lubricate the hair. During active growth, the root is tightly surrounded by live tissue called the hair bulb. The bulb contains a layer of dividing cells. As new cells are formed, older ones die and are pushed upwards to form the hair root and shaft. Attached to each hair is a muscle (erector pili), which produces a 'goosebump' when pulled upright.

Your hair texture, colour, curliness, thickness and length are genetically determined. Melanin-producing cells at the base of each hair follicle feed pigments through to the hair root. Red melanin produces blonde, auburn or red hair, while black melanin produces shades of brown or black depending on its concentration. In blonde hairs, melanin pigment is pale and found only in the middle layer of the hair shaft (cortex). In people with dark hair, pigments are found in both the cortex and the inner core (medulla) to give a greater depth of colour.

SWEAT GLANDS

These are long, coiled hollow tubes. The sweat is produced in the coiled part deep in the dermis and is carried to the skin surface in the tube. There are two types: eccrine sweat glands are distributed over nearly all of the body, with the greatest density being on the palms and soles. They secrete water, salt and other waste products. Apocrine sweat glands are found on hair-bearing skin such as your armpits, groin and scalp. They become active at puberty and secrete sweat, containing proteins, fats and sugars, into hair follicles rather than onto the skin surface. This type of sweat is broken down by skin bacteria to produce a characteristic and unpleasant body odour.

SEBACEOUS GLANDS

These are found all over your skin (except the eyelids) and are especially concentrated on your palms and soles. They secrete sebum, an oily compound containing fatty substances, which enables the skin to retain water.

NAILS

Nails, specialized skin structures, are made of a tough protein called keratin. Your nails strengthen the tips of your fingers and toes and protect them from damage and improve your grip on small objects.

Each nail consists of three parts: the root, the nail plate and the free edge at the tip. The lunula is the visible, crescent-shaped part of the nail root that produces new nail. The lunula is pronounced on the thumbnail but barely visible on that of the little finger. Over the lunula, a thin fold of cuticle is usually pulled up from the enclosing skin as the nail grows. Nail growth starts from the root to the tip of the finger, with additional nutrition supplied from the nail bed.

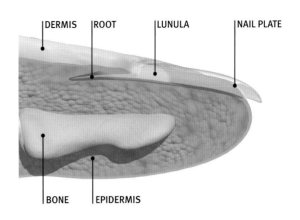

DERMIS | ROOT | LUNULA | NAIL PLATE

BONE | EPIDERMIS

Fingerprints

Your fingertips have ridges of skin that help to increase your grip on slippery surfaces. These ridges and valleys make unique patterns of whorls, loops and discontinuous lines that are unique for every individual. The ridges contain sweat ducts and leave marks called fingerprints when an object is touched. Your fingerprints form when you are an embryo, and reflect genetic influences, as well as blood flow and nutrition in the womb. No two people have the same fingerprints – even identical twins – and comparison of minutiae points, such as those indicated below, mean an individual can be identified by the fingerprints they leave behind.

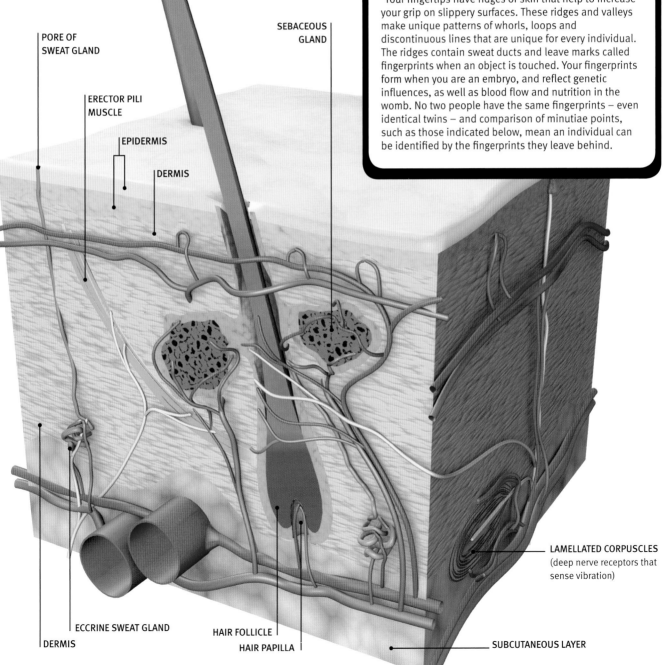

HAIR

SEBACEOUS GLAND

PORE OF SWEAT GLAND

ERECTOR PILI MUSCLE

EPIDERMIS

DERMIS

LAMELLATED CORPUSCLES
(deep nerve receptors that sense vibration)

DERMIS

ECCRINE SWEAT GLAND

HAIR FOLLICLE

HAIR PAPILLA

SUBCUTANEOUS LAYER

SKELETAL SYSTEM

PRIMAL PELVIS
Coloured X-ray of the pelvic region – the largest structure in the skeletal system. The pelvic girdle is firmly attached to the base of the spinal column to increase stability and help transfer body weight more evenly through the lower limbs. The female pelvis is slightly deeper and wider than the average male pelvis to support the fetus in pregnancy.

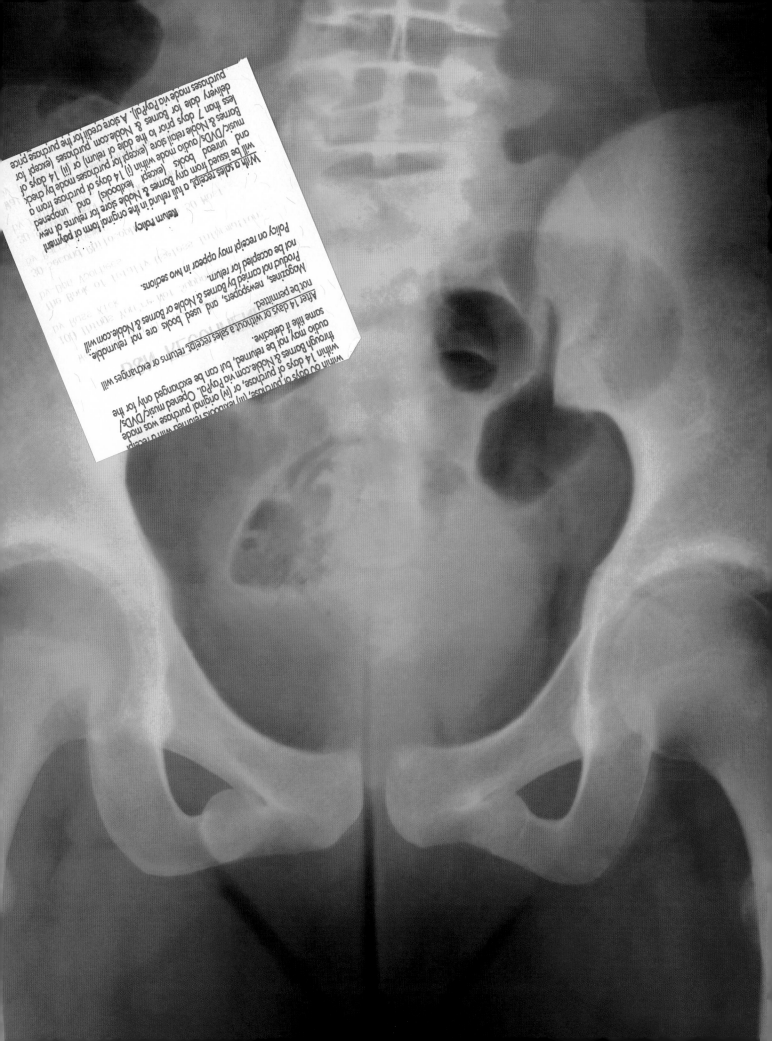

Bones of the body

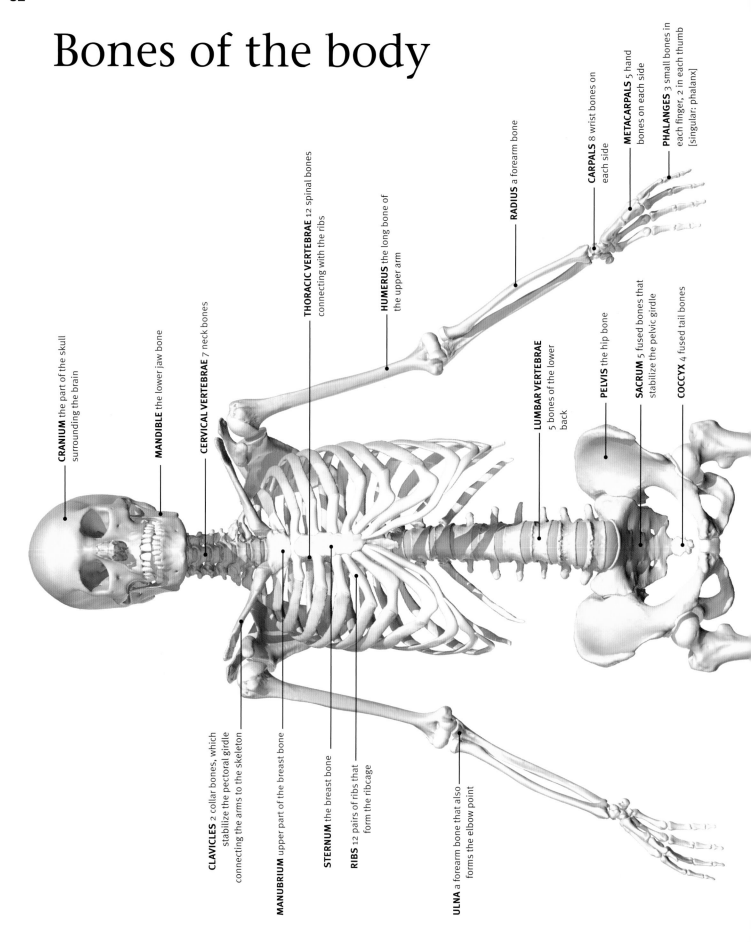

CRANIUM the part of the skull surrounding the brain

MANDIBLE the lower jaw bone

CERVICAL VERTEBRAE 7 neck bones

THORACIC VERTEBRAE 12 spinal bones connecting with the ribs

HUMERUS the long bone of the upper arm

RADIUS a forearm bone

CARPALS 8 wrist bones on each side

METACARPALS 5 hand bones on each side

PHALANGES 3 small bones in each finger, 2 in each thumb [singular: phalanx]

LUMBAR VERTEBRAE 5 bones of the lower back

PELVIS the hip bone

SACRUM 5 fused bones that stabilize the pelvic girdle

COCCYX 4 fused tail bones

CLAVICLES 2 collar bones, which stabilize the pectoral girdle connecting the arms to the skeleton

MANUBRIUM upper part of the breast bone

STERNUM the breast bone

RIBS 12 pairs of ribs that form the ribcage

ULNA a forearm bone that also forms the elbow point

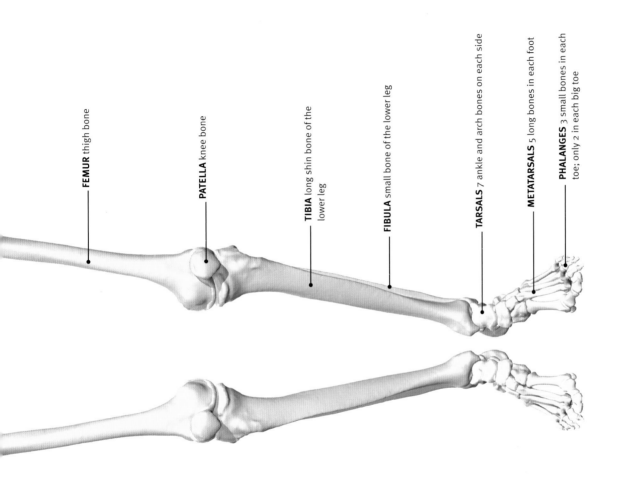

FEMUR thigh bone

PATELLA knee bone

TIBIA long shin bone of the lower leg

FIBULA small bone of the lower leg

TARSALS 7 ankle and arch bones on each side

METATARSALS 5 long bones in each foot

PHALANGES 3 small bones in each toe; only 2 in each big toe

Bone structure

Your bones are living tissues in which a network of collagen fibres is filled with the mineral calcium phosphate. The hard outer layer is called cortical bone. This is made up of tiny tubes of bone called osteons, which form a strong outer shell. Inside the cortical bone is a spongy, central filling called cancellous bone, whose honeycomb of struts (trabeculae) provides the bone with strength while remaining relatively lightweight.

BODY FACT

Our wonderful bones

- Compact or cortical bone is the second hardest material in the body after tooth enamel.
- Some 80 per cent of the body's bone weight comes from dense cortical bone.
- Trabecular bone accounts for only 20 per cent of bone weight but has a surface area that is 10 times greater.
- Bone is five times stronger than a steel bar of the same weight.

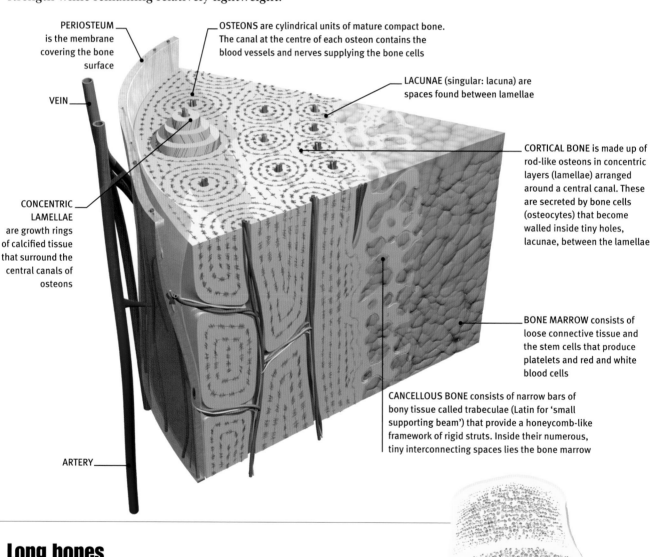

PERIOSTEUM is the membrane covering the bone surface

OSTEONS are cylindrical units of mature compact bone. The canal at the centre of each osteon contains the blood vessels and nerves supplying the bone cells

LACUNAE (singular: lacuna) are spaces found between lamellae

VEIN

CONCENTRIC LAMELLAE are growth rings of calcified tissue that surround the central canals of osteons

CORTICAL BONE is made up of rod-like osteons in concentric layers (lamellae) arranged around a central canal. These are secreted by bone cells (osteocytes) that become walled inside tiny holes, lacunae, between the lamellae

BONE MARROW consists of loose connective tissue and the stem cells that produce platelets and red and white blood cells

CANCELLOUS BONE consists of narrow bars of bony tissue called trabeculae (Latin for 'small supporting beam') that provide a honeycomb-like framework of rigid struts. Inside their numerous, tiny interconnecting spaces lies the bone marrow

ARTERY

Long bones

Each long bone is made up of a shaft (diaphysis) and two ends (epiphyses). The shaft consists of a thick outer layer of cortical bone surrounding cancellous bone, within which is a central cavity containing bone marrow. The ends consist mainly of cancellous bone covered by a thin outer layer of cortical bone. Near the end of the long bones is the epiphyseal plate where bones lengthen during periods of growth. Once the epiphyseal plate fuses, growth in height stops.

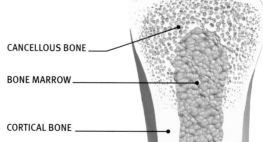

CANCELLOUS BONE

BONE MARROW

CORTICAL BONE

Five main types of bone shape

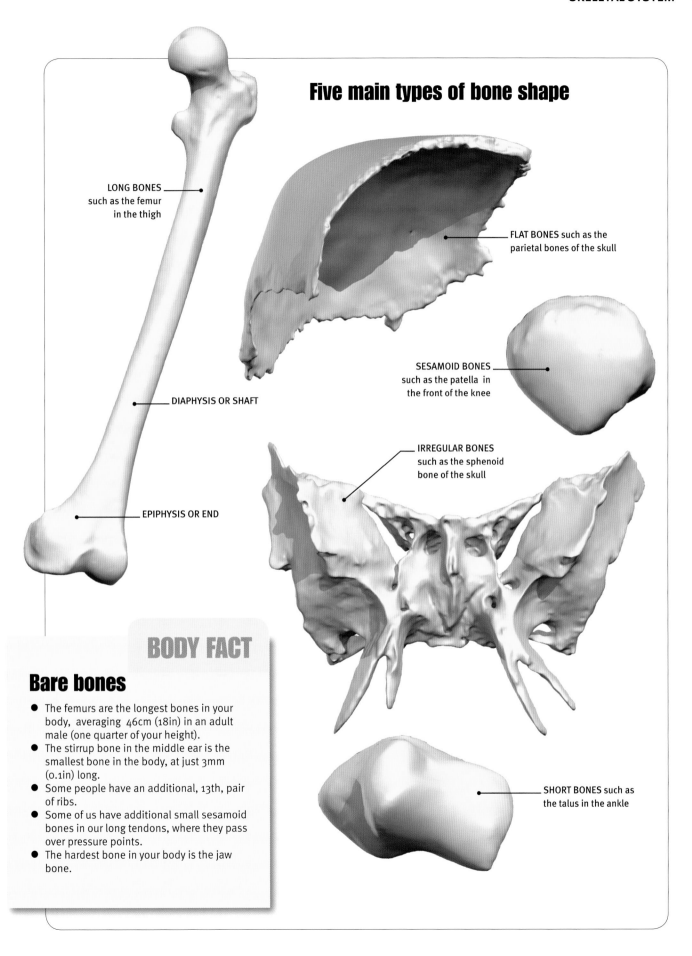

LONG BONES
such as the femur
in the thigh

FLAT BONES such as the
parietal bones of the skull

DIAPHYSIS OR SHAFT

SESAMOID BONES
such as the patella in
the front of the knee

IRREGULAR BONES
such as the sphenoid
bone of the skull

EPIPHYSIS OR END

SHORT BONES such as
the talus in the ankle

BODY FACT

Bare bones

- The femurs are the longest bones in your body, averaging 46cm (18in) in an adult male (one quarter of your height).
- The stirrup bone in the middle ear is the smallest bone in the body, at just 3mm (0.1in) long.
- Some people have an additional, 13th, pair of ribs.
- Some of us have additional small sesamoid bones in our long tendons, where they pass over pressure points.
- The hardest bone in your body is the jaw bone.

Joints

A joint forms at the point where two bones meet. Some joints are fixed, meaning the bones are locked together. Most joints in your body can, however, move more freely. Each joint has a fixed range of movement depending on the shape of the bones involved and the way the bones are held together.

MOBILE JOINTS

The bone surfaces within a mobile joint are coated with slippery cartilage and oiled with synovial fluid. Your joints are held together by bands of connective tissue that form ligaments. Some joints, such as the knee, also have internal stabilizing ligaments that prevent the bones from moving back and forth or from side to side while bending.

PIVOT JOINT such as the one between the radius and ulna in your elbow, allows one bone to swivel inside another bone. The elbow joint allows pronation and supination of the forearm (the ability to turn your palm upwards or downwards) and that between your two upper neck vertebrae enables your head to turn from side to side

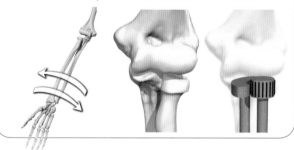

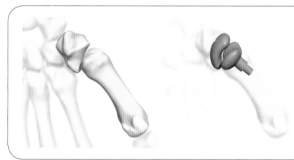

SADDLE JOINT such as the thumb, consists of two U-shaped bone surfaces that fit together at right angles to rock back and forth and from side to side. This type of joint gives a limited amount of rotation

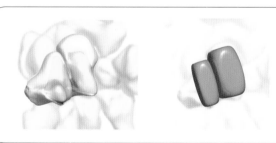

GLIDING JOINT is formed when two, almost flat, joint surfaces slide over each other. Some of the joints in the feet and hands and in the vertebral column are of this kind; strong ligaments limit their range of movement

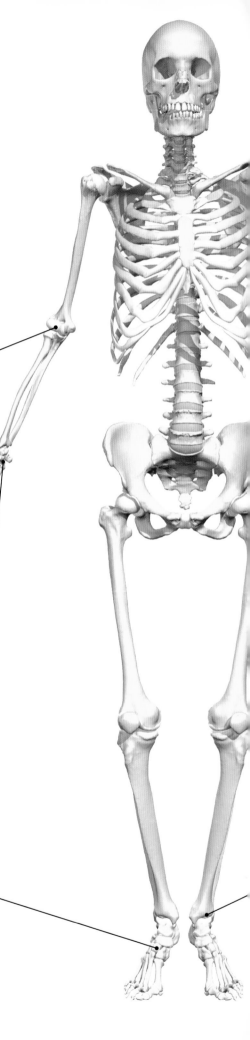

BALL-AND-SOCKET JOINT such as the hip, occurs where a round-shaped surface of one bone fits inside a cup-shaped socket in another one. This type of joint has the greatest range of movement. The shoulder ball-and-socket joint, known as a multiaxial joint, has the widest range of movement. It allows your arm to move in more than two planes: up and down as well as backwards and forwards. It also allows some rotation at the side of the body

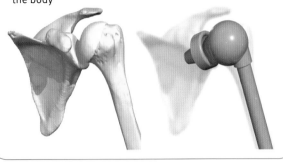

CONDYLOID (ELLIPSOID) JOINT occurs where an oval-shaped bone surface fits into an oval-shaped cup in another bone. An example is your wrist, which can move backwards and forwards or from side to side, although rotation is limited

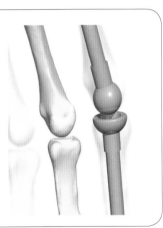

HINGE JOINT such as the ankle, is formed where a cylindrical surface on one bone sits inside the curve of another bone and movement is allowed in one plane only. Your elbow and knee are modified hinge joints and have limited rotation, too

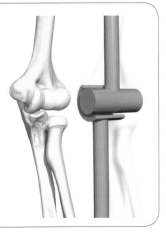

Joint with limited movement

Some joints, such as that between the lower ulna and radius at the wrist have a limited amount of movement as the bony surfaces are bound together by a ligament. This type of joint is known as a syndemosis.

RADIUS

SYNDESMOSIS JOINT is a joint of limited movement between the lower arm bones and the wrist bones; the joint surfaces are bound together by ligaments

ULNA

BONES OF THE WRIST

BODY FACT

JOINT ACTION

- Your hand movements are delicate or strong depending on the coordination of the 29 separate bones and their variety of joints.
- Joints move when skeletal muscles act on them.
- When joints are pulled apart they are said to be dislocated or subluxed.
- People who are 'double jointed' have less stable joints that dislocate easily.
- The shoulder joint allows the greatest degree of movement in the body. It often lies in the impact zone in contact sport injuries, so is prone to injury.

Skull

All of the bones that make up your skull, except the lower jaw (mandible), are firmly locked together at rigid points called suture joints. The space called the cranial vault supports and encases your brain, while your facial bones anchor the muscles you use to produce facial expressions, as well as to talk and chew.

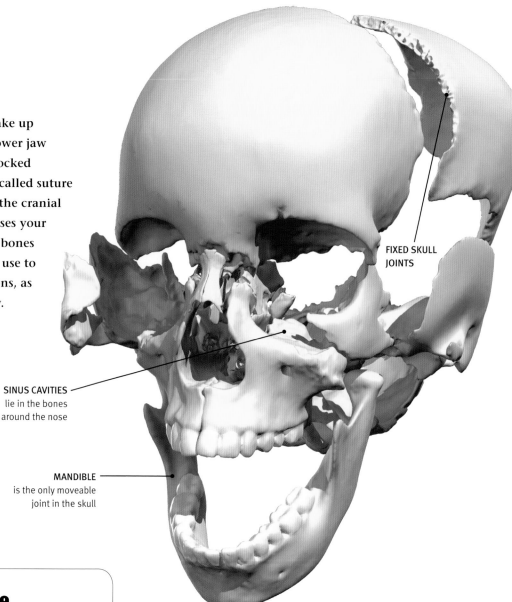

FIXED SKULL JOINTS

SINUS CAVITIES
lie in the bones around the nose

MANDIBLE
is the only moveable joint in the skull

Ossicles of the middle ear

The middle ear contains three ossicles (bones): the malleus (hammer), incus (anvil) and stapes (stirrup), which are named after their shapes. The inner ear is filled with fluid, which helps maintain balance, and the ossicles amplify sound vibrations as they are passed on through a membrane-covered opening known as the oval window.

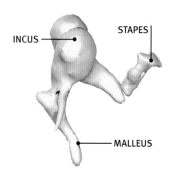

INCUS

STAPES

MALLEUS

BODY FACT

Bags of bones

- Your skull contains 22 bones, which, apart from the mandible (lower jaw) are joined by sutures.
- The cranial vault consists of eight bones that protect your brain: the frontal bone, two parietal bones, the occipital bone, the sphenoid bone, two temporal bones and the ethmoid bone.
- Your face is made up of 14 bones: two nasal bones, two lacrimal bones, two zygomatic bones, two maxillae (singular: maxilla), two palatine bones, two inferior concha bones, the vomer and the hyoid bone (see the tongue, pages 108–109).
- Your skull also houses three tiny bones (ossicles) within each middle ear.
- When you blow your nose, most of the secretions have come from your eight sinuses.

SUTURE LINE

SKULL BONE

FIXED JOINTS

In fixed joints (left), the bony edges are close together and may interlock. This type of joint is designed to allow force to pass easily from one bone to another, reducing the risk of injury. Fixed joints are found between the bones of the skull and are known as sutures.

Fontanelles

The eight skull bones of the cranium (skull) encase the brain. Before and at birth they are connected by bands of fibrous tissue, which are flexible and allow skull distortion during birth. The largest fibrous areas are known as fontanelles, which remain, to some degree, until the brain stops growing at the age of five.

Temporomandibular joint

A combined hinge and gliding joint, the temporomandibular joint (TMJ) is where the jaw bone (mandible) and the temporal bone meet on each side of the skull. This joint contains a disc of cartilage that allows the bones to glide from side to side and to protrude forwards and backwards during chewing and grinding.

MANDIBULAR FOSSA

ARTICULAR CAPSULE

STYLOID PROCESS

STYLOMANDIBULAR LIGAMENT

LOWER JAW (MANDIBLE)

Skull continued

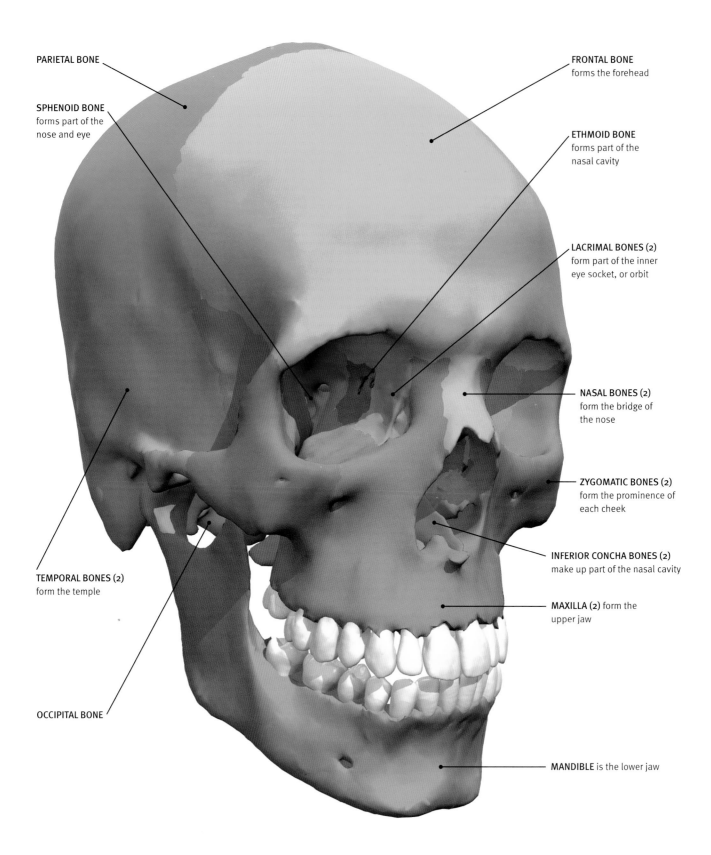

PARIETAL BONE

SPHENOID BONE
forms part of the
nose and eye

TEMPORAL BONES (2)
form the temple

OCCIPITAL BONE

FRONTAL BONE
forms the forehead

ETHMOID BONE
forms part of the
nasal cavity

LACRIMAL BONES (2)
form part of the inner
eye socket, or orbit

NASAL BONES (2)
form the bridge of
the nose

ZYGOMATIC BONES (2)
form the prominence of
each cheek

INFERIOR CONCHA BONES (2)
make up part of the nasal cavity

MAXILLA (2) form the
upper jaw

MANDIBLE is the lower jaw

Paranasal sinuses

There are eight air-filled cavities in the bones surrounding the nose that help to lighten the bones of your skull, improve the resonance of your voice and act as a safety 'crumple zone' to absorb blows to the face. Each sinus is lined by a membrane that secretes a thin, watery mucus. This traps airborne particles, such as pollen or dust, and drains them away along narrow channels opening into your nose.

There are:
- two frontal bone sinuses in the forehead,
- two maxillary sinuses, one in each cheek bone,
- two ethmoid sinuses in the small bones between the orbits of the eyes,
- two sphenoidal sinuses, in the winged sphenoid bone, behind your nose in the roof of the nasal cavity (not seen).

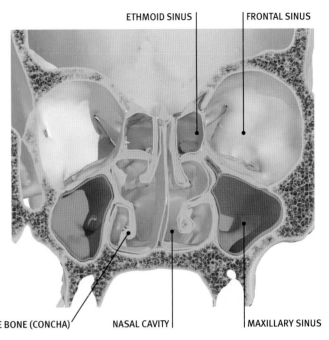

ETHMOID SINUS | FRONTAL SINUS

TURBINATE BONE (CONCHA) | NASAL CAVITY | MAXILLARY SINUS

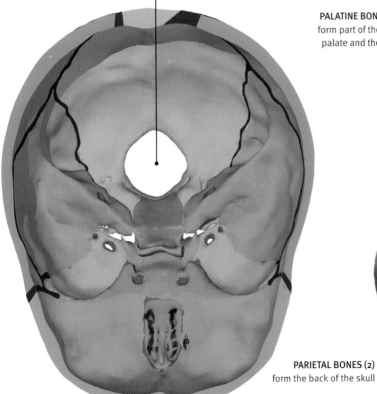

FORAMEN MAGNUM (LARGE HOLE)
in the occipital bone at the base of your brain is where your spinal cord passes down from the brain into the spinal column

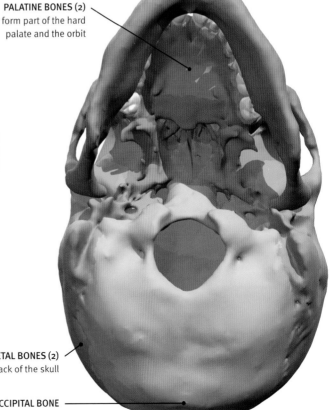

PALATINE BONES (2)
form part of the hard palate and the orbit

PARIETAL BONES (2)
form the back of the skull

OCCIPITAL BONE
forms the base of the skull

Spinal column

The spine is a column of small bones, and it supports the head and upper body. It contains 33 bones called vertebrae (single: vertebra) that surround and protect your spinal cord (see pages 86–88). The shape of the vertebrae allows you to bend and twist your back. The joints between the bones allow forward movement, while the small processes on the rear of each bone prevent you from bending too far back.

STRUCTURE OF THE SPINE

The vertebrae interlock in a series of sliding joints, giving the backbone its flexibility. The bones are aligned to form an 'S-shape' with four gentle curves, each formed by a different group of vertebrae (cervical, thoracic, lumbar and sacral). This S-shape provides strength and stability.

Each vertebra contains a weight-bearing region, the centrum, attached to a ring of bone called the neural arch. This forms a central hole (the vertebral foramen) through which the spinal cord passes. The arch has a number of bony projections – two transverse processes and a single spinous process – that attach to the ligaments and muscles. Between each vertebra is an intervertebral disc of cartilage with a jelly-like core, which acts as a shock-absorbing cushion.

BODY FACT

Your body's support

- Your spinal column is made up of 33 vertebrae. These form 26 moveable joints; the remainder are fixed.
- Your neck contains seven cervical vertebrae.
- There are 12 thoracic vertebrae in your chest.
- You have five lumbar vertebrae in the lower spine.
- Your sacrum contains five fused vertebrae.
- Although the coccyx usually contains four fused vertebrae, some people have three and some have five.

CERVICAL REGION There are seven vertebrae in this region, normally referred to as C1 to C7. The first two are known as the atlas and axis, see opposite.

THORACIC REGION The vertebrae in this part of the body connect to the ribs via ligaments and muscles to form the protective rib cage. The ends of the ribs fit into hollows in the sides of the vertebrae. There are 12 thoracic vertebrae, referred to as T1 at the top down to T12 at the bottom.

LUMBAR REGION These are the largest and strongest vertebrae as they have to stabilize and support the weight of the whole upper body. There are five lumbar vertebrae – L1 to L5.

SACRUM This region comprises two groups of fused bones. There is limited movement between the two groups. The nerves at the base of the spinal cord pass through the holes in the sacrum.

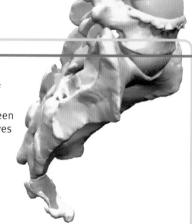

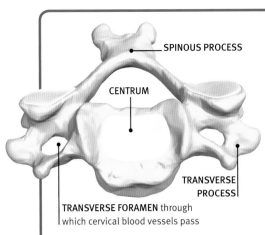

CERVICAL VERTEBRA These are the smallest and lightest bones of the spinal column. The first two, the axis and atlas, are shaped to allow the start of the spinal cord, see right. The first six of these vertebrae also have holes in the transverse processes through which the cervical arteries and veins can pass. This is C6, a typical cervical vertebra.

SPINOUS PROCESS

CENTRUM

TRANSVERSE PROCESS

TRANSVERSE FORAMEN through which cervical blood vessels pass

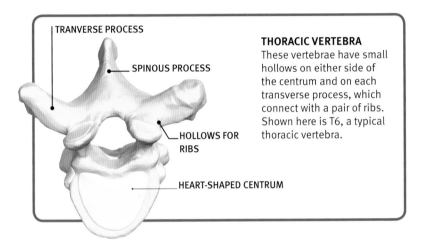

TRANVERSE PROCESS

SPINOUS PROCESS

HOLLOWS FOR RIBS

HEART-SHAPED CENTRUM

THORACIC VERTEBRA These vertebrae have small hollows on either side of the centrum and on each transverse process, which connect with a pair of ribs. Shown here is T6, a typical thoracic vertebra.

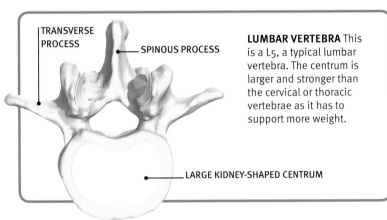

TRANSVERSE PROCESS

SPINOUS PROCESS

LARGE KIDNEY-SHAPED CENTRUM

LUMBAR VERTEBRA This is a L5, a typical lumbar vertebra. The centrum is larger and stronger than the cervical or thoracic vertebrae as it has to support more weight.

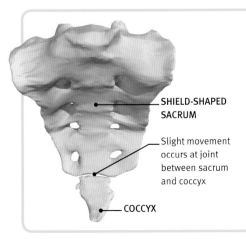

SHIELD-SHAPED SACRUM

Slight movement occurs at joint between sacrum and coccyx

COCCYX

SACRUM AND COCCYX The sacrum contains five vertebrae that are separate at birth, but which are fused together by adulthood to form a strong, rigid anchor for the pelvic bones. Lower down, the coccyx or tailbone contains four vertebrae that fuse during the first few years of life. The coccyx provides attachments for the muscles of the buttocks and the pelvic floor.

Head movement

The first two cervical vertbrae, the atlas and the axis, sit directly under the skull and interlock with each other to allow you to move your head in a side-to-side movement and to nod. They are a different shape to the remaining cervical vertebrae. They are supported by the nuchal, or neck, muscles and ligaments. They have a larger foramen in the centre to allow for the fact that the spinal cord is widest as it emerges from the brain.

ATLAS (C1)

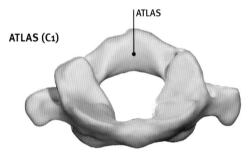

ATLAS

The first cervical vertebra (C1) is called the atlas. It has no centrum, but forms a ring of bone that supports the skull. The atlas allows the head to nod up and down on top of the spinal column.

AXIS (C2)

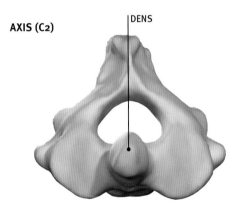

DENS

The second cervical vertebra (C2) is called the axis. It has a small broad centrum, and a small process (dens) that projects from the body, against the rear wall of the vertebral foramen of C1 to form a pivot that allows side-to-side movement. The joint is held in place by the transverse ligament.

Thorax

Your ribcage forms part of what is called the axial skeleton. As well as supporting your upper body, the ribcage encloses your thoracic cavity, protecting the vital organs in your chest (your heart, lungs and major blood vessels); it also plays an important role in your breathing mechanism (see pages 110–117). Your lower ribs protect the organs in your upper abdominal cavity (your liver, spleen and stomach).

The thoracic cavity is separated from the abdominal cavity by a sheet of muscular tissue called the diaphragm (see page 117).

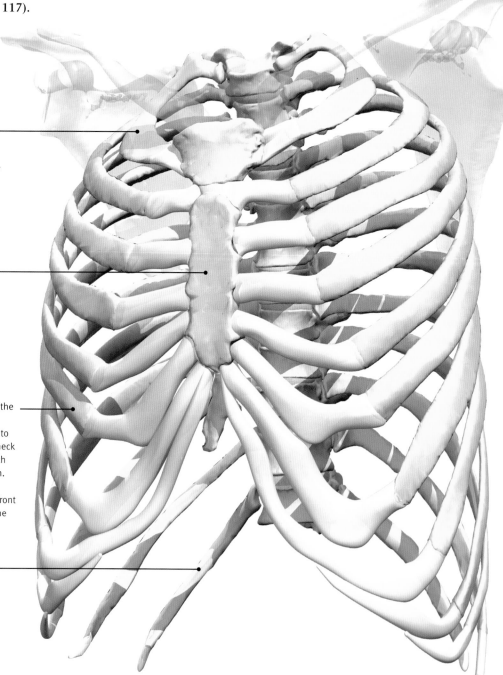

FIRST RIB is short, flat and broad, and its head and tubercle form joints with the first thoracic vertebra (T1). Its neck attaches to the costo-transverse ligaments, which firmly connect the rib to T1. The front of the rib is attached to the 1st costal cartilage, which joins to the manubrium of the sternum

STERNUM (BREAST BONE) at the front of the ribcage is made up of three bones: the upper manubrium, the middle body and the lower xiphoid cartilage (also known as the xiphisternum). The xiphoid process is made of cartilage during childhood, and turns into bone (that is, it becomes 'ossified') by adulthood

SIXTH RIB is a typical rib. Its head joins with the fifth thoracic vertebra (T5) above, the sixth thoracic vertebra (T6) below, and it attaches to the intervertebral disc between the two. Its neck attaches to costo-transverse ligaments, which firmly connect the rib to the vertebral column. The point where the rib shaft starts to curve forwards and twists is called the angle. The front edge of the rib attaches to the sternum via the 6th costal cartilage

TWELFTH RIB is unusual. It has a head but no neck, tubercle or angle. The head is attached to the middle of the twelfth thoracic vertebra (T12), and the floating front end has a protective cap of cartilage

Ribs

The upper seven pairs of ribs are each joined directly to a thoracic vertebra and to the sternum by strips of costochondral cartilage. They are known as the true ribs. The first pair of ribs connects with the manubrium; the second pair connects with the notch between the manubrium and the sternum; the third to sixth pairs connect with the body of the sternum; and the seventh pair connects with the notch between the body and the xiphoid process.

The eighth, ninth and tenth ribs also connect to the costal cartilage at the front, but this cartilage then connects to the rib above, not to the sternum. These are known as the false ribs.

The eleventh and twelfth pairs of ribs do not form any connections at the front and are thus called the floating ribs.

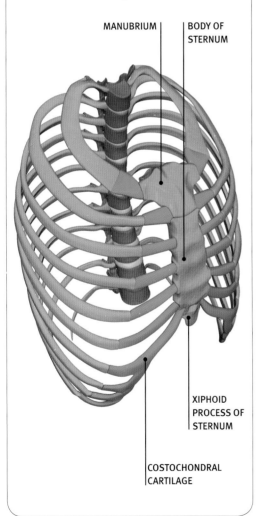

MANUBRIUM

BODY OF STERNUM

XIPHOID PROCESS OF STERNUM

COSTOCHONDRAL CARTILAGE

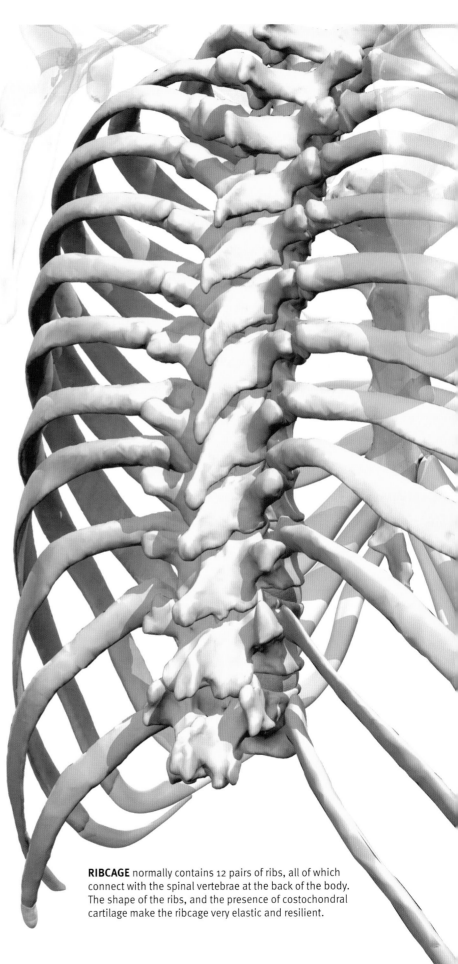

RIBCAGE normally contains 12 pairs of ribs, all of which connect with the spinal vertebrae at the back of the body. The shape of the ribs, and the presence of costochondral cartilage make the ribcage very elastic and resilient.

Shoulder and upper limbs

The upper limbs form part of your appendicular skeleton. They attach to the axial skeleton via your pectoral girdle – the ring of bone made up of your clavicles (collar bones) and scapulae (singular: scapula), or shoulder blades, on each side.

BODY FACT

Movement

- Your shoulder has a greater range of movement than any other joint in the body.
- The shoulder is referred to as a multiaxial joint, which means your arm can move in more than two planes. It can move up and down, to the side, backwards and forwards and can also rotate to swing in a circle.
- Your arm span is usually similar to your height.

Elbow joint

The elbow is a hinge joint between the humerus, ulna and radius. It is capable of two types of movement: extension and flexion (up and down) and pronation and supination (side to side).

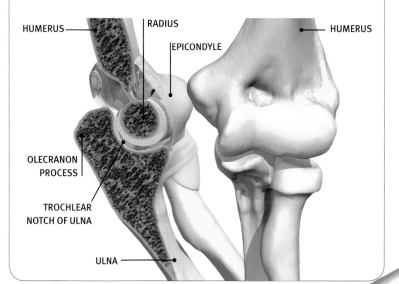

HUMERUS

RADIUS

EPICONDYLE

HUMERUS

OLECRANON PROCESS

TROCHLEAR NOTCH OF ULNA

ULNA

WRIST JOINT

RADIUS extends from the elbow to the wrist, on the same side as the thumb (lateral, or outside of the forearm). The head is a circular disc that forms a joint with the humerus, above, and the ulna on the inside. At the wrist, the radius forms a joint with the scaphoid and lunate bones

ULNA runs from the elbow to the wrist, on the same side as the little finger (medial, or inside of the forearm). The upper end has a hook-like projection called the trochlear notch, which forms a hinge joint with the humerus. The back of the trochlear notch is the tip of the elbow. Beside the trochlear notch is the radial notch, which forms a pivot joint (see page 36) with the head of the radius. The gap between the ulna and the wrist is filled with a triangular disc of cartilage

HUMERUS is the largest and longest bone in the upper limb. The rounded head of the hurmerus articulates medially with the glenoid cavity of the scapula. The lower end of the humerus has two curved areas, called distal (meaning farthest away from the body) condyles. The lateral (outside) distal condyle forms a joint with the radius. The medial (inside) distal condyle forms a hinge joint (see page 37) with the ulna

CLAVICLE connects with the manubrium of the sternum at the front, and with one of the scapulae at the back

SHOULDER JOINT

ELBOW JOINT

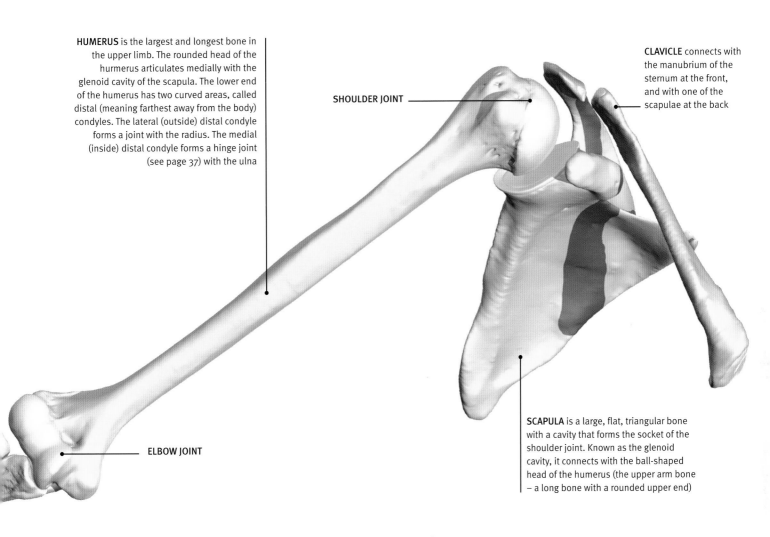

SCAPULA is a large, flat, triangular bone with a cavity that forms the socket of the shoulder joint. Known as the glenoid cavity, it connects with the ball-shaped head of the humerus (the upper arm bone – a long bone with a rounded upper end)

Shoulder joint

The shoulder, or glenohumeral, joint is a ball-and-socket joint (see page 37) in which the head of the humerus articulates with the glenoid cavity of the scapula.

Like other moveable joints, the shoulder joint is bound together by strong ligaments, and is lined with a synovial membrane that secretes lubricating synovial fluid.

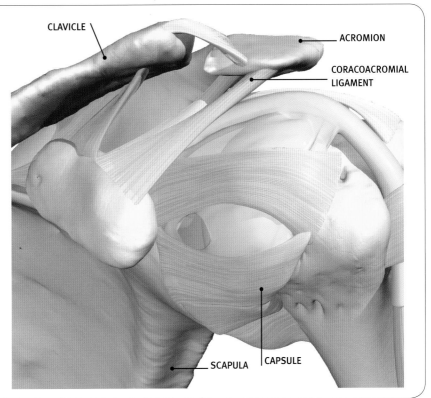

CLAVICLE

ACROMION

CORACOACROMIAL LIGAMENT

SCAPULA

CAPSULE

Pelvis and lower limbs

Your lower limbs form part of your appendicular skeleton. They are attached to your axial skeleton via your pelvic girdle – a ring of bone made up of the sacrum and coccyx at the back, and the hip bones on each side.

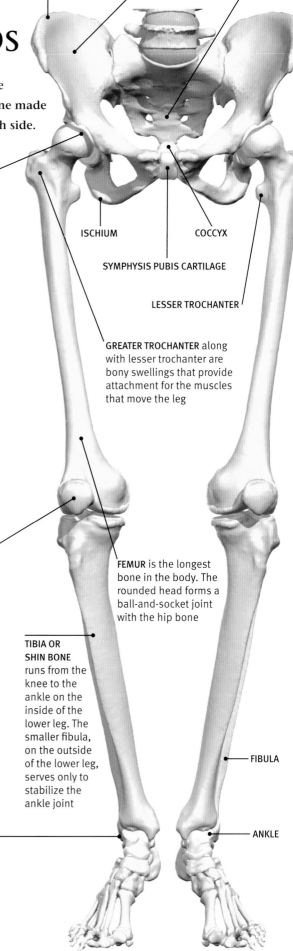

ILIAC CREST ILIUM SACRUM

ISCHIUM COCCYX

SYMPHYSIS PUBIS CARTILAGE

LESSER TROCHANTER

GREATER TROCHANTER along with lesser trochanter are bony swellings that provide attachment for the muscles that move the leg

FEMUR is the longest bone in the body. The rounded head forms a ball-and-socket joint with the hip bone

TIBIA OR SHIN BONE runs from the knee to the ankle on the inside of the lower leg. The smaller fibula, on the outside of the lower leg, serves only to stabilize the ankle joint

FIBULA

ANKLE

HIP JOINT

This is a ball-and-socket joint that connects the head of the femur (the ball) to the acetabulum of the pelvic bone (socket). It is extremely strong and stable because of the massive capsule, which encloses the femoral head and neck and keeps the ball in its socket. The acetabulum contains a rim of fibrous cartilage, the acetabular labrum, and the capsule is thickened to form three ligaments while other ligaments cross the joint to improve stabilization.

The hip has a wide range of movement: flexion, extension, adduction, abduction and rotation.

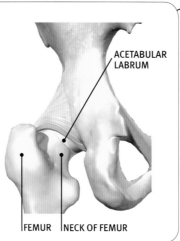

ACETABULAR LABRUM

FEMUR NECK OF FEMUR

KNEE JOINT

Your knee is a hinge joint between the upper end of the tibia (shin bone), the lower end of the femur (thigh bone) and the patella (knee bone) at the front. Strong fibrous bands of tissue hold the knee joint together, including the collateral ligaments at the sides, plus two cruciate (crossed) ligaments inside the joint itself. These maintain stability and allow the joint to bend while stopping the ends of the bones from moving excessively back and forth or from side to side. The knee is lined with a synovial membrane that secretes a thick, cushioning synovial fluid.

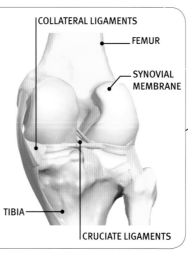

COLLATERAL LIGAMENTS

FEMUR

SYNOVIAL MEMBRANE

TIBIA

CRUCIATE LIGAMENTS

ANKLE JOINT

Also known as the talocrural joint, this is a hinge joint formed by articulations (touching points) between the tibia, fibula and talus. The primary weightbearing articulation is the tibiotalar joint, between the distal tibia and the trochlea of the talus.

The ankle joint allows limited dorsiflexion and plantar flexion (ankle extension).

The front and back of the ankle capsule are thin, but the medial and lateral parts are thick, reinforced by stout ligaments. The malleoli ligaments prevent the ankle bones from sliding from side to side.

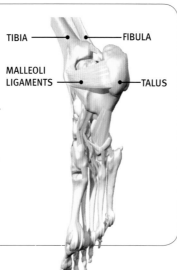

TIBIA FIBULA

MALLEOLI LIGAMENTS TALUS

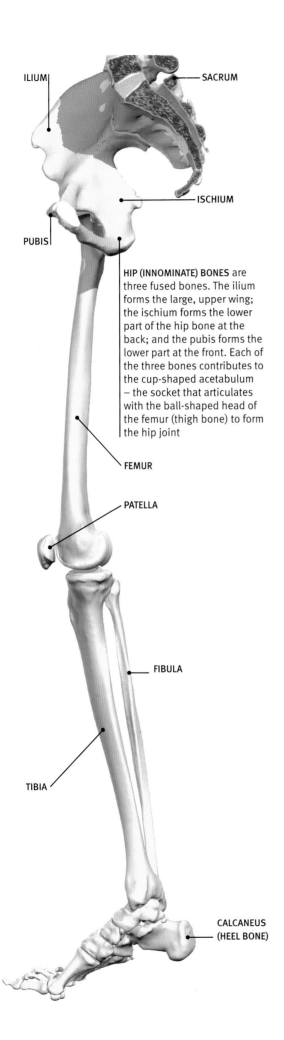

ILIUM

SACRUM

ISCHIUM

PUBIS

HIP (INNOMINATE) BONES are three fused bones. The ilium forms the large, upper wing; the ischium forms the lower part of the hip bone at the back; and the pubis forms the lower part at the front. Each of the three bones contributes to the cup-shaped acetabulum – the socket that articulates with the ball-shaped head of the femur (thigh bone) to form the hip joint

FEMUR

PATELLA

FIBULA

TIBIA

CALCANEUS (HEEL BONE)

Female pelvis

The pelvis is formed by the hip bones, sacrum and coccyx and connects the lower limbs to the axial skeleton. A disc of cartilage called the symphysis pubis separates the left and right pubic bones. At the joint where the sacrum and ilium meet, there is limited movement. The pelvis is designed to protect the bladder, a portion of the reproductive organs and part of the large intestine. It forms the fixed axis of the birth canal in females. The male (shown opposite) and female pelvises differ in shape in a number of ways.

Most noticeably, the female pelvis is lighter, wider and more shallow, and the pelvic inlet and outlets are larger and rounder. This shape of the pelvis is better at allowing a baby to pass through during childbirth.

Each ilium is less sloped, so the bony prominences you can feel at the front (the anterior superior iliac spines) are wider apart.

The female sacrum is shorter, wider and less curved and the coccyx is more flexible. The hip sockets are smaller and point more towards the front. The female pubic angle is broader compared with the sharper male angle.

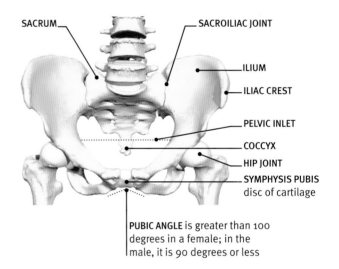

SACRUM

SACROILIAC JOINT

ILIUM

ILIAC CREST

PELVIC INLET

COCCYX

HIP JOINT

SYMPHYSIS PUBIS disc of cartilage

PUBIC ANGLE is greater than 100 degrees in a female; in the male, it is 90 degrees or less

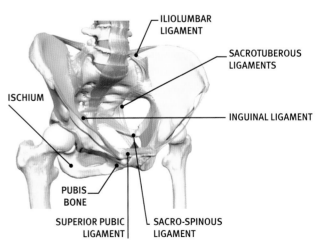

ILIOLUMBAR LIGAMENT

SACROTUBEROUS LIGAMENTS

ISCHIUM

INGUINAL LIGAMENT

PUBIS BONE

SUPERIOR PUBIC LIGAMENT

SACRO-SPINOUS LIGAMENT

PELVIC LIGAMENTS support the bones of the pelvic girdle. Throughout pregnancy the ligaments soften to allow for the birth of the baby.

Hands and feet

The many bones in your hands and feet are divided into three groups: those in the main joint (the wrist or ankle), those in the flat of the hand or foot (palm or sole) and those in the fingers and toes.

HANDS

Each of your hands contains 27 bones: eight bones in the wrist (carpus), five metacarpals in the palm and 14 phalanges (singular: phalanx) in the fingers and thumb.

OPPOSABLE THUMB

This opposable thumb, made possible by the carpometacarpal joint, means the human hand can grasp objects and is very important in terms of human evolution.

CARPAL BONES form gliding joints (see page 36) that give the wrist a good range of movement. There are eight in the wrist and they are arranged in two rows.

BODY FACT

Amazing bones

- More than half of the bones in your body (106 out of 206) are found in your hands and feet.
- Additional sesamoid bones can form inside the tendons in the hands and feet to protect the pressure points. Two are usually found beneath the head of the first metatarsal bone in the foot. They often also develop in the thumb.
- The thumbs and big toes have only two phalanges, while the other fingers and toes have three.
- Each of your hands has 14 knuckles – joints formed between the metacarpals and phalanges (metacarpophalangeal joints), and between the phalanges themselves (interphalangeal joints). These give the hand great flexibility.
- Your feet are among the hardest-working parts of your body, carrying your weight for an average of 5,000 steps a day – over 80,000 miles during your lifetime.

THE FIRST CARPOMETACARPAL JOINT is the only saddle joint (see page 36) in the body. It is formed by the first metacarpal and the first phalanx of the thumb. This allows the thumb to oppose, or turn back against, the finger.

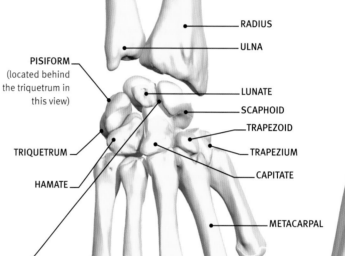

FRONT VIEW OF LEFT HAND

RADIUS

ULNA

PISIFORM
(located behind the triquetrum in this view)

LUNATE

SCAPHOID

TRAPEZOID

TRIQUETRUM

TRAPEZIUM

HAMATE

CAPITATE

METACARPAL

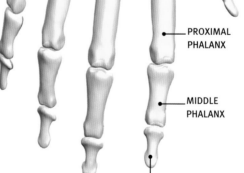

PROXIMAL PHALANX

MIDDLE PHALANX

DISTAL PHALANX

FOOT

Each of your feet contains 26 bones: seven tarsal bones in the ankle (tarsus), five metatarsals in the body of the foot and 14 phalanges in the toes.

JOINTS OF THE FOOT

There are four groups. The first two are gliding joints permitting limited sliding and twisting movements – the intertarsal and tarsometatarsal joints. The other two are ellipsoidal joints that allow flexion and extension – the metatarsophalangeal and interphalangeal joints.

ANKLE

This has seven tarsal bones. These are the talus (which forms the ankle joint with the tibia and fibula), the calcaneus (heel bone), the navicular, cuboid and first, second and third cuneiforms.

Arches of the foot

The bones and joints that give your foot flexibility are arranged into arches to support your body's weight. There are three arches in the foot. The medial longitudinal arch is the highest and most important, and is made up of the calcaneus, talus, navicular, cuneiforms and the first three metatarsals. The lateral longitudinal arch, which is lower and flatter, is formed from the calcaneus, cuboid and the fourth and fifth metatarsals. The transverse (crosswise) arch is made from the cuneiforms, the cuboid and the base of each metatarsal.

THE MEDIAL LONGITUDINAL ARCH OF THE FOOT is maintained by the shape of the bones, by strong ligaments and by the action of muscles and tendons.

RIGHT FOOT FROM ABOVE

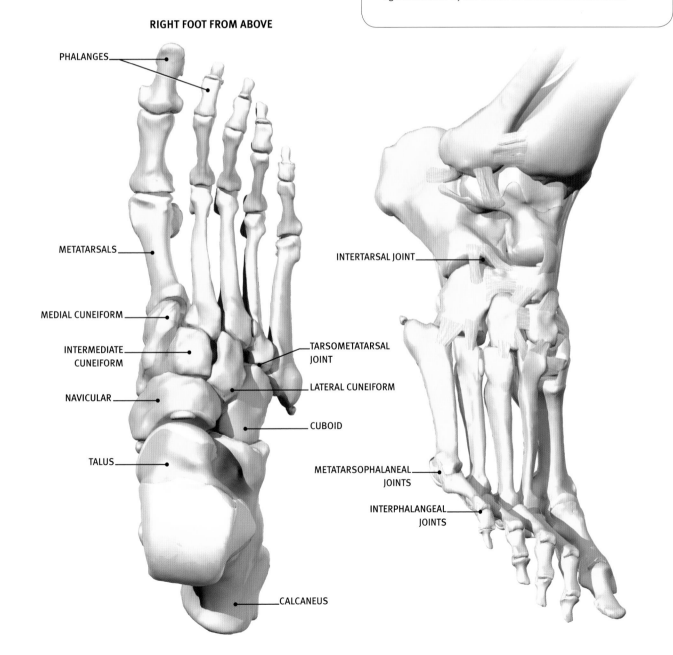

PHALANGES

METATARSALS

MEDIAL CUNEIFORM

INTERMEDIATE CUNEIFORM

NAVICULAR

TALUS

CALCANEUS

TARSOMETATARSAL JOINT

LATERAL CUNEIFORM

CUBOID

INTERTARSAL JOINT

METATARSOPHALANEAL JOINTS

INTERPHALANGEAL JOINTS

MUSCULAR SYSTEM

CRUCIAL CARDIAC MUSCLE
Found only in the heart, this muscle type is not under conscious control. It begins to function quite soon in the developing fetus, making rapid rhythmical contractions that pump blood around the body.

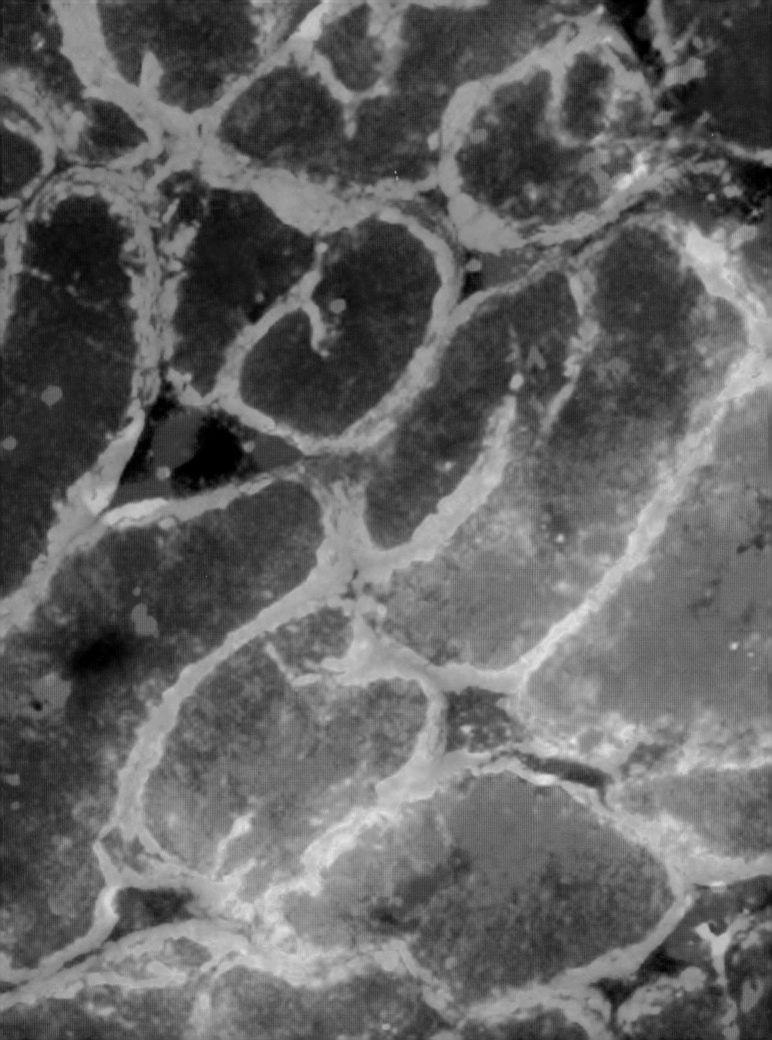

Major muscles

Your body contains somewhere
around 650 voluntary skeletal muscles.
Many are hidden deep inside your
body, others lie just under the outer,
superficial layer of muscle.

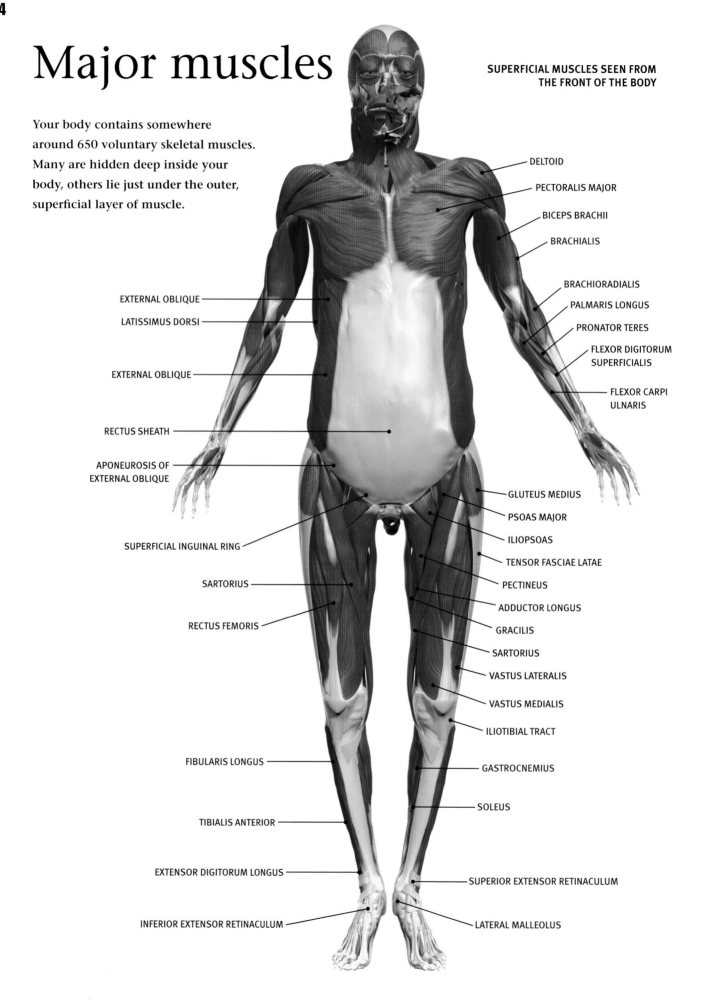

DELTOID

PECTORALIS MAJOR

BICEPS BRACHII

BRACHIALIS

BRACHIORADIALIS

PALMARIS LONGUS

PRONATOR TERES

FLEXOR DIGITORUM
SUPERFICIALIS

FLEXOR CARPI
ULNARIS

EXTERNAL OBLIQUE

LATISSIMUS DORSI

EXTERNAL OBLIQUE

RECTUS SHEATH

APONEUROSIS OF
EXTERNAL OBLIQUE

GLUTEUS MEDIUS

PSOAS MAJOR

ILIOPSOAS

TENSOR FASCIAE LATAE

PECTINEUS

ADDUCTOR LONGUS

GRACILIS

SARTORIUS

VASTUS LATERALIS

VASTUS MEDIALIS

ILIOTIBIAL TRACT

SUPERFICIAL INGUINAL RING

SARTORIUS

RECTUS FEMORIS

FIBULARIS LONGUS

GASTROCNEMIUS

SOLEUS

TIBIALIS ANTERIOR

EXTENSOR DIGITORUM LONGUS

SUPERIOR EXTENSOR RETINACULUM

INFERIOR EXTENSOR RETINACULUM

LATERAL MALLEOLUS

**SUPERFICIAL MUSCLES SEEN FROM
THE BACK OF THE BODY**

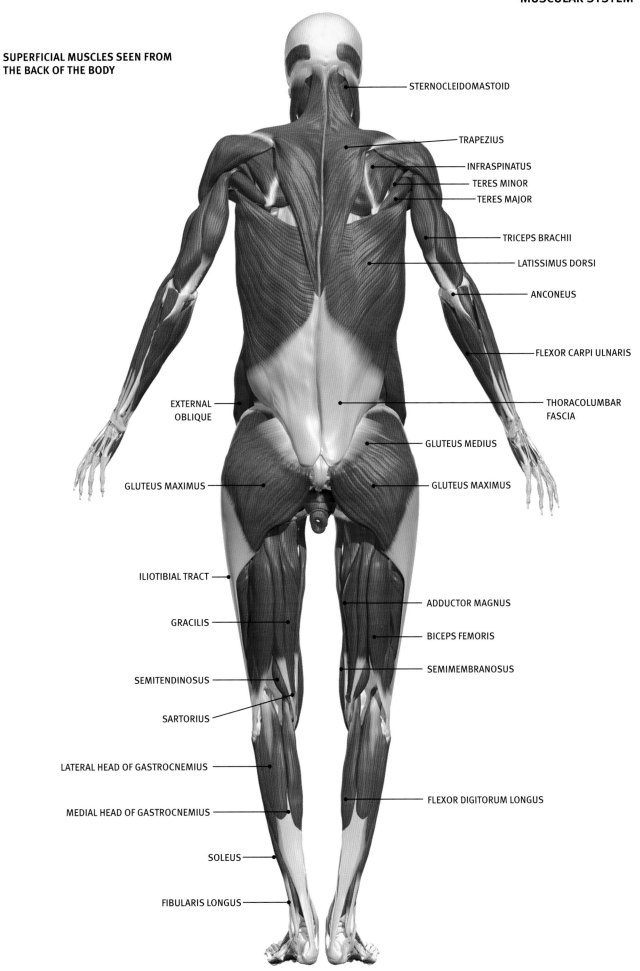

STERNOCLEIDOMASTOID

TRAPEZIUS

INFRASPINATUS

TERES MINOR

TERES MAJOR

TRICEPS BRACHII

LATISSIMUS DORSI

ANCONEUS

FLEXOR CARPI ULNARIS

THORACOLUMBAR
FASCIA

GLUTEUS MEDIUS

GLUTEUS MAXIMUS

ADDUCTOR MAGNUS

BICEPS FEMORIS

SEMIMEMBRANOSUS

FLEXOR DIGITORUM LONGUS

EXTERNAL
OBLIQUE

GLUTEUS MAXIMUS

ILIOTIBIAL TRACT

GRACILIS

SEMITENDINOSUS

SARTORIUS

LATERAL HEAD OF GASTROCNEMIUS

MEDIAL HEAD OF GASTROCNEMIUS

SOLEUS

FIBULARIS LONGUS

Muscle tissue

Without your muscles there would be no movement. Your muscle cells are designed to contract and move parts of your body. They are divided into three main types, shown below.

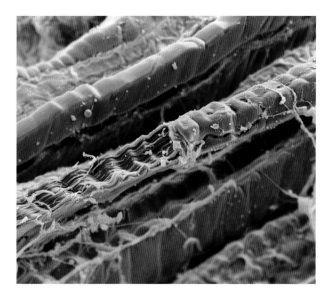

SKELETAL MUSCLE Skeletal muscle cells have a striped appearance under a microscope and are therefore referred to as striated. They have multiple cell nuclei that are located around the periphery of the cell. Attached to your skeleton at one or more ends, this muscle type is mostly under your voluntary control, though some is controlled automatically, such as in the chest wall, that expand and contract when you breathe.

Muscle matters

- You have at least 650 skeletal muscles in your body – the exact number depends on whether certain muscles are classed as individual muscles or as part of a more complex muscle.
- Most of your muscles have an identical 'twin' on the other side of the body.
- Muscle usually makes up between 30 per cent and 50 per cent of body weight, depending on your level of fitness and the size of your body's fat stores.
- Smooth muscle is unstriated (non-striped) because the actin and myosin filaments are arranged in a different pattern from those in striated muscle cells.
- If voluntary muscle contracts involuntarily, it may cause cramp.
- Muscle contraction and relaxation is fast enough to allow you to drum your fingers on a table many times per second.
- Your muscles are always slightly contracted to offset the effects of gravity.

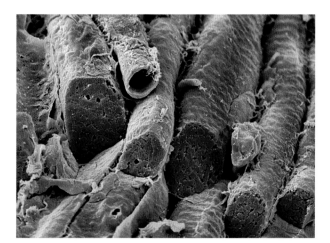

SMOOTH MUSCLE Non-striated and non-voluntary, smooth muscle performs automatic tasks regulated by your nervous system, such as dilating and constricting your arteries. Smooth muscle cells are shaped like spindles; they narrow almost to a point at both ends and have only one nucleus, in the cell's centre.

CARDIAC (HEART) MUSCLE Striated, but non-voluntary, cardiac muscle has branched fibres designed to transmit electric messages quickly and efficiently. This ensures the heart beats in an ordered fashion. It has one or two nuclei in the centre of each cell.

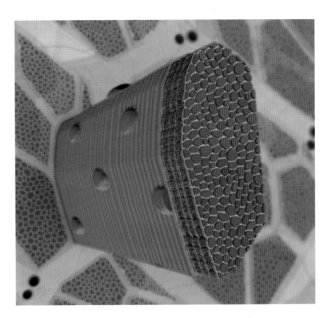

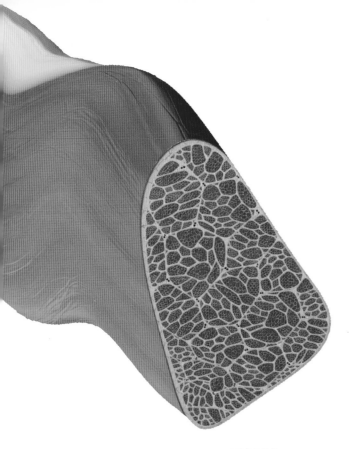

SKELETAL MUSCLE ANATOMY

A single myofibre (muscle cell), seen above and right increasingly magnified, rises out of a bundle of myofibres. Multiple cell nuclei are located at the outside while a sheath of connective tissue surrounds it. This sheath electrically insulates each muscle cell allowing selective contraction of muscle fibres so the strength and extent of the muscle contraction can be fully controlled. All the connective tissue sheaths converge at both ends of the muscle to form the tendons. A single myofibre contains many myofibrils – these are cylindrical bundles of contractile proteins. Each myofibril contains two different contractile proteins known as myofilaments, which overlap each other. The thicker myofilaments contain a protein called myosin, and the thinner myofilaments contain a protein called actin. The interlocking myofilaments of actin and myosin give the myofibrils a striped, or striated, appearance.

MUSCLE CONTRACTION AND RELAXATION

When a muscle cell (myofibre) burns glucose or fatty acids as a fuel, it releases both heat and energy. This energy is used to power the movement of actin and myosin filaments, which slide past each other to shorten the cell, a process initiated by the nervous system. A motor impulse from a motor nerve causes the release of calcium, which floods into the muscle cells and triggers myofibril contraction. This shortens the muscle, and moves the part of the body to which the muscle is attached. As the actin and myosin filaments slide apart again, the muscle relaxes.

Skeletal muscle types

The majority of the body's muscles are skeletal; they connect the bones and through contraction, shortening and thickening, enable the body to move. Skeletal muscles can be classified according to their shape. Each has three main zones: a middle belly; a sinewy origin, where it connects to a bone at one end; and a sinewy insertion at the other end, where it connects to another bone, ligament or similar structure, such as the fibrous linea alba in the midline of the abdomen (see page 60).

TRIANGULAR MUSCLES have fibres that form a fan shape, converging to a common site of attachment to achieve the maximum force of contraction. The temporalis muscle in the temple is a good example.

A 3-HEADED PARALLEL MUSCLE splits at the end nearest the body to attach at three different places. The triceps brachii is one example.

QUADRATE MUSCLE forms a flat, four-sided shape, such as the pronator quadratus in the forearm.

FUSIFORM MUSCLES have fibres that run parallel to each other in the middle, before converging to form a tendon at one or both ends. These muscles can contract over a long distance, and have excellent staying power, but are not very strong. Muscles that move the fingers, such as the flexor pollicis longus, are of this type.

PENNATE MUSCLES have very dense fibres, making them strong, but they tend to become fatigued quickly. Pennate means 'feather-like' and the muscle fibres look rather like the vane of a feather. These come in three types: unipennate, such as the extensor digitorum longus in the shin; bipennate such as the rectus femoris in the leg; and multipennate such as the deltoid muscle in the shoulder.

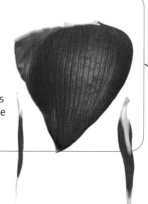

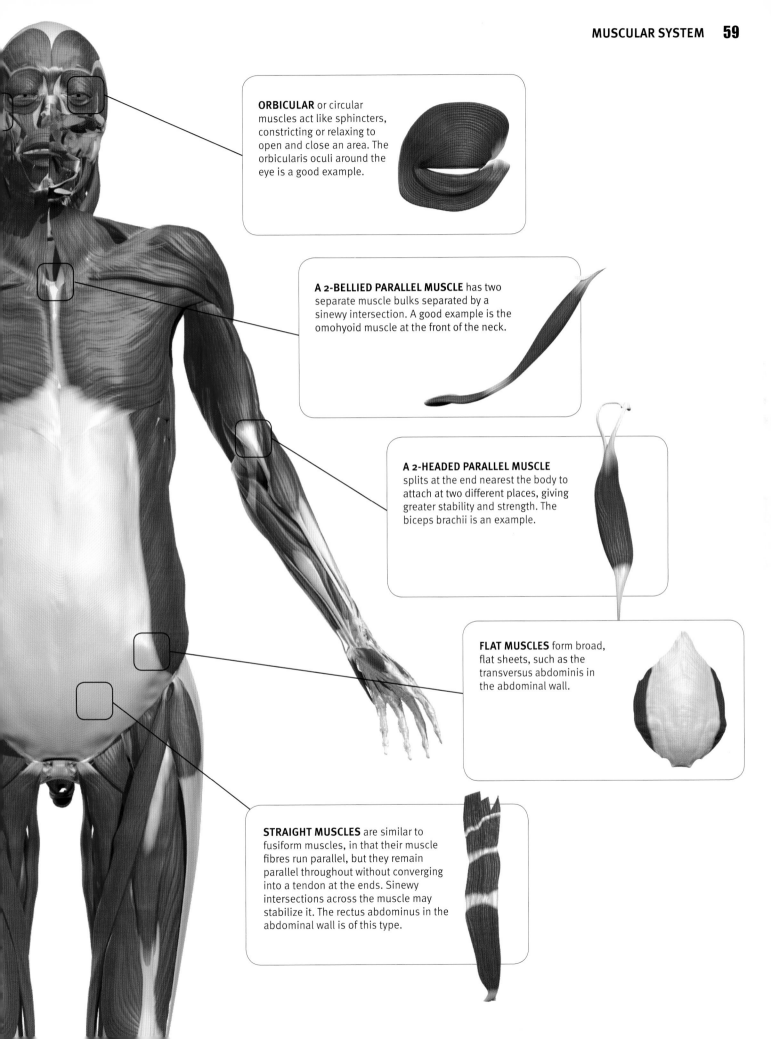

ORBICULAR or circular muscles act like sphincters, constricting or relaxing to open and close an area. The orbicularis oculi around the eye is a good example.

A 2-BELLIED PARALLEL MUSCLE has two separate muscle bulks separated by a sinewy intersection. A good example is the omohyoid muscle at the front of the neck.

A 2-HEADED PARALLEL MUSCLE splits at the end nearest the body to attach at two different places, giving greater stability and strength. The biceps brachii is an example.

FLAT MUSCLES form broad, flat sheets, such as the transversus abdominis in the abdominal wall.

STRAIGHT MUSCLES are similar to fusiform muscles, in that their muscle fibres run parallel, but they remain parallel throughout without converging into a tendon at the ends. Sinewy intersections across the muscle may stabilize it. The rectus abdominus in the abdominal wall is of this type.

Muscle types continued

The large white expanse of connective tissue at the front of the abdomen is an example of what is called an 'aponeurosis'. This is similar to a large, flat tendon, and is an extension of the connective tissue that separates muscle fibres from one another. The midline of this aponeurosis, known as the linea alba (literally, a 'white line') is a fibrous structure where the aponeuroses of all the abdominal wall muscles fuse together.

Muscles in the abdominal wall form three layers in which the fibres run in different directions.

TOPMOST LAYER

This is made up of the external oblique (obliquus externus) muscle. Its fibres slope downwards and forwards from the edges of the 5th–12th ribs, to the front half of the iliac crest, and to the linea alba. This muscle contracts to pull the ribcage down. The aponeurosis at the front of the abdomen is that of the obliquus externus muscle.

MIDDLE LAYER

This consists of the internal oblique (obliquus internus) muscle. Its fibres run at an angle from the iliac crest and inguinal ligament, up to insert in the linea alba. This muscle contracts to rotate the ribcage and pull it down towards the hip and lower back on the same side (side bend). It also pulls the ribcage down during breathing.

LOWEST LAYER

This is made up of the transverse abdominal (transversus abdominis) muscle. Its fibres run horizontally across the belly, from the inguinal ligament, iliac crest (the upper part of the hip bone) and lower six costal cartilages to insert in the midline linea alba. This is one of the core body muscles, compressing the intestinal organs and helping to stabilize the thorax and the abdominal and pelvic organs.

Muscles work in pairs

When muscles contract, they can only pull, not push. Muscles therefore have to work in pairs, so that contraction of one muscle moves the joint in one direction, while contraction of the other muscle moves it in the opposite direction. For example, contraction of the biceps bends the elbow, while contraction of the triceps straightens the elbow out again, as the biceps relaxes.

During something called isotonic contraction, such as when picking up a weight, a muscle produces a steady pull as it gets shorter. For example, when holding a weight above the ground, the muscle stays the same length. Instead of contracting, it produces a strong pulling force, or tension.

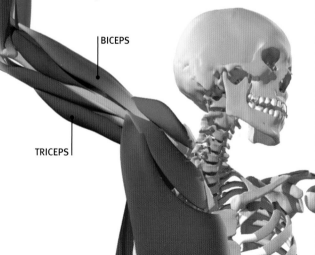

BICEPS

TRICEPS

Ligaments and tendons

While the ligaments join the bones together, it is tendons that attach skeletal muscles to bone.

Tendons are made up of connective tissues that form when the collagen fibres coating each individual muscle cell (see page 24) come together. Collagen fibres from the tendons pass right through the outer bone membrane (the periosteum) to become firmly embedded within the outer cortex of a bone. This forms a strong attachment that is not easily pulled away. Tendons are elastic and act like a spring to help modify forces produced during movement.

The thickest and strongest tendon in the body is the calcaneal (Achilles) tendon, which connects the calf muscles to the heel. The Achilles tendon can support more than 10 times your body weight during sprinting.

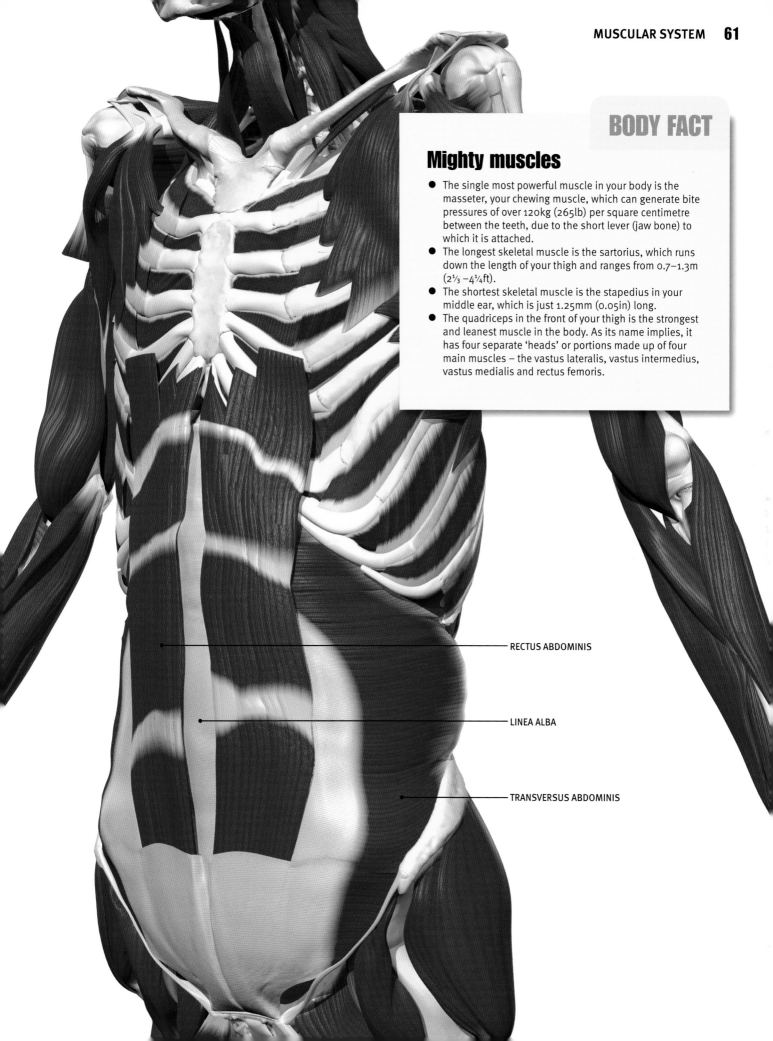

BODY FACT

Mighty muscles

- The single most powerful muscle in your body is the masseter, your chewing muscle, which can generate bite pressures of over 120kg (265lb) per square centimetre between the teeth, due to the short lever (jaw bone) to which it is attached.
- The longest skeletal muscle is the sartorius, which runs down the length of your thigh and ranges from 0.7–1.3m (2⅓ –4¼ft).
- The shortest skeletal muscle is the stapedius in your middle ear, which is just 1.25mm (0.05in) long.
- The quadriceps in the front of your thigh is the strongest and leanest muscle in the body. As its name implies, it has four separate 'heads' or portions made up of four main muscles – the vastus lateralis, vastus intermedius, vastus medialis and rectus femoris.

RECTUS ABDOMINIS

LINEA ALBA

TRANSVERSUS ABDOMINIS

Muscles of the head and neck

The muscles of the head and neck are responsible for moving the face and its associated structures, tongue and larynx. They are therefore responsible for verbal and nonverbal communication through sound and facial expression, feeding involving chewing and swallowing (see pages 157 and 160) and controlling the eyes (see page 65). Sound is produced in the throat by the action of the muscles. Some muscles involved with sight and hearing originate on the skull, along with those associated with the ear and hearing. The anterior muscles of the neck are concerned primarily with altering the position of the larynx, hyoid bone and floor of the mouth.

Throat

Extending from the back of the nasal cavity to the top of the trachea and the entrance to the oesophagus, the throat is made up of two cavities or spaces, the larynx and pharynx. The pharynx is the larger of the two cavities (12–14cm/4.5–5.5in). It has three divisions: nasopharynx, oropharynx and laryngopharynx. The shorter larynx, commonly known as the 'voice box' sits in front and houses the vocal cords (see page 113).

BODY FACT

Face facts

Your facial muscles are made of striated voluntary muscle fibres, like skeletal (striated) muscle, but there are subtle differences between them.

- The facial muscles attach to connective tissues in your skin.
- Your facial muscles are relatively flat, difficult to separate from surrounding connective tissue and share fibres so they attach to one another.
- The facial muscles do not work in pairs with opposite actions – facial tissue returns to its original position due to its tone rather than the action of an opposing muscle.
- Where muscles do produce opposite expressions, such as raising or lowering the corners of the lip, they are attached to different bones and tissues, rather than to the same bones, as with skeletal muscles working in pairs.
- The risorius muscle does not attach to bone, but arises from connective tissue (fascia) overlying the parotid salivary gland, and inserts into the skin at the angle of the mouth.
- Anatomists recently discovered that the risorius muscle is found in only two-thirds of the population; other muscles can perform its role if it is missing.

MUSCLES OF FACIAL EXPRESSION

The human face can produce a number of expressions, such as anger, contempt, disgust, fear, happiness, sadness, confusion and surprise. Facial expressions are produced by the contraction or relaxation of around 40 facial, or mimetic, muscles. Other skull muscles, such as the masseter, the chewing muscle, also contribute towards expressions. Interestingly, the left side of the face is usually more expressive than the right. The muscles that enable facial expression are highly developed for communication skills. A tiny degree of muscle contraction can produce facial skin movement, changing your expression.

OCCIPITOFRONTALIS draws back the scalp to wrinkle the forehead when frowning, and raises the eyebrows when surprised

ORBICULARIS OCULI closes the eyelids and allows you to wink

NASALIS compresses the nasal cartilage when flaring the nostrils

LEVATOR LABII SUPERIORIS lifts the upper lip during smiling

ORBICULARIS ORIS purses the lips, such as when whistling or blowing

BUCCINATOR pulls back the angle of the mouth and flattens the cheek when sucking in your cheeks

DEPRESSOR LABII INFERIORIS depresses the lower lip

DEPRESSOR ANGULI ORIS draws down the corner of the mouth when showing doubt

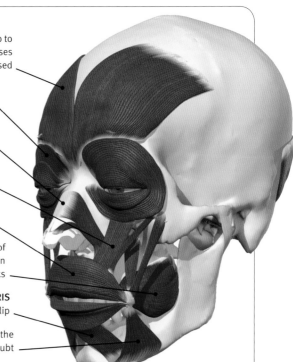

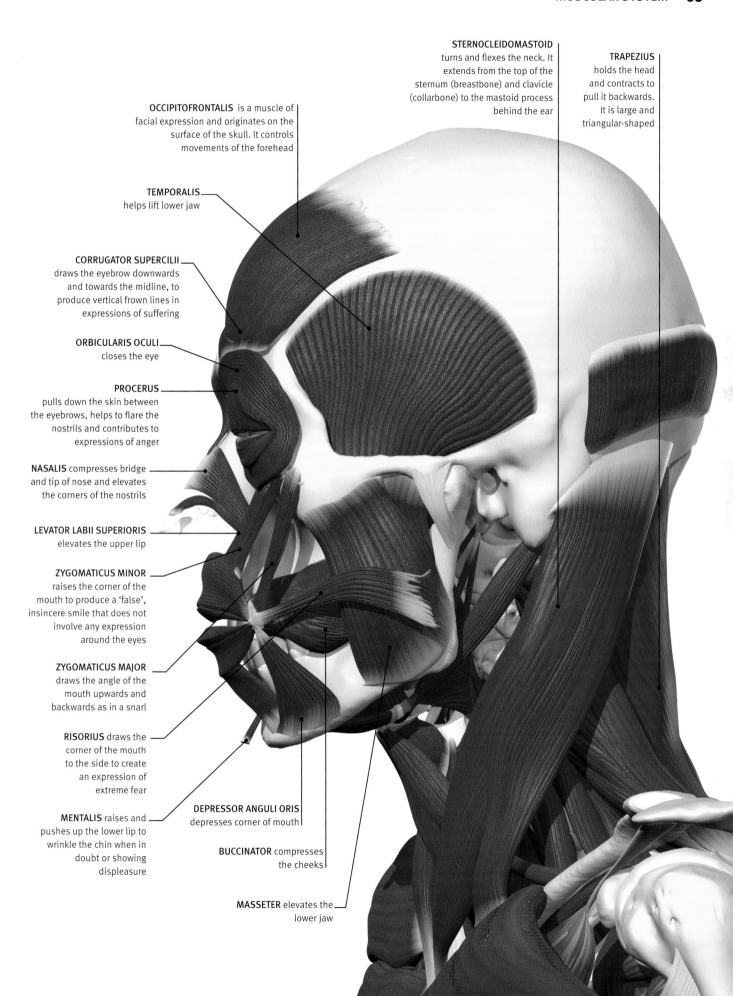

STERNOCLEIDOMASTOID turns and flexes the neck. It extends from the top of the sternum (breastbone) and clavicle (collarbone) to the mastoid process behind the ear

TRAPEZIUS holds the head and contracts to pull it backwards. It is large and triangular-shaped

OCCIPITOFRONTALIS is a muscle of facial expression and originates on the surface of the skull. It controls movements of the forehead

TEMPORALIS helps lift lower jaw

CORRUGATOR SUPERCILII draws the eyebrow downwards and towards the midline, to produce vertical frown lines in expressions of suffering

ORBICULARIS OCULI closes the eye

PROCERUS pulls down the skin between the eyebrows, helps to flare the nostrils and contributes to expressions of anger

NASALIS compresses bridge and tip of nose and elevates the corners of the nostrils

LEVATOR LABII SUPERIORIS elevates the upper lip

ZYGOMATICUS MINOR raises the corner of the mouth to produce a 'false', insincere smile that does not involve any expression around the eyes

ZYGOMATICUS MAJOR draws the angle of the mouth upwards and backwards as in a snarl

RISORIUS draws the corner of the mouth to the side to create an expression of extreme fear

MENTALIS raises and pushes up the lower lip to wrinkle the chin when in doubt or showing displeasure

DEPRESSOR ANGULI ORIS depresses corner of mouth

BUCCINATOR compresses the cheeks

MASSETER elevates the lower jaw

Muscles moving the eye

Each eye has six muscles – superior and inferior recti, which enable the eye to look sideways; the superior and inferior oblique permit the eye to roll and to look up and sideways, and the medial and lateral rectus enable the eye to look up and down. These muscles work in three opposing pairs to enable a full range of external eye movements (see page 98). If the muscles act asymmetrically, then a squint can arise. The intrinsic eye muscles, which are inside the eyeball, control the diameter of the pupil and the shape of the lens.

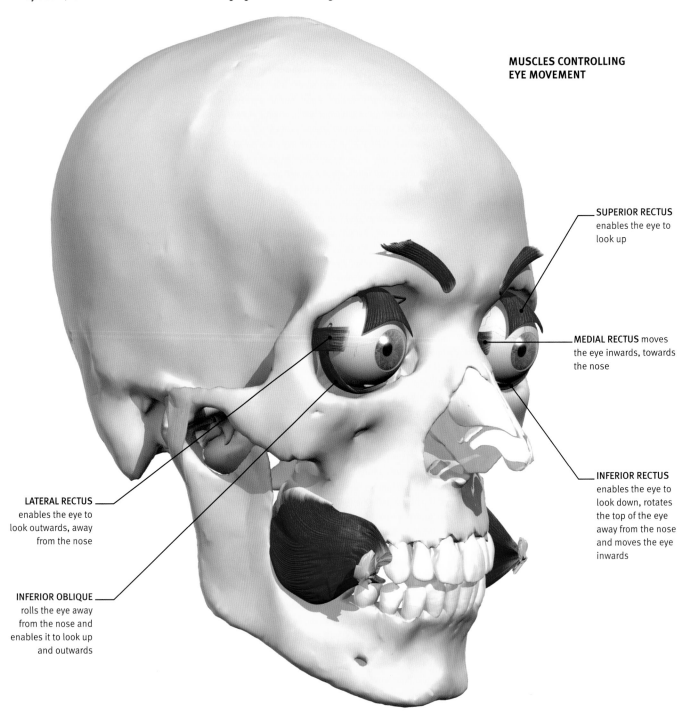

**MUSCLES CONTROLLING
EYE MOVEMENT**

SUPERIOR RECTUS
enables the eye to
look up

MEDIAL RECTUS moves
the eye inwards, towards
the nose

INFERIOR RECTUS
enables the eye to
look down, rotates
the top of the eye
away from the nose
and moves the eye
inwards

LATERAL RECTUS
enables the eye to
look outwards, away
from the nose

INFERIOR OBLIQUE
rolls the eye away
from the nose and
enables it to look up
and outwards

MUSCLES IN EYE MOVEMENT

The outer sclera of each eye is attached to six extraocular muscles that allow the eyeball to move within its socket. Each muscle is supplied with nerves ('innervated') by a specific cranial nerve (see pages 89–91). Movements are coordinated so that both eyes look in the same direction.

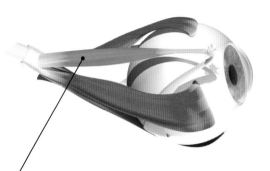

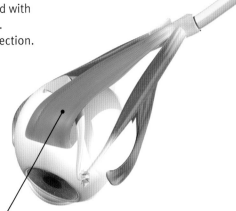

SUPERIOR OBLIQUE MUSCLE rotates the top of the eye towards the nose, moves the eye downwards and outwards; this muscle passes through the trochlea – a ring-like tendon that acts as a pulley – before it attaches to the eye.

SUPERIOR RECTUS MUSCLE moves the eye upwards, rotates the top of the eye towards the top of the nose and moves the eye inwards.

LATERAL RECTUS MUSCLE moves the eye outwards, away from the nose.

MEDIAL RECTUS MUSCLE moves the eye inwards, towards the nose.

INFERIOR OBLIQUE MUSCLE rotates the top of the eye away from the nose, moves the eye upwards and outwards.

INFERIOR RECTUS MUSCLE moves the eye downwards, rotates the top of the eye away from the nose and moves the eye inwards.

NERVOUS SYSTEM

NECESSARY NEURONS
The building blocks of the entire nervous system, over 100 billion nerve cells or neurons, make up the brain and are found elsewhere in the body, particularly in the spinal cord and its branching nerves.

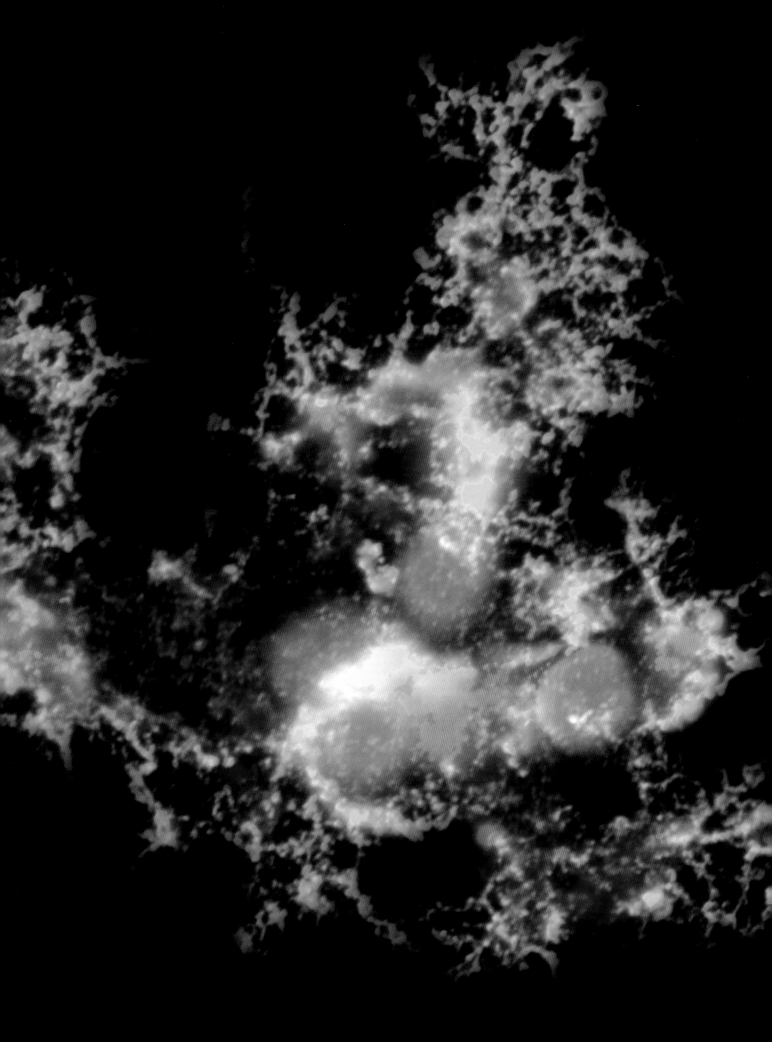

Nervous system

Your nervous system controls and coordinates all the body systems. It is divided into two main parts: the central nervous system (CNS), which consists of the brain and spinal cord, and the peripheral nervous system, which forms a network throughout the rest of the body.

The nervous system forms a communication network made up of all the neural tissue in the body. Structurally, the central nervous system (CNS) is the brain and spinal cord. The peripheral nervous system includes all neural tissue outside the CNS. It delivers sensory information to the brain and spinal cord and carries commands back to the body.

CENTRAL NERVOUS SYSTEM

The brain and spinal cord are complex organs that include not just neural tissue, but also blood vessels and connective tissue cells. They are responsible for integrating, processing and coordinating sensory data and motor commands. For example when you trip, your nervous system integrates information about your balance, and the position of your limbs, and in the same instant sends commands to the appropriate limbs to enable you to right yourself. In addition, it is also the centre of higher intellectual and emotional functions.

PERIPHERAL NERVOUS SYSTEM

Nerve fibres outside the brain and spinal cord are collected together in bundles along with blood vessels and connective tissue. Fibres from many different nerve cells (neurons) run together to form the cable-like peripheral nerves. Cables come together to form nerve trunks, which branch into smaller and smaller nerves. Some nerves group together to form a nerve plexus (see page 92). One group of nerves is connected directly to the brain: the cranial nerves. Those attached to the spinal cord are known as spinal nerves.

The peripheral nervous system sends information from your body back to your brain via the sensory nerves in the spinal cord. Your brain processes this information and sends back any necessary instructions via the motor nerves. There are two main divisions:
SOMATIC NERVOUS SYSTEM carries sensory and motor information to and from receptors all over the body. It is mainly concerned with your skeletal muscles, co-ordinating voluntary movements, for example, and instructing your skeletal muscles during walking.
AUTONOMIC NERVOUS SYSTEM (visceral nervous system) regulates the activity of all involuntary, or automatic, functions. It controls your organs and blood vessels and regulates your heart rate and blood pressure. Part of this system, the enteric nervous system, is embedded in the lining of your gastrointestinal tract and regulates the process of digestion.

The autonomic nervous system supplies two opposing types of instruction. For example, one instruction may cause a blood vessel to constrict, but another opposing instruction is needed to cause the blood vessel to dilate. These opposing instructions are carried in two sub-divisions of the autonomic nervous system, referred to as the sympathetic nervous system and the parasympathetic nervous system. The sympathetic nervous system tends to speed things up, preparing the body for action such as the fight-or-flight stress response (see page 150), while the parasympathetic system tends to slow things down, regulating general maintenance responses while the body is at rest.

A group of nerve cell bodies located outside the brain and spinal cord is known as a ganglion (plural: ganglia). Nerve cell bodies within the sympathetic nervous system form a chain of ganglia along each side of the vertebral column.

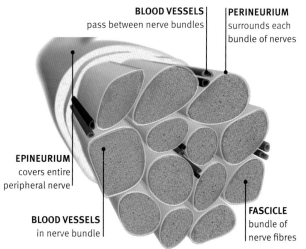

Anatomy of a peripheral nerve

CROSS SECTION OF PERIPHERAL NERVE

BLOOD VESSELS
pass between nerve bundles

PERINEURIUM
surrounds each bundle of nerves

EPINEURIUM
covers entire peripheral nerve

BLOOD VESSELS
in nerve bundle

FASCICLE
bundle of nerve fibres

A peripheral nerve is made up of lots of nerve axons grouped together in bundles called fascicles, which contain blood vessels. Each fascicle is surrounded by an insulating sheath called a perineurium. Bundles of fascicles are, in turn, wrapped up in an outer insulating layer called the epineurium, which also contains blood vessels and fat.

All of the cell bodies of the neurons within a peripheral nerve cluster together to form a swelling called a ganglion.

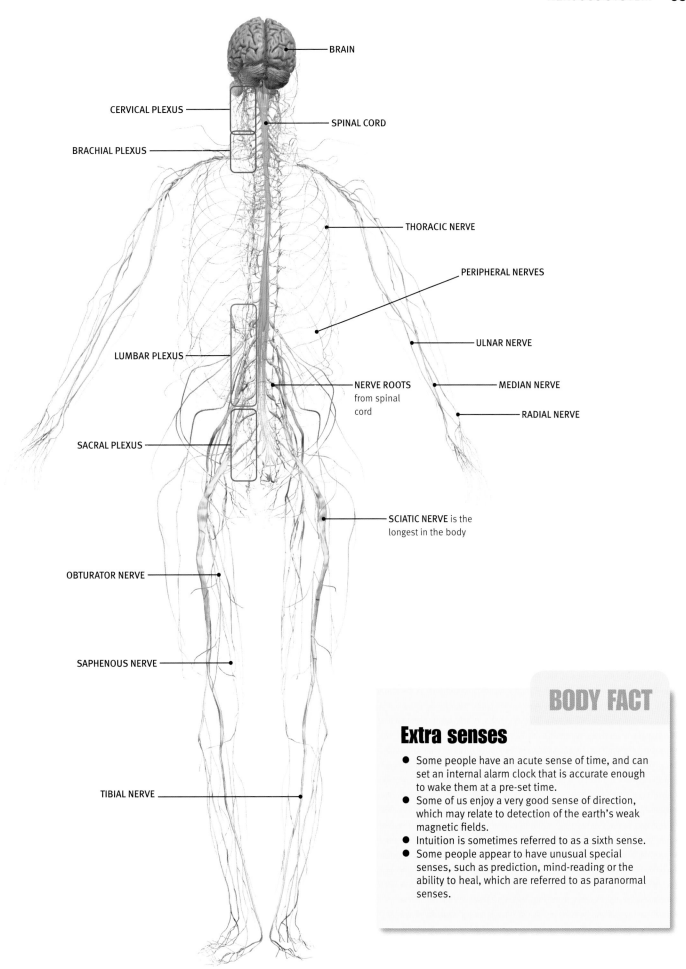

BRAIN

CERVICAL PLEXUS

SPINAL CORD

BRACHIAL PLEXUS

THORACIC NERVE

PERIPHERAL NERVES

ULNAR NERVE

LUMBAR PLEXUS

NERVE ROOTS
from spinal
cord

MEDIAN NERVE

RADIAL NERVE

SACRAL PLEXUS

SCIATIC NERVE is the
longest in the body

OBTURATOR NERVE

SAPHENOUS NERVE

TIBIAL NERVE

BODY FACT

Extra senses

- Some people have an acute sense of time, and can set an internal alarm clock that is accurate enough to wake them at a pre-set time.
- Some of us enjoy a very good sense of direction, which may relate to detection of the earth's weak magnetic fields.
- Intuition is sometimes referred to as a sixth sense.
- Some people appear to have unusual special senses, such as prediction, mind-reading or the ability to heal, which are referred to as paranormal senses.

Nerve cells

Your nervous system contains specialized cells, called neurons, which are capable of generating and transmitting electrical impulses. There are three main types of nerve cells: motor, sensory and association neurons. Motor neurons carry signals from the central nervous system to the body to control voluntary and involuntary actions. Sensory neurons gather information and carry signals back to your brain and spinal cord from all over the body. Association neurons act as connectors between different neurons, passing signals between them so that information can be sorted, compared and processed.

STRUCTURE OF A NEURON

Each neuron has a cell body that contains the nucleus, plus a number of projections known as dendrites and axons. Dendrites are short, and allow a neuron to communicate with other nerve cells close by. Axons are longer and carry signals away from the cell body, allowing the neuron to communicate with nerves or muscle cells farther afield.

TYPES OF NEURON

Neurons are classified according to the number of axons and dendrites they possess:

● a unipolar neuron has one short process that immediately divides into two very long processes. These are found in the dorsal root ganglia of the spinal nerves (see page 92) and send sensory information to the central nervous system.
● a bipolar neuron has a single axon and a single dendrite; these are rare and mainly found in the eye and ear.
● a multipolar neuron has a single long axon plus varying numbers of dendrites; these are the most common type.

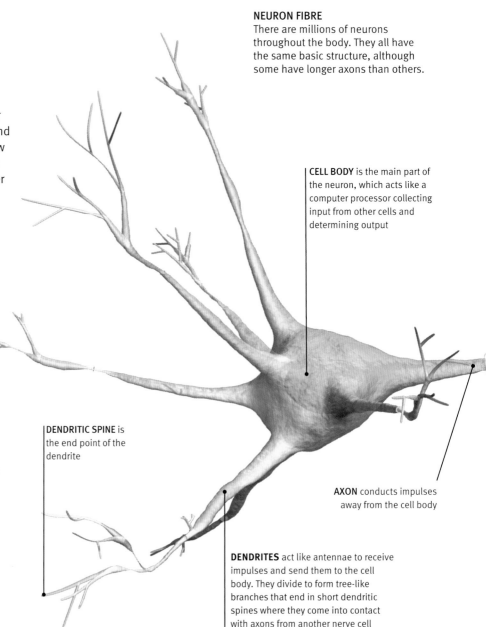

NEURON FIBRE
There are millions of neurons throughout the body. They all have the same basic structure, although some have longer axons than others.

CELL BODY is the main part of the neuron, which acts like a computer processor collecting input from other cells and determining output

DENDRITIC SPINE is the end point of the dendrite

AXON conducts impulses away from the cell body

DENDRITES act like antennae to receive impulses and send them to the cell body. They divide to form tree-like branches that end in short dendritic spines where they come into contact with axons from another nerve cell

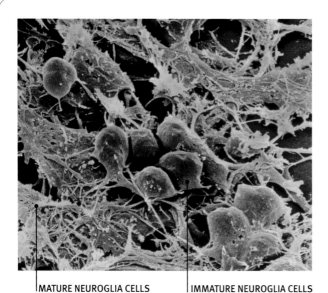

MATURE NEUROGLIA CELLS   IMMATURE NEUROGLIA CELLS

Neuroglia

These are special 'glue' cells that support and nourish the nerve fibres, rather than transmit signals. They make up about half the mass of the central nervous sytem. Your brain contains between 10 and 50 times more neuroglia than neurons. There are several different types of neuroglia cell:

- Oligodendrocytes insulate axons within the central nervous system.
- Astrocytes, the most common type, remove communication chemicals (neurotransmitters) released by neurons.
- Satellite cells coat the outer surface of the peripheral neurons to maintain a constant environment.
- Radial cells act like scaffolding to guide migrating neurons within an embryo.
- Schwann cells insulate the peripheral nerve axons and form the myelin sheath.
- Ependymal cells line the fluid-filled spaces within the brain.

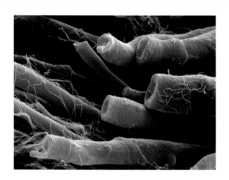

MYELIN SHEATH This is a layer of tissue that surrounds the axons of larger peripheral nerve cells. It is formed by neuroglial (Schwann) cells that wrap around the axon rather like beads on a string.

AXON TERMINALS form at the axon and subdivide into several smaller axonal terminals

SYNAPTIC TERMINALS occur where a neuron makes contact with other nerve, muscle or gland cells

MYELIN SHEATH

NODES OF RANVIER are the gaps between each neuroglia cell in the myelin sheath along the axon

BODY FACT

Neurons and neuroglia at work

- The human body contains billions of neurons.
- Most of your brain cells are multipolar neurons.
- Some neurons in the central nervous system and in the retina of the eye have dendrites but no axons.
- Many neurons in your brain have axons that are only a millionth of a centimetre long as their only purpose is to send messages to neighbouring cells.
- The axons may connect with the dendrite of another nerve cell, with a cell body or occasionally end directly on the axon of another neuron (axo-axonal endings).
- Schwann cells wrap around only a small section of a single peripheral nerve axon.
- An oligodendrocyte puts out processes that can wrap around a small section of up to 50 different axons within the central nervous system.

How nerve cells communicate

Your nerve cells are specialized to generate and transmit electrical impulses. But how does it all work? Pumps in all of your cell membranes force positively charged potassium ions out of the cell, so the inside of a cell becomes negatively charged compared with the outside. This is known as the membrane potential. All of the body's cells generate a membrane potential, but it is greatest in your muscle and nerve cells, where it is between minus-70 and minus-100 millivolts (mV).

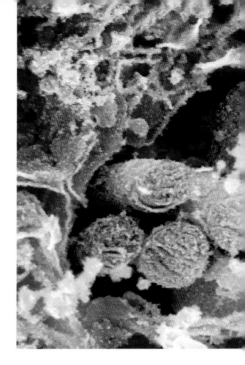

NERVE STIMULI

A neuron produces an electrical impulse only when it receives a stimulus. Stimuli may be external (for example, pressure, sound, light, smell, taste, temperature) or internal (for example, changes in hormone or salt levels).

An electrical impulse arriving at a synaptic knob triggers the release of stored neurotransmitters. These diffuse across the synapse to interact with protein receptors on the opposite membrane. This opens up pores in the receiving neuron, allowing electrically charged ions to flood in and out of the cell. If enough stimulation occurs, and enough pores are opened, the next neuron in the chain depolarizes and generates an electrical current to pass the impulse on. The image above right shows the release of neurotransmitters in the cells (yellow), and the mitochondria that supply the cell with energy (blue/yellow).

Most synapses transmit information using communication chemicals called neurotransmitters. These are made in the nerve cell body and transported down the length of the axon in microtubules.

The neurotransmitters released into the synaptic cleft are quickly taken up again and recycled, or broken down, so that the synapse is ready to respond to the next electrical signal it receives.

The axons terminate in swellings known as synaptic knobs, which act as nerve cell transmitters. The axons of larger peripheral nerve cells are coated in a fatty, myelin sheath. This is formed by neuroglial (Schwann) cells that wrap around the axon rather like beads on a string. The electrical impulse 'jumps' along the spaces (nodes of Ranvier) between the neuroglial cells to speed the rate of transmission.

On the other side of a synapse, the membrane of the second neuron thickens to form the dendritic spines that act as receivers. Information passes from one neuron to another at connection points called synapses. If the stimulus is large enough, it triggers the sudden opening of pores in the nerve cell membrane. Electrically charged ions flood in and out of the cell so that the membrane potential is momentarily reversed. Known as depolarization, this electrial charge is propagated down the nerve axon as a wave of electricity called the action potential, or nerve impulse.

TRANSMISSION BETWEEN NERVE CELLS

The electric signal in the first nerve cell causes vesicles to release their neurotransmitters into the synapse, where they diffuse across the gap to stimulate receptors on the next cell.

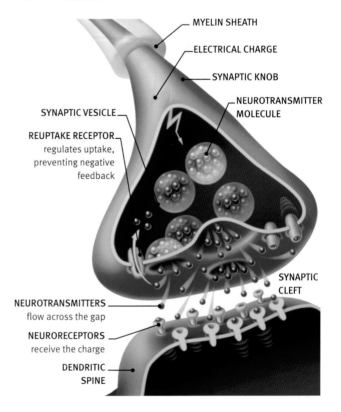

MYELIN SHEATH

ELECTRICAL CHARGE

SYNAPTIC KNOB

NEUROTRANSMITTER MOLECULE

SYNAPTIC VESICLE

REUPTAKE RECEPTOR
regulates uptake, preventing negative feedback

SYNAPTIC CLEFT

NEUROTRANSMITTERS
flow across the gap

NEURORECEPTORS
receive the charge

DENDRITIC SPINE

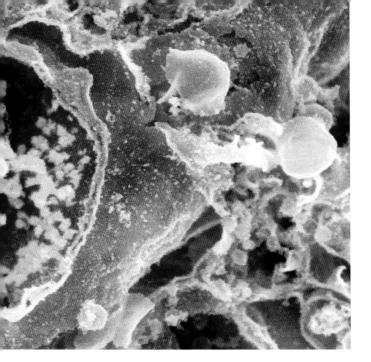

Speedy synapses

- Typical neurons make between 1,000 and 10,000 synaptic connections.
- Around 98 per cent of the synapses are between the axon of one cell and the dendritic spines of another (axodendritic synapses).
- Most of the remaining synapses form between the axon of one neuron and the cell body of another (axosomatic synapses).
- Synapses between two axons (axoaxonal synapses) are rare.
- The electrical impulse (action potential) travels down nerve axons at speeds of up to 120m (nearly 400ft) per second.

SYNAPTIC DELAY

The delay between an electric impulse arriving at a synaptic knob and the triggering of a response in the target neuron is around 0.5 milliseconds – the time it takes for enough chemicals to diffuse across the synaptic cleft. This synaptic delay means that transmission of a signal through a nerve pathway becomes slower as more and more synapses are involved.

A few synapses pass information in the form of an electrical impulse, which jumps from one neuron to the other with very little delay.

Some synapses are capable of passing messages both chemically and electrically, so there is an initial, rapid transmission of a direct electric signal, followed up with a slower chemical signal. These are known as conjoint synapses.

ONE-WAY CONDUCTION

Most synapses in the brain are chemical synapses. Although this form of transmission is slower than electrical transmission, it ensures that messages pass only in one direction from one cell to another, as neurotransmitters are stored at only one side of the synaptic cleft. This valve-like function is essential to prevent information chaos.

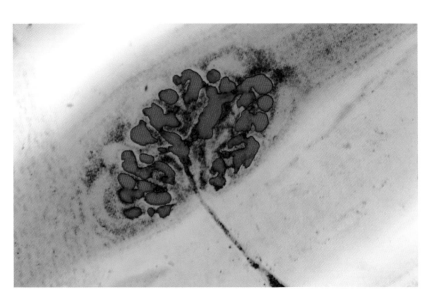

NEUROMUSCULAR JUNCTION
A special synaptic connection forms between the synaptic knob at the end of an axon and a muscle cell. This connection is known as a neuromuscular junction. An electrical impulse arriving at the neuromuscular junction is converted into a chemical signal, as occurs at most synapses between two nerve cells. When the chemical signal diffuses across the neuromuscular synaptic cleft, it triggers contraction of the connecting muscle fibre.

External views of the brain

The adult human brain weighs around 1.4kg (3lb). It contains an estimated hundred billion neurons plus up to five trillion (thousand billion) supporting glial cells (neuroglia). Over 85 per cent of your neuronal cell bodies are concentrated in the outer part of the hemispheres – this is your so-called grey matter.

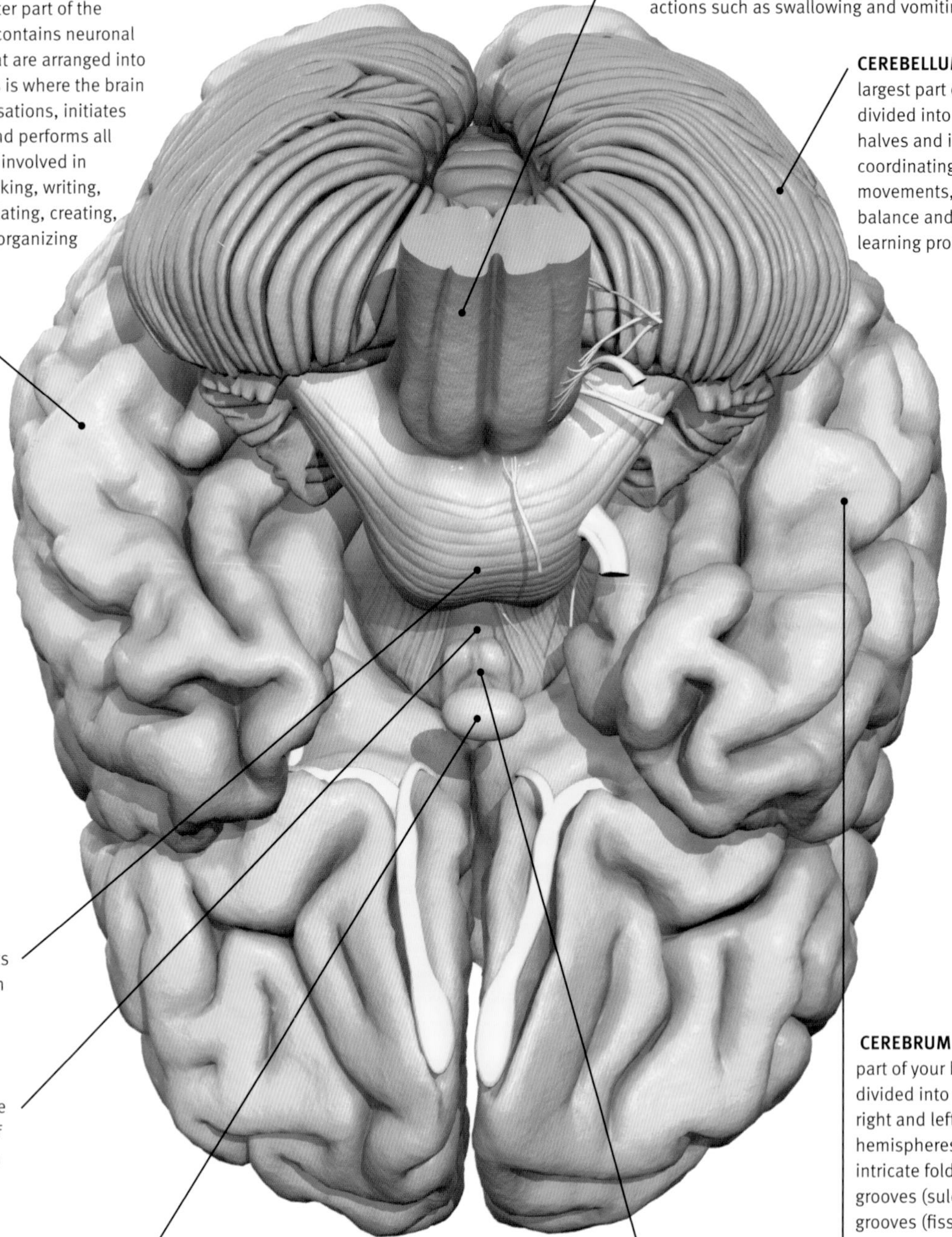

BRAINSTEM connects the brain to the spinal cord. It regulates automatic activities that are vital for survival, such as breathing, heart rate, blood pressure, sleeping and waking, as well as reflex actions such as swallowing and vomiting

CORTEX or outer part of the hemispheres contains neuronal cell bodies that are arranged into six layers. This is where the brain interprets sensations, initiates movements and performs all the processes involved in thinking, speaking, writing, singing, calculating, creating, planning and organizing

CEREBELLUM is the second largest part of the brain. It is divided into two tightly folded halves and is responsible for coordinating muscle movements, maintaining balance and helping in some learning processes

PONS connects the cerebellum to the brain stem

MID BRAIN the highest part of the brain stem

CEREBRUM is the largest part of your brain and is divided into two halves: the right and left cerebral hemispheres. These form intricate folds (gyri), small grooves (sulci) and deeper grooves (fissures) that increase the total surface area of the brain

PITUITARY GLAND

HYPOTHALAMUS

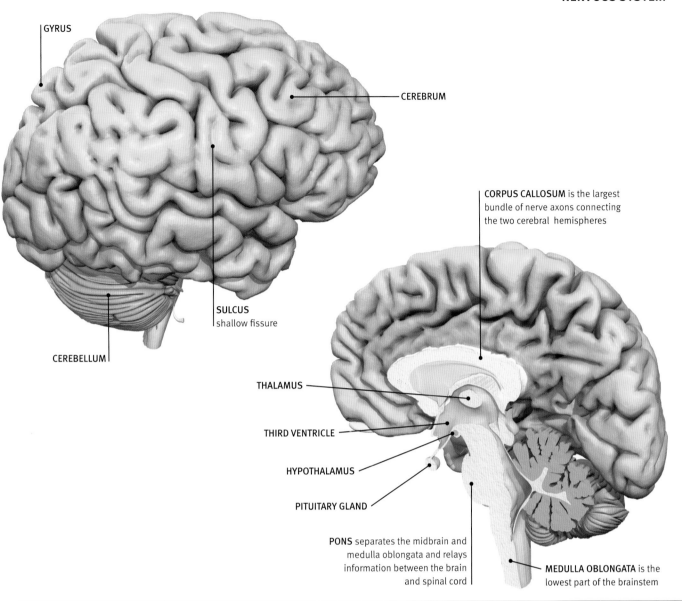

GYRUS

CEREBRUM

CORPUS CALLOSUM is the largest bundle of nerve axons connecting the two cerebral hemispheres

SULCUS
shallow fissure

CEREBELLUM

THALAMUS

THIRD VENTRICLE

HYPOTHALAMUS

PITUITARY GLAND

PONS separates the midbrain and medulla oblongata and relays information between the brain and spinal cord

MEDULLA OBLONGATA is the lowest part of the brainstem

Cerebral hemisphere

Each cerebral hemisphere is divided into four lobes. Each lobe is divided into different regions that have their own important functions.

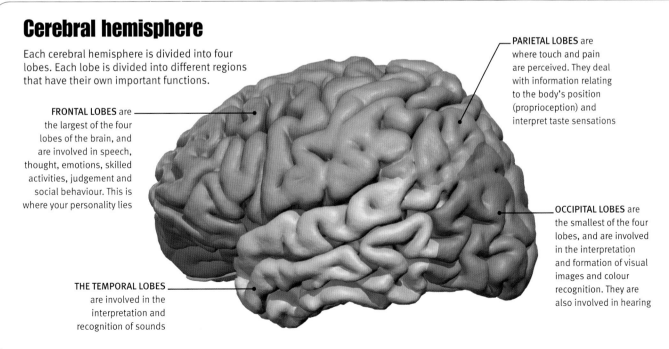

FRONTAL LOBES are the largest of the four lobes of the brain, and are involved in speech, thought, emotions, skilled activities, judgement and social behaviour. This is where your personality lies

PARIETAL LOBES are where touch and pain are perceived. They deal with information relating to the body's position (proprioception) and interpret taste sensations

OCCIPITAL LOBES are the smallest of the four lobes, and are involved in the interpretation and formation of visual images and colour recognition. They are also involved in hearing

THE TEMPORAL LOBES are involved in the interpretation and recognition of sounds

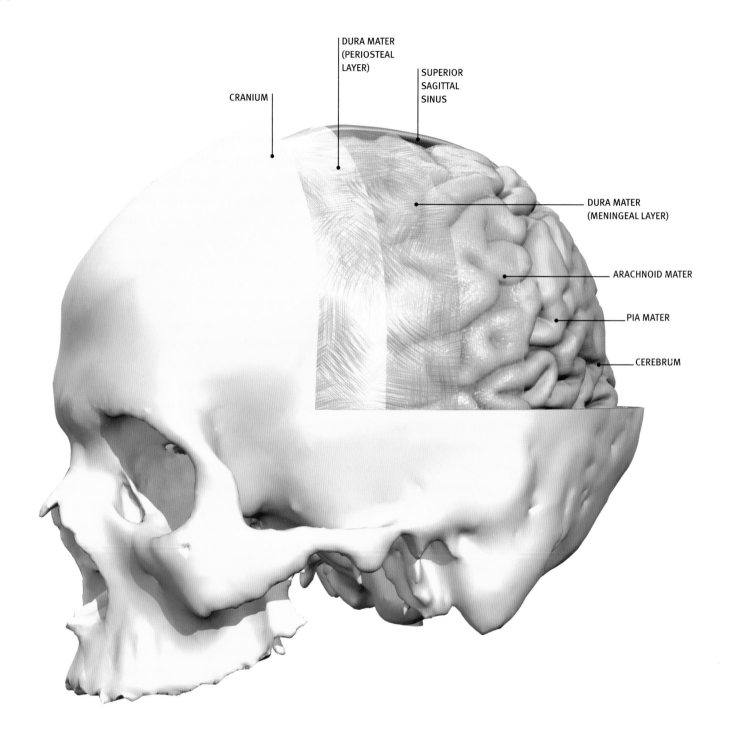

CRANIUM

DURA MATER
(PERIOSTEAL
LAYER)

SUPERIOR
SAGITTAL
SINUS

DURA MATER
(MENINGEAL LAYER)

ARACHNOID MATER

PIA MATER

CEREBRUM

MENINGES

The entire brain and spinal cord are protected by three membranes, called the meninges (singular: meninx). The meninges extend down through the opening at the base of the skull, the foramen magnum, to reach the level of the second sacral vertebra.

OUTER DURA MATER

This is made up of dense fibrous tissue. It contains two layers: the outer periosteal layer attached to the skull, and the inner meningeal layer that is loosely attached to the underlying arachnoid mater. The two layers of the dura run together throughout most of the skull. They separate where the inner layer folds into the brain to separate the two hemispheres, and to separate the cerebellum and brain stem from the occipital lobes of the cerebrum.

Where the two layers of the dura mater separate, the space between them forms large drainage channels, called dural sinuses, which take venous blood and cerebrospinal fluid away from the brain.

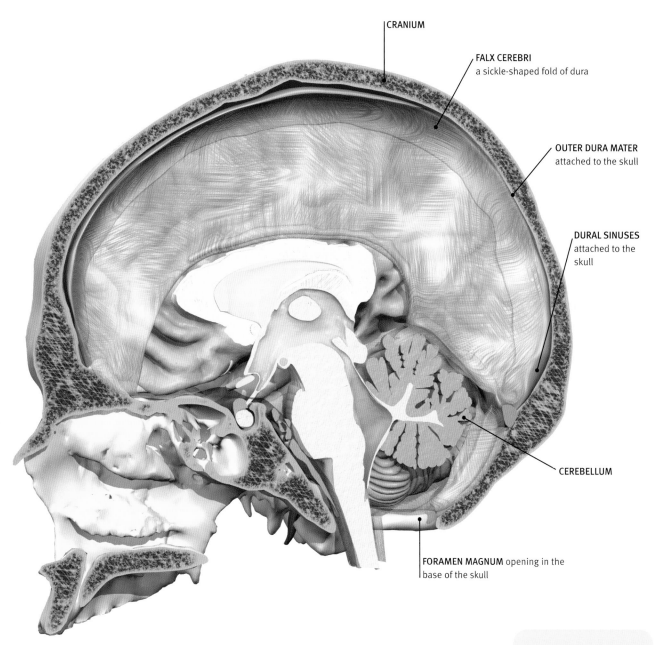

CRANIUM

FALX CEREBRI
a sickle-shaped fold of dura

OUTER DURA MATER
attached to the skull

DURAL SINUSES
attached to the
skull

CEREBELLUM

FORAMEN MAGNUM opening in the
base of the skull

MIDDLE ARACHNOID MATER

This is a thin, transparent membrane that forms a loose
layer, which helps to cushion the brain and spinal cord.

PIA MATER

The delicate inner pia mater is attached to the outer
surface of the brain and spinal cord. It closely follows the
contours of the gyri and sulci, and contains blood vessels
and capillaries that supply the brain.

BODY FACT

Brain truths

- In adults, the thickness of the grey matter in the cortex
  averages just 1.6mm (0.06in).
- The brain is the least sensitive organ in your body.
- The most sensitive parts of your brain are the meninges.
- Laid end to end, all the dendrites and axons in your
  brain would measure around 160,000 km (nearly
  100,000 miles).
- The nerve cell fibres cross over so that the right side
  of your brain controls the left side of your body and
  vice versa.

Internal views of the brain

Beneath the grey matter of your brain, which contains your neuron cell bodies, is the white matter. This is made up of axons surrounded by glial cells (neuroglia), which form their white, myelinated sheath. Large tracts of white matter link the different parts of each half of your brain (the hemispheres) to each other and to other parts of the brain.

CEREBELLUM

Embedded in the white matter are clusters of grey matter known as the basal ganglia. These include the thalamus, globus pallidus, putamen and caudate nucleus, which are involved in the control of complex movements such as walking.

The thalamus sorts, interprets and directs sensory nerve signals from the sense organs to the sensory areas of the cortex.

The internal capsule is a fan-shaped collection of myelinated axons (white matter) that connects the cerebral cortex to the brainstem and spinal cord. It carries information that controls movements in the upper and lower limbs.

The corpus callosum contains myelinated axons that connect the left and right cerebral hemispheres.

The hypothalamus is situated between the thalamus and pituitary gland. It regulates certain automatic functions such as body temperature, food intake, water and salt balance, sleep/wake cycles and secretion of some hormones. It also generates primitive emotions such as anger and fear.

PITUITARY GLAND

This small gland is protected in the sphenoid bone, hanging below the hypothalamus. It is divided into three lobes – the anterior, intermediate and posterior – and produces different peptide hormones. Secretion is regulated by messenger chemicals from the hypothalamus. Important functions of the pituitary include regulation of the thyroid gland, the ovary and testis.

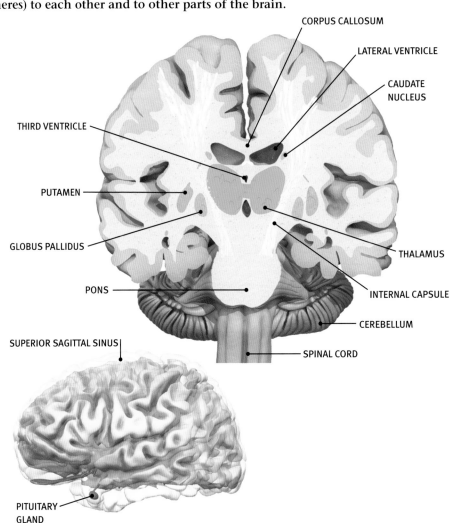

BODY FACT

The busy brain

- The arrangement of the Circle of Willis (see opposite) varies, with two out of three people having different arteries in its formation. Because it forms a circle, other arteries help to maintain blood flow to the brain if one vessel becomes blocked.
- Blood flow through the adult brain averages 1000ml (1.7 pints)/min.
- The volume of cerebrospinal fluid (CSF) averages 125–150ml (4–5 fl oz).
- Production of CSF is around 500ml (0.8 pints) a day.
- Normal CSF is crystal-clear and colourless.
- A collection of neurons within the basal ganglia, called the nucleus accumbens, acts as the brain's pleasure centre, playing a role in sexual arousal and drug 'highs'.

VENTRICLES

Your brain contains four fluid-filled cavities called ventricles. These are filled with cerebrospinal fluid. The left and right lateral ventricles each communicate with the midline third ventricle via a small gap called the interventricular foramen. The third ventricle links with the fourth ventricle via a narrow channel, the cerebral aqueduct.

CEREBROSPINAL FLUID

This is secreted by the choroid plexus of the capillaries inside each ventricle. The cerebrospinal fluid is found in the ventricles and between the pia mater and arachnoid mater meninges (see page 77). It cushions and protects the brain as well as providing it with nourishment.

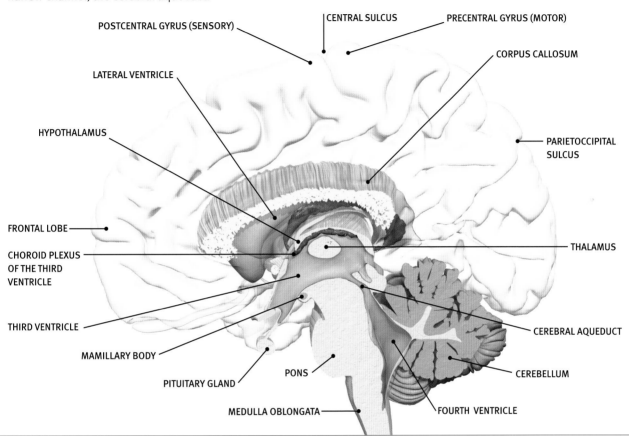

POSTCENTRAL GYRUS (SENSORY)
CENTRAL SULCUS
PRECENTRAL GYRUS (MOTOR)
CORPUS CALLOSUM
LATERAL VENTRICLE
PARIETOCCIPITAL SULCUS
HYPOTHALAMUS
FRONTAL LOBE
THALAMUS
CHOROID PLEXUS OF THE THIRD VENTRICLE
THIRD VENTRICLE
CEREBRAL AQUEDUCT
MAMILLARY BODY
CEREBELLUM
PITUITARY GLAND
PONS
MEDULLA OBLONGATA
FOURTH VENTRICLE

Blood supply to the brain

A circle of arteries, known as the Circle of Willis, supplies blood to the brain. It consists of the anterior communicating artery, the left and right anterior cerebral arteries, the left and right internal carotid arteries, the left and right posterior cerebral arteries and the left and right posterior communicating arteries. From the Circle of Willis, arteries branch out to supply the brain tissues.

Tight junctions between cells in the walls of the brain capillaries allow oxygen, glucose and water to pass through to the brain tissues, but prevent bacteria and some drugs getting through. This protective mechanism is known as the blood-brain barrier.

Blood flows back from the brain via the cerebral veins into the sinuses between the two layers of the dura mater (see page 76). Together with spent cerebrospinal fluid, blood is discharged into the internal jugular veins.

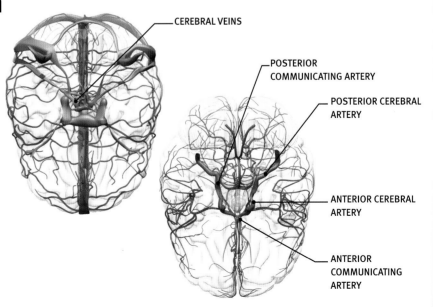

CEREBRAL VEINS
POSTERIOR COMMUNICATING ARTERY
POSTERIOR CEREBRAL ARTERY
ANTERIOR CEREBRAL ARTERY
ANTERIOR COMMUNICATING ARTERY

Brain function

Your cerebral cortex contains sensory areas, motor areas and association areas. The sensory areas receive and interpret information from the sense organs and other receptors throughout your body. Your motor areas control the skeletal muscles involved in voluntary movements, while your association areas analyze information from the sensory areas and fine-tune the instructions sent to the motor areas. The association areas are involved in thought and comprehension; they analyze experiences and interpret them in a logical and artistic way to make you fully conscious and aware.

BRAIN CONNECTIONS

Your two cerebral hemispheres communicate with each other, and the rest of your body, through bundles of nerve fibres that cross from one side of the body to the other.

The left cerebral cortex receives sensory information from the right side of the body, and sends motor information that controls movement on the right side. Similarly, the right side of the brain relates to the left side of the body.

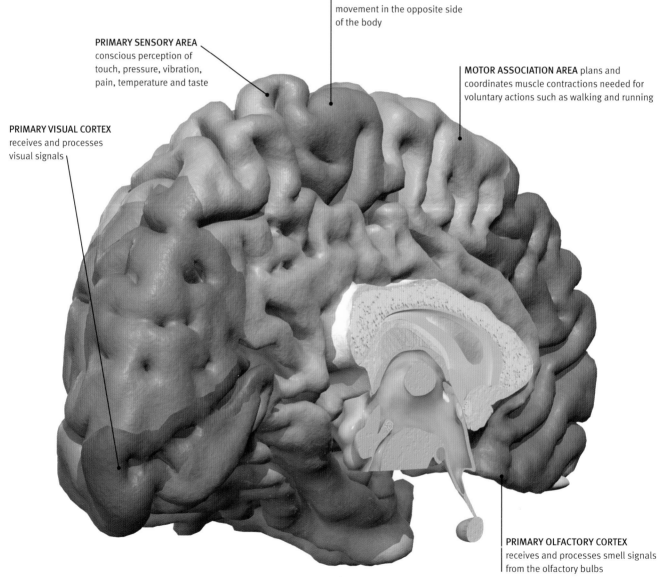

PRIMARY MOTOR AREA controls movement in the opposite side of the body

PRIMARY SENSORY AREA conscious perception of touch, pressure, vibration, pain, temperature and taste

MOTOR ASSOCIATION AREA plans and coordinates muscle contractions needed for voluntary actions such as walking and running

PRIMARY VISUAL CORTEX receives and processes visual signals

PRIMARY OLFACTORY CORTEX receives and processes smell signals from the olfactory bulbs

Boundless brain

- At birth, a baby's brain contains over 200 billion brain cells – as many stars as there are in the Milky Way.
- Each brain cell is wired to its neighbours through up to 20,000 different branches resulting in trillions of connections – more than the number of stars in all the galaxies.
- The neurons within the brain can form more possible connections than the total number of atoms in the universe.
- The two hemispheres of your brain generate different patterns of brainwave frequency and amplitude from one another.
- During meditation, profound feelings of serenity are associated with synchronization of brainwave patterns.

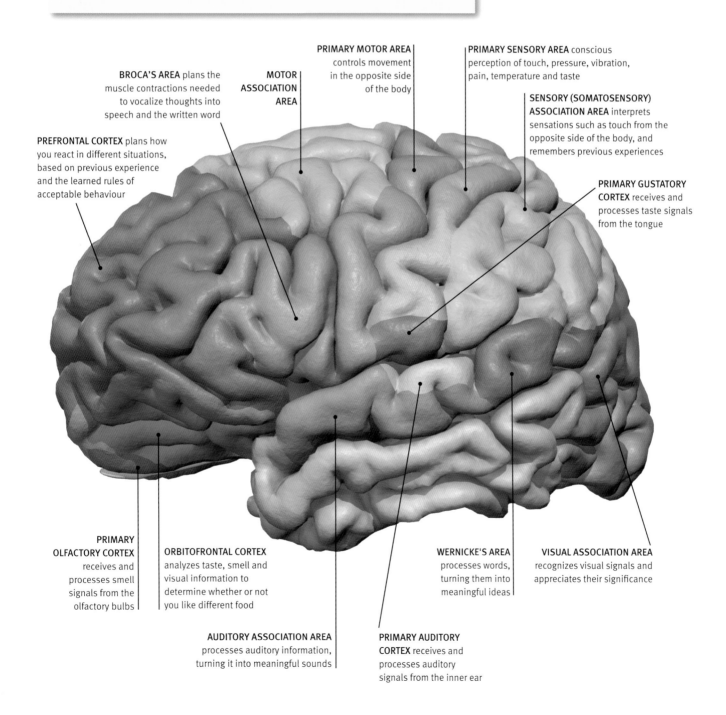

PRIMARY MOTOR AREA controls movement in the opposite side of the body

PRIMARY SENSORY AREA conscious perception of touch, pressure, vibration, pain, temperature and taste

BROCA'S AREA plans the muscle contractions needed to vocalize thoughts into speech and the written word

MOTOR ASSOCIATION AREA

SENSORY (SOMATOSENSORY) ASSOCIATION AREA interprets sensations such as touch from the opposite side of the body, and remembers previous experiences

PREFRONTAL CORTEX plans how you react in different situations, based on previous experience and the learned rules of acceptable behaviour

PRIMARY GUSTATORY CORTEX receives and processes taste signals from the tongue

PRIMARY OLFACTORY CORTEX receives and processes smell signals from the olfactory bulbs

ORBITOFRONTAL CORTEX analyzes taste, smell and visual information to determine whether or not you like different food

WERNICKE'S AREA processes words, turning them into meaningful ideas

VISUAL ASSOCIATION AREA recognizes visual signals and appreciates their significance

AUDITORY ASSOCIATION AREA processes auditory information, turning it into meaningful sounds

PRIMARY AUDITORY CORTEX receives and processes auditory signals from the inner ear

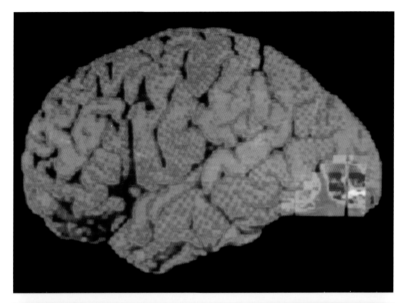

Centres of brain activity

Coloured positron emission tomography (PET) scans are able to show which areas of the brain are activated by different tasks.

The occipital cortex in the back of the brain contains the visual area and is stimulated by sight.

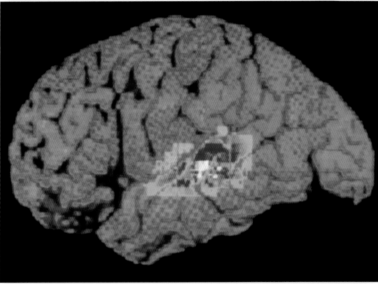

The superior temporal cortex contains the auditory area, which is activated by hearing.

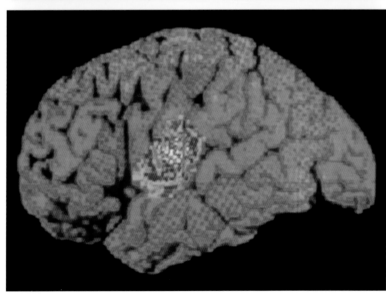

The insula and motor cortex contain the speech centres of the brain, which are stimulated by speaking.

Homunculi

Some parts of the body are connected to the motor and sensory cortex by more neurons than other parts. If the body is drawn to reflect the relative space these neurons occupy within the brain, the resulting figures are known as the sensory and motor hormunculi. In the figure, below right, the relative proportions of the body reflect the space these neurons occupy within the brain. The resulting figure shows for example that the hands and facial muscles are richly supplied with motor neurons to control their complex movements. The sensory neurons supply the lips, hands, feet and genitals (see page 102).

   Handedness is also controlled by the cerebral cortex. Nine out of 10 people have a preference for using their right hand for actions involving careful coordination. The remaining 10 per cent are either left-handed, or able to use their left and right hands equally well (ambidextrous). In a right-handed person, there are an estimated 186 million more neurons on the left side of the brain than on the right. In left-handed people, this pattern of function is usually reversed.

PREFRONTAL GYRUS is the primary motor area of the brain

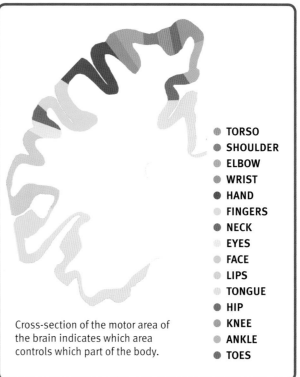

- TORSO
- SHOULDER
- ELBOW
- WRIST
- HAND
- FINGERS
- NECK
- EYES
- FACE
- LIPS
- TONGUE
- HIP
- KNEE
- ANKLE
- TOES

Cross-section of the motor area of the brain indicates which area controls which part of the body.

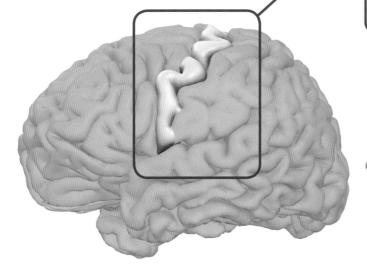

MOTOR HUMUNCULUS

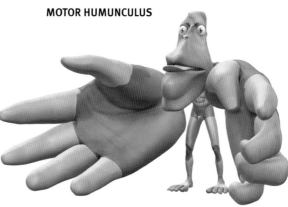

Brainwaves

The millions of nerve impulses generated in the brain per second produce an electrical field that can be measured to produce a recording known as an electro-encephalogram (EEG). This shows different wave patterns depending on the activity level of the brain. The top row, right, shows brainwaves in a brain that is awake. There are four main patterns of brainwave:

- Alpha waves (frequency 8–13Hz) occur during waking periods when the eyes are closed and you are relaxed, see second row, right.
- Beta waves (frequency 13–30Hz) are associated Theta waves (frequency 4–7Hz) are associated with meditation and creative thought. The third trace shows these waves as a person falls asleep, and the fourth shows complex theta waves.
- Delta waves (frequency 0.5–4Hz) occur during deep sleep, seen with the last trace.

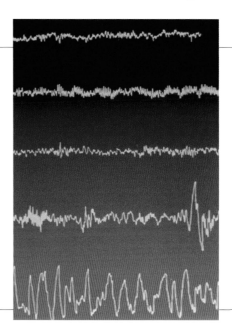

Brain function continued

Each of the billions of nerve cells within your brain form connections with between 1,000 and 20,000 other neurons. The number of possible routes an electrical impulse can take through your brain is therefore astronomically large and measured in trillions of trillions. It is these connections that control the higher functions of the brain, the aspects that make us uniquely human, including intelligence, consciousness and personality. Many subconscious processes are controlled by the limbic system.

INTELLIGENCE

The word 'intelligence' means 'understanding'. It refers to the mental ability to reason, plan, solve problems, weigh up options, predict outcomes and think in abstract terms about complex concepts, such as time and the future. It also involves the use of language and the ability to learn quickly and from experience. These higher functions all occur within the brain, and they appear to relate to individual anatomical structures, such as dendrite branching and cortical convolutions.

The dendrites on a neuron cell body divide to form six, and sometimes seven or eight, successive layers, or orders, of branching (see page 70). These branches are an important determinant of intelligence. The first, second and third levels of branching are determined by our genes. The fourth to eighth higher orders of branching are partly determined by genes, and partly by the level of stimulation and interaction experienced during early life – including within the womb. The more of the higher-order branchings that someone has, the more intelligent they are likely to be.

The cerebral cortex is folded into convolutions called gyri. Intelligence is also linked with the degree of cortical folding occurring in certain regions, especially within the temporo-occipital lobe in an area called the posterior cingulate gyrus.

MEMORY

The basic biological function underpinning intelligence is that of memory, without which every new experience and item of information would have to be processed as if it were totally unique. Memory is the ability to store, retain and subsequently retrieve information. It allows us to reason by analogy – learning how to solve new problems by thinking about similar situations in which we achieved a desired outcome. Memory is poorly understood, but many different areas of the brain, such as the hippocampus, amygdala and mammillary bodies are thought to be involved. Each is related to a different type of memory, such as working (short-term) memory, long-term memory, spatial memory and emotional memory.

EMOTIONS

Human beings experience a number of different emotions, including anger, fear, sadness, disgust, surprise, curiosity, acceptance and joy. But these are by no means the only ones – there's also confusion, envy, excitement, guilt,

Brainstem

This is one the hardest working areas of the brain. It initiates and coordinates the hundreds of subconscious body processes that enable your body to function. The brainstem is situated under the cerebrum and leads into the top of the spinal cord. All nerve signals into and out of the brain from every part of the body pass through the brainstem, and the nerves that connect the right and left side of the brain cross over at this point. The main structures in the brainstem are the midbrain, medulla and the reticular formation (not visible in this illustration).

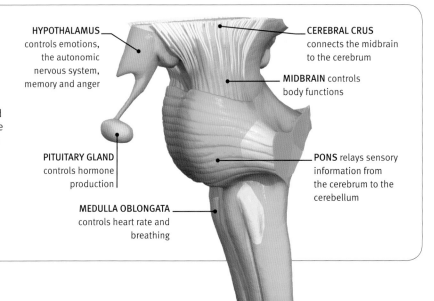

HYPOTHALAMUS controls emotions, the autonomic nervous system, memory and anger

CEREBRAL CRUS connects the midbrain to the cerebrum

MIDBRAIN controls body functions

PITUITARY GLAND controls hormone production

PONS relays sensory information from the cerebrum to the cerebellum

MEDULLA OBLONGATA controls heart rate and breathing

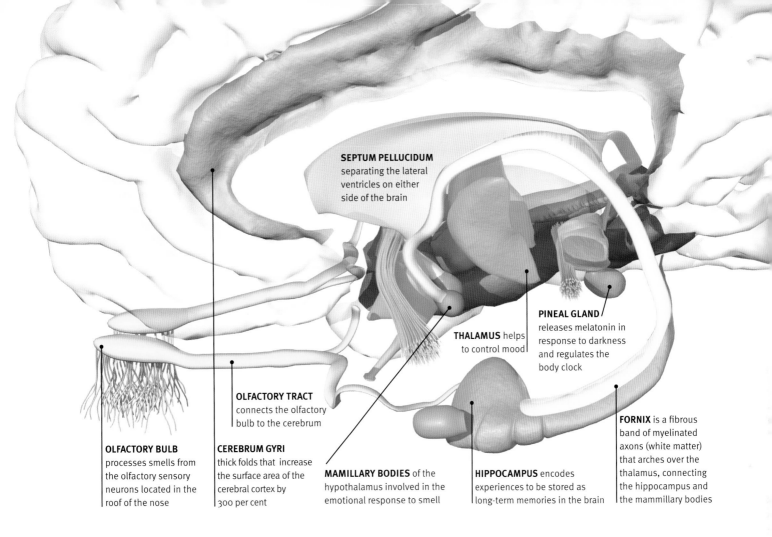

SEPTUM PELLUCIDUM separating the lateral ventricles on either side of the brain

PINEAL GLAND releases melatonin in response to darkness and regulates the body clock

THALAMUS helps to control mood

OLFACTORY TRACT connects the olfactory bulb to the cerebrum

OLFACTORY BULB processes smells from the olfactory sensory neurons located in the roof of the nose

CEREBRUM GYRI thick folds that increase the surface area of the cerebral cortex by 300 per cent

MAMILLARY BODIES of the hypothalamus involved in the emotional response to smell

HIPPOCAMPUS encodes experiences to be stored as long-term memories in the brain

FORNIX is a fibrous band of myelinated axons (white matter) that arches over the thalamus, connecting the hippocampus and the mammillary bodies

compassion, anxiety, grief, embarrassment, caution, loneliness, jealousy, shyness, pleasure, love and lust, among others. Emotions appear to result from the interaction of bodily and mental responses. Many different parts of the brain are involved in the processing of emotions, especially the hypothalamus and the structures within the limbic system, such as the amygdala and hippocampus.

PHEROMONES

Pheromones are volatile substances secreted by the apocrine sweat glands (see page 28) in the armpits and around the genitals and nipples. These odourless chemicals are detected by specialized cells (the vomeronasal organ) within the mucous lining of the nasal septum. Pheromones are related to the master sex hormone, DHEA (dehydroepiandrostenedione), and have subconscious effects on others – especially those of the opposite sex. Pheromones influence both physical sexual responses, such as ovulation and the length of the menstrual cycle, and emotional responses, promoting feelings of warmth, cuddliness, attentiveness and attraction. Interestingly, while the effects of female pheromones can diffuse over large distances, male pheromones seem to require close-up contact.

LIMBIC SYSTEM

The limbic system influences subconscious, instinctive behaviour related to survival as well as our moods and emotions. Many of these instincts become modified by learned moral, social and cultural traditions. One part of the limbic system, the hippocampus, is involved with learning, recognition of new experiences and memory – especially of physical, three-dimensional relationships. The limbic system is also closely linked to the detection of smell within the olfactory tract, which is why some odours trigger strong memories and emotions.

BODY FACT

Fight, flight and pleasure

- In evolutionary terms, the limbic system is one of the oldest parts of your brain.
- Your limbic system developed to regulate the 'fight-or-flight' stress response, and influences your endocrine system and autonomic nervous system.
- The limbic system is also linked with the pleasure centre of the brain within the basal ganglia.

Spinal cord

The adult spinal cord measures about 45cm (18in) long extending from the lower brain to the lumbar vertebrae. It is structurally and functionally integrated with the brain, although many nerve impulses coming from the peripheral nervous system are processed in the spinal cord without ever reaching the brain.

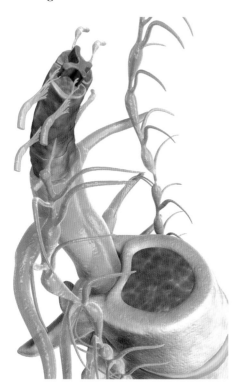

STRUCTURE OF THE CORD

In the spinal cord, unlike the brain, the central part consists of grey matter (cell bodies of neurons and supporting neurological cells), surrounded by white matter and a central canal. The grey matter forms projections at each corner called horns. White matter consists of tracts of myelinated and unmyelinated axons that travel up and down the cord.

Integration of impulses and command initiation occur in the grey matter. The white matter carries information from place to place.

Nerves extend from the spinal cord to the different parts of the body. Each vertebra is associated with its own pair of spinal nerves that supply a specific part of the body with somatic, sensory and sympathetic nerves.

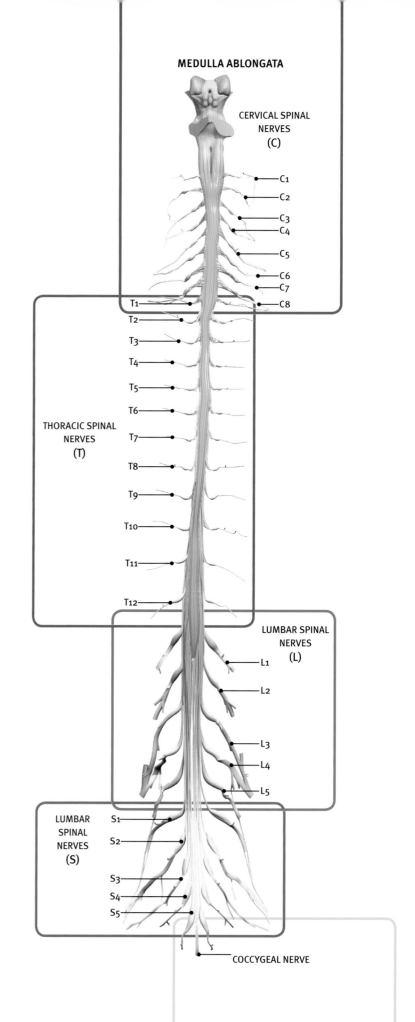

MEDULLA ABLONGATA

CERVICAL SPINAL NERVES (C)

C1
C2
C3
C4
C5
C6
C7
C8

THORACIC SPINAL NERVES (T)

T1
T2
T3
T4
T5
T6
T7
T8
T9
T10
T11
T12

LUMBAR SPINAL NERVES (L)

L1
L2
L3
L4
L5

LUMBAR SPINAL NERVES (S)

S1
S2
S3
S4
S5

COCCYGEAL NERVE

Neural reflex arc

Reflexes are rapid automatic responses to stimuli to preserve the internal status quo. These are activated, for example, when your hand touches a hot pan and instinctively pulls away. There are set neurons involved in this process known as the reflex arc. Most spinal reflexes have the sensory nerve cell body in the dorsal root ganglion. The order of function is as follows:

The stimulus arrives – a hand touches hot object,

⋮

The sensory neuron is activated,

⋮

Information is processed in the central nervous system, normally the spinal cord,

⋮

Motor neuron is activated,

⋮

Response occurs – the hand is moved.

BODY FACT

Your spinal cord

- The spinal cord is an extension of your brain.
- The adult spinal cord weighs around 35g (1⅕ oz) and contains an estimated one billion neurons.
- Your spinal cord stops growing in childhood, but the vertebral column continues to lengthen. As a result, an adult spinal cord extends only two-thirds of the way down your vertebral column, to around the level of L1 or L2 (see page 42).
- Your spinal cord is approximately 45cm (18in), whereas your vertebral column is around 70cm (28in).
- The 10 lower pairs of spinal nerve roots extend below the spinal cord to emerge lower down the spinal column. These form a bundle of nerve fibres called the cauda equina, which is Latin for 'horse's tail'.
- The spinal cord tapers to form a slender filament, the filum terminale, that is around 20cm (8in) long. Composed mainly of fibrous tissue, it is a continuation of your pia mater, and tethers the cord within the vertebral canal.

Protection for the spine

The spinal cord is surrounded and protected by three layers of meningeal membranes (the pia, dura and arachnoid mater). Blood vessels branching within these layers deliver oxygen and nutrients to the spinal cord. Between the arachnoid mater and the spinal cord is the subarachnoid space, which is filled with the cerebrospinal fluid (csf) that acts as a shock absorber, and a diffusion medium for nutrients, waste products and gases. The membranes and csf together protect the delicate neural tissue of the cord from knocks and bumps from the external world. The cord and the meninges are further protected by the vertebrae.

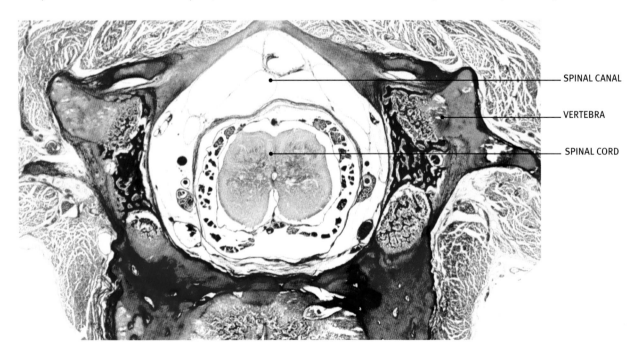

SPINAL CANAL

VERTEBRA

SPINAL CORD

Spinal cord continued

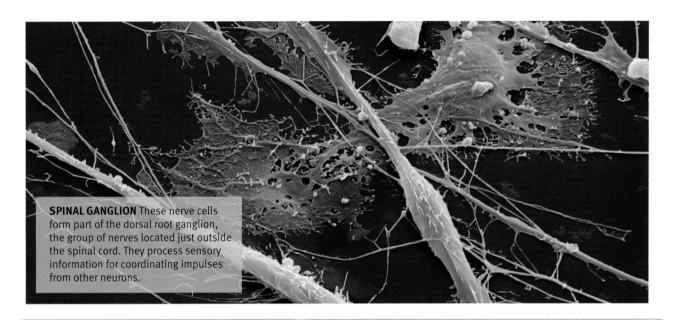

SPINAL GANGLION These nerve cells form part of the dorsal root ganglion, the group of nerves located just outside the spinal cord. They process sensory information for coordinating impulses from other neurons.

CROSS SECTION OF THE CORD

In cross section, the spinal cord has an internal area of grey matter that contains neuron cell bodies, and an outer coat of white matter that contains myelinated axons. Seen like this, the grey matter forms a shape similar to two butterfly wings joined by a narrow bridge. Each wing is made up of three triangular areas known as horns.

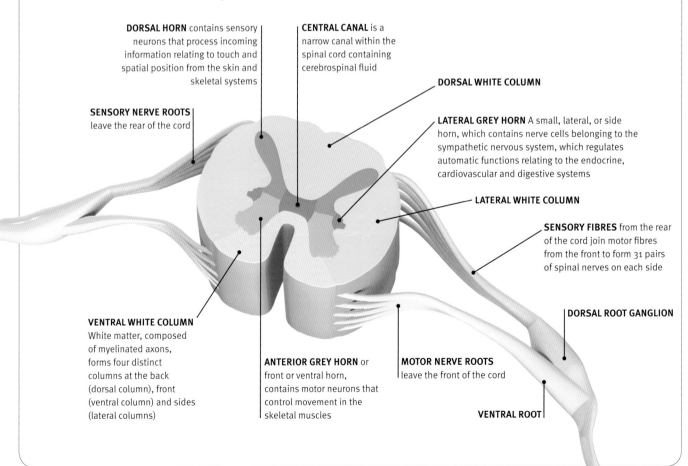

DORSAL HORN contains sensory neurons that process incoming information relating to touch and spatial position from the skin and skeletal systems

CENTRAL CANAL is a narrow canal within the spinal cord containing cerebrospinal fluid

DORSAL WHITE COLUMN

SENSORY NERVE ROOTS leave the rear of the cord

LATERAL GREY HORN A small, lateral, or side horn, which contains nerve cells belonging to the sympathetic nervous system, which regulates automatic functions relating to the endocrine, cardiovascular and digestive systems

LATERAL WHITE COLUMN

SENSORY FIBRES from the rear of the cord join motor fibres from the front to form 31 pairs of spinal nerves on each side

VENTRAL WHITE COLUMN White matter, composed of myelinated axons, forms four distinct columns at the back (dorsal column), front (ventral column) and sides (lateral columns)

ANTERIOR GREY HORN or front or ventral horn, contains motor neurons that control movement in the skeletal muscles

MOTOR NERVE ROOTS leave the front of the cord

DORSAL ROOT GANGLION

VENTRAL ROOT

Cranial nerves

Twelve pairs of cranial nerves emerge symmetrically from your brain and brainstem. These are traditionally numbered using the Roman numerals I to XII. Nerve pairs I and II emerge from the brain, while pairs III to XII emerge from the brainstem.

NERVES OF THE SENSES

Your cranial nerves are involved in sight, hearing, balance, smell, taste sensation, control of facial expressions and regulation of certain automatic functions such as heart rate, breathing and the secretion of intestinal juices. Some cranial nerves (pairs III, IV, VI, XI, XII) carry motor signals that control movement in muscles of the head and neck; some (I, II, VIII) carry sensory information back to the brain; and some carry both types of signal (V, VII, IX, X, known as the sensorimotor nerves).

BODY FACT

Nerve centre

- A controversial pair of nerves, known as cranial nerves zero, may also exist, but they are so fine that they are difficult to find without an electron microscope.
- Cranial nerves zero are believed to emerge from the nasal cavity close to the olfactory nerves and allow you to detect pheromones – odourless chemicals involved in human bonding and lust.
- The olfactory nerves (I) are the shortest of your 12 cranial nerves.
- The optic nerves (II) develop as out-pouchings from the brain during embryonic development and, strictly speaking, form part of the central nervous system.
- The trochlear nerves (IV) are the only cranial nerves that cross to the other side before reaching their target, and the only cranial nerves to emerge from the back of your brainstem.
- The trigeminal nerves (V) are your largest cranial nerves.
- Your vagus nerves (X) are the longest cranial nerves.
- The accessory nerves (XI) are the only cranial nerves to both enter and exit your skull through its base.

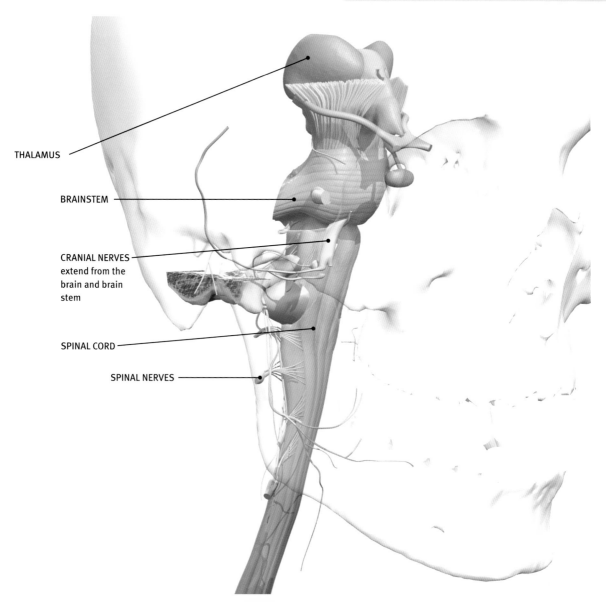

THALAMUS

BRAINSTEM

CRANIAL NERVES extend from the brain and brain stem

SPINAL CORD

SPINAL NERVES

Cranial nerve function

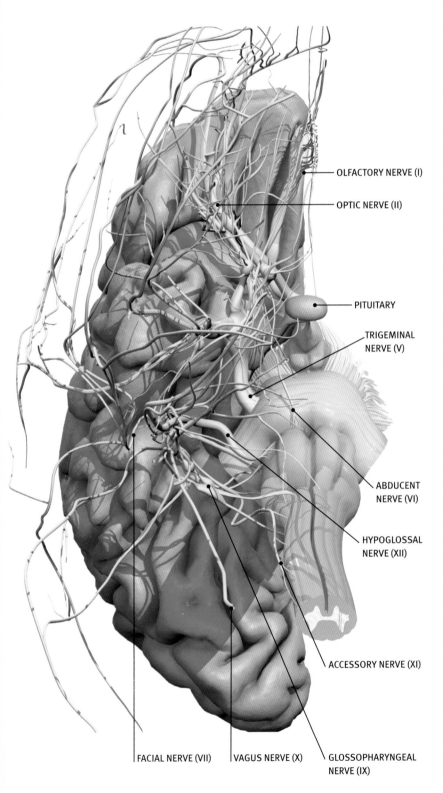

OLFACTORY NERVE (I)

OPTIC NERVE (II)

PITUITARY

TRIGEMINAL NERVE (V)

ABDUCENT NERVE (VI)

HYPOGLOSSAL NERVE (XII)

ACCESSORY NERVE (XI)

FACIAL NERVE (VII)

VAGUS NERVE (X)

GLOSSOPHARYNGEAL NERVE (IX)

FIRST CRANIAL NERVES The olfactory nerves (sensory) consist of 15–20 delicate sensory nerve fibres that carry information from the smell receptors in the upper part of the nasal cavity to the smell centre (olfactory bulbs) of the brain. The sensory nerve fibres pass through the sieve-like openings of the cribriform plate in the ethmoid bone of the skull.

SECOND CRANIAL NERVES The optic nerves (sensory) carry information from light receptors in the retina of the eye, through the optic canal of the sphenoid bone, and are relayed on to the visual cortex.

THIRD CRANIAL NERVES The oculomotor nerves (motor) control voluntary movements of the eye muscles (the superior rectus, medial rectus, inferior rectus, inferior oblique), open the eyelids (via the levator palpebrae superioris muscle) and constrict the pupil and lens. They divide into two branches that enter the orbit through the superior orbital fissure.

FOURTH CRANIAL NERVES The trochlear nerves (motor) control voluntary movements of a single eye muscle, the superior oblique, on each side. They enter the orbit via the superior orbital fissure.

FIFTH CRANIAL NERVES The trigeminal nerves (sensorimotor) each have three branches (the ophthalmic, maxillary and mandibular nerves). These carry sensations from the face and control muscles involved in mastication (chewing), biting and swallowing. The branches leave the skull through the superior orbital fissure (the ophthalmic nerve), and through small holes in the sphenoid bone – the foramen rotundum (maxillary nerve) and the foramen ovale (the mandibular nerve).

SIXTH CRANIAL NERVES The abducens nerves (motor) control the voluntary movements of a single eye muscle, the lateral rectus, on each side. They enter the orbit via the superior orbital fissure.

SEVENTH CRANIAL NERVES The facial nerves (sensorimotor) carry information from the taste buds on the anterior (front) two-thirds of the tongue to the brain, and regulate saliva production in the salivary glands (except the parotid). They also regulate production of tears in the lacrimal glands. They also control the facial muscles and the stapedius – a tiny muscle that stabilizes the stapes bone in the middle ear. They run through the internal acoustic canal and facial canal of the temporal bone, to exit at the stylomastoid foramen.

EIGHTH CRANIAL NERVES The vestibulocochlear nerves (sensory), also known as the auditory or acoustic nerves, carry information about hearing and balance from sense organs in the ear to the brain, allowing detection of head position and movements. These nerves pass through the internal acoustic canal of the temporal bone on each side, and split into two large branches – the cochlear nerve and the vestibular nerve.

NINTH CRANIAL NERVES The glossopharyngeal nerves (sensorimotor) control a muscle used in swallowing (the stylopharyngeus) and carry sensory information relating to taste from the posterior (rear) third of the tongue, and to touch, temperature and pain, from the mouth and middle ear. They carry parasympathetic fibres that regulate salivary secretion in the parotid gland, and pass through the jugular foramen in the base of the skull.

TENTH CRANIAL NERVES The vagus nerves (sensorimotor) are the only cranial nerves to pass below the head to the neck, chest and abdomen. They regulate many automatic functions such as heart rate, breathing, and the secretion of digestive juices in the upper intestines and the first two-thirds of the colon (as far as the splenic flexure). They supply nerves to the palatoglossus muscle of the tongue and are involved in speech and taste sensation from taste buds on the epiglottis. They pass through the jugular foramen in the base of the skull.

ELEVENTH CRANIAL NERVES The accessory nerves (motor) control two skeletal muscles that move the head, neck and shoulders (the sternocleidomastoid and trapezius muscles). They enter the skull through its base, via the foramen magnum, and exit the skull via the jugular foramen.

TWELTH CRANIAL NERVES The hypoglossal nerves (motor) control movement of muscles in the tongue (except the palatoglossus) and other muscles used in swallowing and speech. They pass through the hypoglossal canal in the occipital bone of the skull.

Nerve roots

The cranial nerves emerge from both sides of the brain and brainstem.

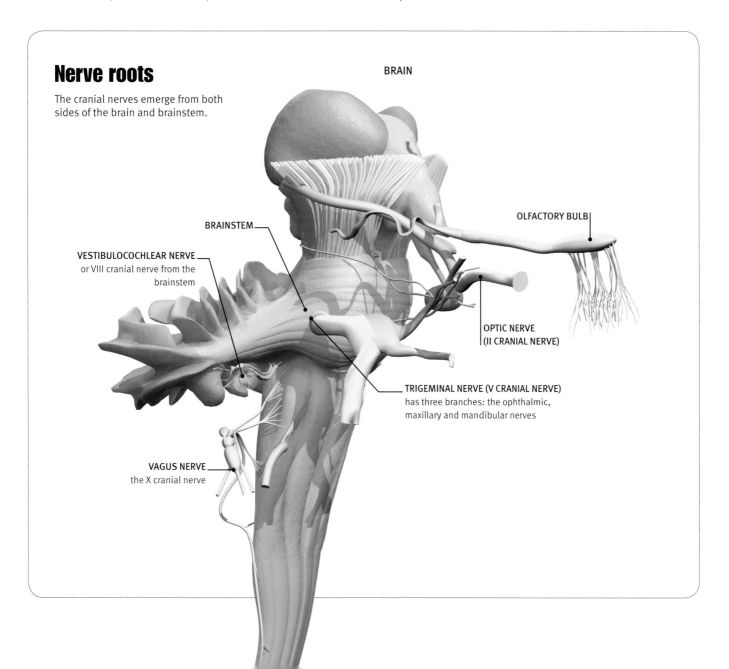

BRAIN

OLFACTORY BULB

BRAINSTEM

VESTIBULOCOCHLEAR NERVE
or VIII cranial nerve from the brainstem

OPTIC NERVE
(II CRANIAL NERVE)

TRIGEMINAL NERVE (V CRANIAL NERVE)
has three branches: the ophthalmic, maxillary and mandibular nerves

VAGUS NERVE
the X cranial nerve

Spinal nerves

There are 31 pairs of nerves that emerge from the spinal cord to different parts of the body. Sensory fibres extend from the rear of your spinal cord (dorsal) to join motor fibres (ventral) from the front.

NERVE FUNCTION

The spinal nerves relay sensory information from the body to the brain, and send back motor instructions relating to voluntary and involuntary actions.

NERVE PLEXUSES

The nerves that emerge from the spinal cord (rami) and innervate (supply nerves to) the arms and legs merge to form complex junctions known as plexuses. The cervical plexus forms in the neck, see right; the brachial plexus in the shoulder; the lumbar plexus in the lower back; and the sacral and coccygeal plexuses in the pelvis, see opposite. The plexuses also send messages along secondary nerves.

The brachial plexus supplies the upper limbs. It is usually formed from the ventral nerve rami of the lower four cervical spinal nerves (fifth, sixth, seventh and eighth) and the first thoracic spinal nerve.

REFLEXES

The synaptic delay (see page 73) means that stimuli sent all the way back to the brain produce a slightly delayed response. Survival sometimes requires an instant response, so certain automatic reflex actions occur at the level of the spinal nerves. In this instance, a sensory neuron connects with a motor neuron via a short interneuron to produce a reflex arc. For example, when you instantly withdraw your finger from a flame, a reflex arc is involved – your finger moves milliseconds before the pain signal travels up the spinal cord to reach your brain.

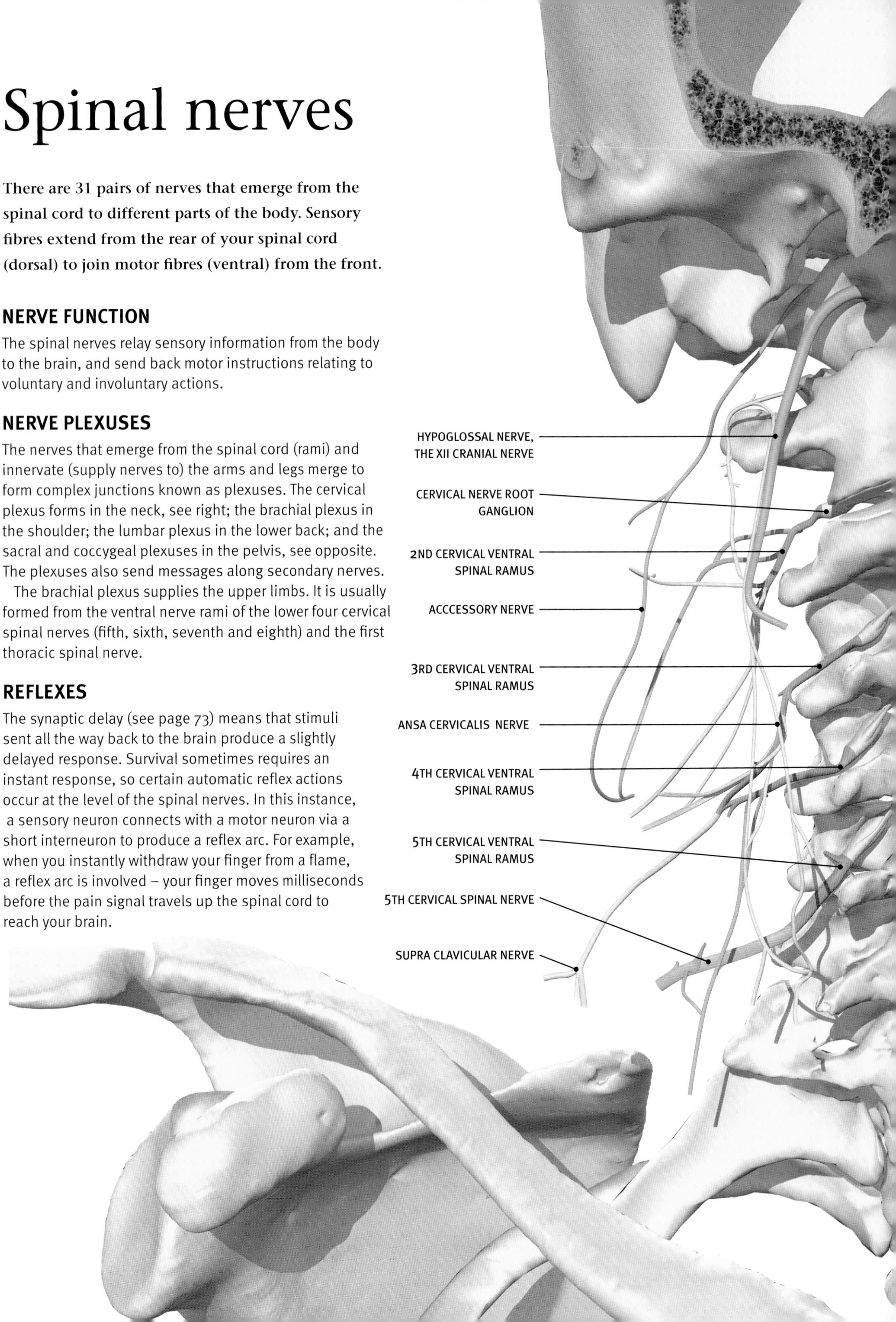

HYPOGLOSSAL NERVE, THE XII CRANIAL NERVE

CERVICAL NERVE ROOT GANGLION

2ND CERVICAL VENTRAL SPINAL RAMUS

ACCCESSORY NERVE

3RD CERVICAL VENTRAL SPINAL RAMUS

ANSA CERVICALIS NERVE

4TH CERVICAL VENTRAL SPINAL RAMUS

5TH CERVICAL VENTRAL SPINAL RAMUS

5TH CERVICAL SPINAL NERVE

SUPRA CLAVICULAR NERVE

Sacral and coccygeal plexuses

There are two complex nerve junctions in this region, the sacral plexus and the coccygeal plexus. These nerves supply the thighs, buttocks and legs, as well as the groin and genital areas. The sciatic nerve runs run down the lower limb and is the longest nerve in the body.

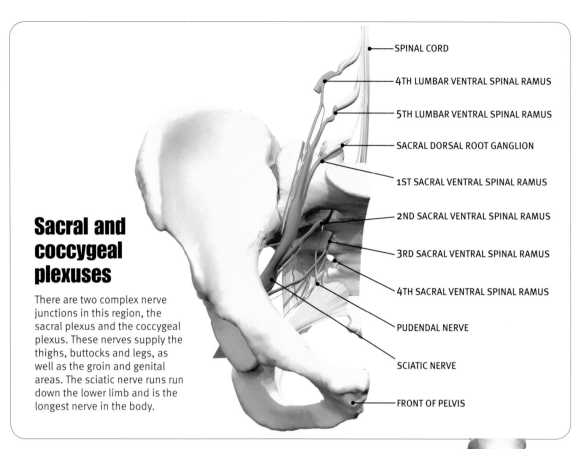

SPINAL CORD

4TH LUMBAR VENTRAL SPINAL RAMUS

5TH LUMBAR VENTRAL SPINAL RAMUS

SACRAL DORSAL ROOT GANGLION

1ST SACRAL VENTRAL SPINAL RAMUS

2ND SACRAL VENTRAL SPINAL RAMUS

3RD SACRAL VENTRAL SPINAL RAMUS

4TH SACRAL VENTRAL SPINAL RAMUS

PUDENDAL NERVE

SCIATIC NERVE

FRONT OF PELVIS

Lumbar nerves

There are five pairs of nerves in the lumbar region. The first four connect to the lumbar plexus. The fourth and fifth lumbar nerves connect to the sacral plexus. These nerves supply the lower abdominal wall and parts of the thighs and lower legs.

1ST LUMBAR VENTRAL SPINAL RAMUS

ILIOHYPOGASTRIC NERVE

ILIO-INGUINAL NERVE

2ND LUMBAR SPINAL NERVE

2ND LUMBAR VENTRAL SPINAL RAMUS

3RD LUMBAR VENTRAL SPINAL RAMUS

4TH LUMBAR VENTRAL SPINAL RAMUS

5TH LUMBAR VENTRAL SPINAL RAMUS

PELVIS

HIP JOINT

SACRUM

COCCYX

BODY FACT

Nerve pairs

You have 31 pairs of spinal nerves:
- eight pairs of cervical spinal nerves,
- 12 pairs of thoracic spinal nerves,
- five pairs of lumbar spinal nerves,
- five pairs of sacral spinal nerves,
- one pair of coccygeal spinal nerves.

Five senses

Ancient philosophers referred to the human senses as the windows to the soul. By that they meant that they allow us to perceive and interact with the realities of the world, while also providing the tools that enable us to visualize, imagine and dream. Life would be much poorer without them.

There are five classic, or 'special', senses: those of smell, taste, sight, hearing and touch. The sense of touch can be further sub-divided into sensations of pain (nocioception), temperature differences (thermoception) and pressure (mechanoreception). Other senses include balance (equilibrioception), plus awareness of the position of different parts of the body relative to each other (proprioception) and of joint movements (kinesthesia).

Smell

Every day, you breathe over 23,000 times, bringing different aromas towards the smell receptors at the top of your nose. Unlike the receptors involved in other senses, smell receptors are directly connected to your brain. Messages are passed to the limbic system, which is involved with learning, memories and emotions. Smell therefore evokes powerful emotional responses. Your sense of smell (olfaction) was strongest at birth – a three-day-old baby can even recognize its own mother's milk. By the age of 20, your sense of smell is only 82 per cent as good as when you were born. By the age of 60, it has fallen to 38 per cent, and by the age of 80, it is only 28 per cent as sensitive as it was at birth.

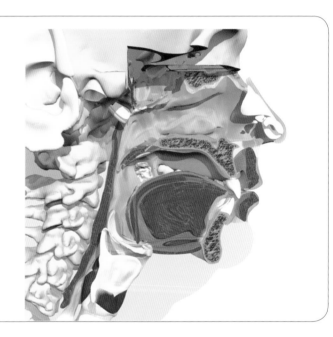

Taste

Your sense of taste (gustation) changes throughout your life. As a baby, you had tastebuds all over the sides and roof of your mouth as well as on your tongue – this helped you to explore the world of taste by sucking and biting new objects. As you grow older, tastebuds disappear from the sides and roof of your mouth, until they are mostly found just on your tongue. These tastebuds become increasingly less sensitive with age, and this may be linked with reduced production of saliva.

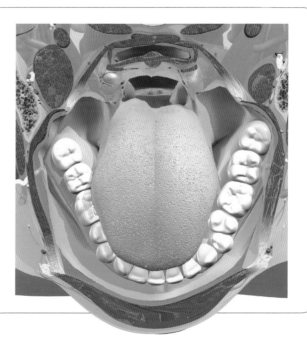

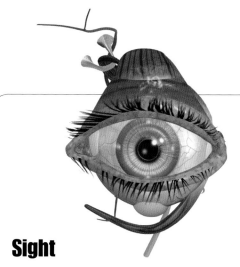

Sight

This is one of your most important senses, allowing you to see and react to the world around you. About 70 per cent of your body's sense receptors are clustered in your eyes and, as well as being able to see in bright sunlight, you can view faint starlight – a brightness range of more than 10 million to one.

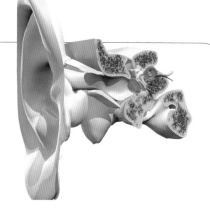

Hearing

Your sense of hearing – and those of motion and balance – involves the stimulation of special receptors within your inner ears. Brain pathways that perceive sound are connected to the primitive limbic system and – like smell – can evoke powerful emotional responses such as those felt by a mother when her baby cries.

Touch

Of all the senses, touch is the one you can least do without. Touch is vital for survival, it enables you to experience the pleasures of kissing through to the mechanisms of reproduction, as well as the simple actions of walking, eating and withdrawing from pain. The sensory receptors within the epidermis and dermis can pick up touch as well as sensations of cold, heat and pain. Touch receptors appear all over the body but some areas of skin, such as the palms, soles and lips, have more receptors than other areas and are therefore more sensitive. Some of these more sensitive spots are known as erogenous zones.

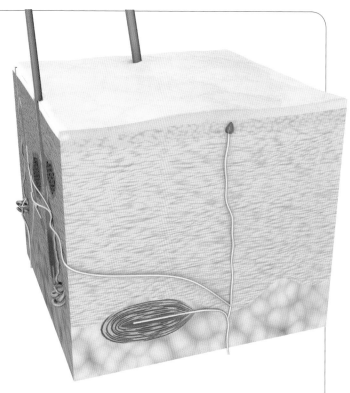

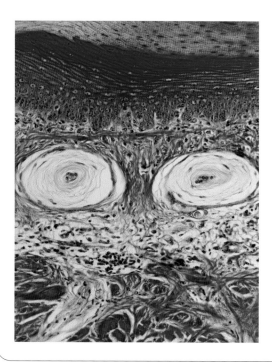

Pacinian Corpuscles. This cross-section of human skin shows the epidermis, in red, and the underlying dermis, in blue. Within the dermis are two Pacinian corpuscles which are oval shaped and approximately 1mm long. Pacinian corpuscles are mechanoreceptors that are responsible for the skin's sensitivity to rough surfaces and to pressure. They resemble small onions and consist of concentric layers of cells, fluid and connective tissue fibres which increase in density towards the single nerve fibre that lies at the core.

Eyes and vision

Your eyes can discriminate between more than 100,000 colours, each of which comes in 150 different hues, meaning you can distinguish as many as 10 million different shades. The brightest and darkest light signals your eyes can sense are a factor of one thousand million apart, and your vision becomes a million times more sensitive as any brightness dims.

SEEING

Light enters your eye through the pupil and is refracted (bent) as it passes through the crystalline lens. The lens changes shape so that an image of what you are looking at is focused, upside-down, onto the retina.

Each of your eyes sees a slightly different image, with the visual fields overlapping. Such binocular, or stereoscopic, vision allows three-dimensional (depth) perception and allows you to judge how far away you are from an object.

Your retina contains two types of cells: one type that detects dim light, but which see only in black or white (rods), and another type that gives colour vision, but only in bright light (cones). When light stimulates these cells, they send signals to the cortex that are interpreted as either dim light, or bright, coloured light.

To see a distant object, the ciliary muscles relax and the lens flattens and thins. To view a nearby object, the ciliary muscles contract and the lens becomes fatter. This is known as accommodation.

Many of the images you perceive are dependent on the brain interpreting information and making assumptions based on prior experience. Optical illusions occur when the brain interprets visual information in a way that differs from reality.

BODY FACT

Visual perception

- The structures involved in visual perception together form the largest system in the brain.
- Neurons within the visual cortex mature at different rates – a newborn baby initially perceives only simple black and white shapes and angles, then becomes able to recognize more complex patterns and colours such as faces.
- Although you have around 126 million rods and cones, only 1.2 million axons pass from your retina to your brain. Each axon therefore carries information processed from around 100 different light-receptor cells.
- Around one person in 30 is colour blind. It is more common in men, affecting as many as one man in 12.

Rods and cones

Light energy stimulates two types of light-sensitive cells (photoreceptors) called rods and cones, which send signals to the visual cortex of the brain for analysis. Rods detect dim light but see only in black and white. They are mainly located in the macula lutea, a yellow spot on the retina (around 1.5mm/0.06in in diameter) that is responsible for fine vision. Cones, which are wider and more rounded than the rods, are responsible for colour vision in bright light. They are distributed throughout the retina and are particularly concentrated within a small pit (the fovea) in the centre of the macula. Cones come in three types, and their pigments respond to either green, red or blue light wavelengths respectively. Different combinations of these three colours allow you to perceive an extraordinary range of different colours.

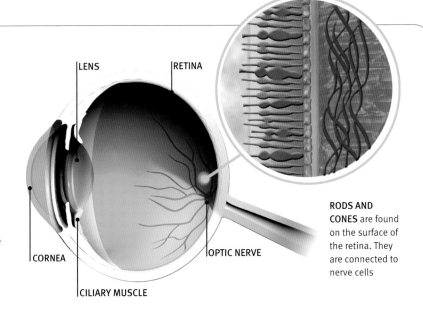

LENS

RETINA

CORNEA

CILIARY MUSCLE

OPTIC NERVE

RODS AND CONES are found on the surface of the retina. They are connected to nerve cells

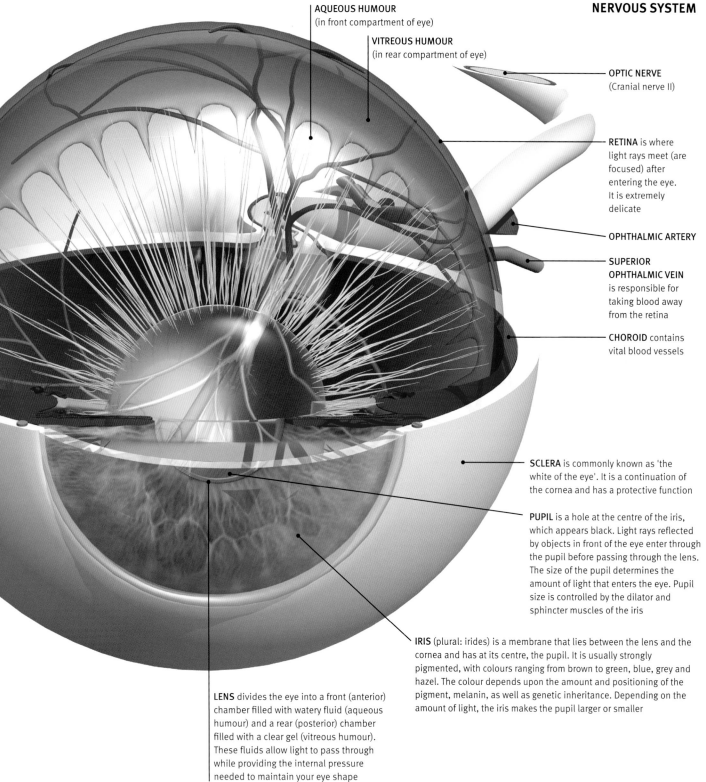

AQUEOUS HUMOUR
(in front compartment of eye)

VITREOUS HUMOUR
(in rear compartment of eye)

OPTIC NERVE
(Cranial nerve II)

RETINA is where light rays meet (are focused) after entering the eye. It is extremely delicate

OPHTHALMIC ARTERY

SUPERIOR OPHTHALMIC VEIN is responsible for taking blood away from the retina

CHOROID contains vital blood vessels

SCLERA is commonly known as 'the white of the eye'. It is a continuation of the cornea and has a protective function

PUPIL is a hole at the centre of the iris, which appears black. Light rays reflected by objects in front of the eye enter through the pupil before passing through the lens. The size of the pupil determines the amount of light that enters the eye. Pupil size is controlled by the dilator and sphincter muscles of the iris

IRIS (plural: irides) is a membrane that lies between the lens and the cornea and has at its centre, the pupil. It is usually strongly pigmented, with colours ranging from brown to green, blue, grey and hazel. The colour depends upon the amount and positioning of the pigment, melanin, as well as genetic inheritance. Depending on the amount of light, the iris makes the pupil larger or smaller

LENS divides the eye into a front (anterior) chamber filled with watery fluid (aqueous humour) and a rear (posterior) chamber filled with a clear gel (vitreous humour). These fluids allow light to pass through while providing the internal pressure needed to maintain your eye shape

EYEBALL

This lies within the orbital cavity of the skull and is a slightly irregular spheroid shape about 24mm (1in) in diameter. The lens divides the eye into two chambers: a front (anterior) chamber filled with watery fluid (aqueous humour) and a rear (posterior) chamber filled with a clear gel (vitreous humour). These fluids allow light to pass through while providing the internal pressure needed to maintain your eye shape.

The eyeball's outer wall has three main layers:
- The outer fibrous layer is made up of the transparent cornea and the white, opaque sclera.
- The middle, vascular layer contains the iris, ciliary body and choroid, whose blood vessels supply oxygen and nutrients to the tissues of the eye.
- The inner retina contains the light-sensitive cells (rods and cones) that detect light.

Eyes and vision continued

The outer part of the eye is designed to protect the whole of the eye, especially the cornea. The tear-producing equipment, eyelids and eyelashes, together form the accessory structures of the eye.

EXTERNAL EYE

Outside the delicate eyeball is a set of structures designed to protect it from damage. The upper and lower eyelids close firmly to protect the conjunctivae. Eyelashes are robust hairs that prevent foreign matter reaching the eye's surface.

The eyelids have a sebaceous (oil producing) gland that produces a lipid-rich substance to prevent the eyelids from sticking together.

The lacrimal apparatus produces, distributes and removes tears. It comprises the lacrimal gland with associated ducts, paired lacrimal canaliculi, a lacrimal sac and a nasolacrimal duct.

The lacrimal gland produces about 1ml of tears each day. Blinking sweeps the tears across the surface of the eye, which accumulate and disappear through the nasolacrimal duct into the nasal cavity. When tears are produced at a faster rate than the duct can cope with, they overflow onto the cheeks.

Tears contain mucus to lubricate the eye, lysozyme (an anti-bacterial substance) and antibodies to prevent infection.

Extra production of tears can be triggered by a foreign body in the eye, pain elsewhere in the body or an outburst of extreme emotion.

BODY FACT

Eyes see

- Your eyes are kept moist, lubricated and free from infection by the washing action of tears.
- You blink around 15 times per minute to spread tears over the eye surface.
- Human beings are the only animals who cry excess tears when they are upset.
- You have around six million cones and 120 million rods in each eye.
- Your eyes are able to detect a lit candle 1.6km (1 mile) away.
- Each eye contains a physiological blind spot, in which light cannot be detected. This is because there are no photoreceptor cells on the optic disc of the retina, where the nerve cells from each rod and cone come together to form the optic nerve.
- Each person has one eye that they use more than the other – the dominant eye. This is the eye you use when looking through a camera's viewfinder or when threading a needle.

Eyelashes

Mainly composed of keratin, eyelashes are hairs that grow from follicles in the eyelids. Their primary function is to provide protection against debris and particles entering the eyes. Because they are sensitive to touch in the same way as a cat's whiskers they offer a warning when an object is very close to the eye, prompting the eyelid to close reflexively.

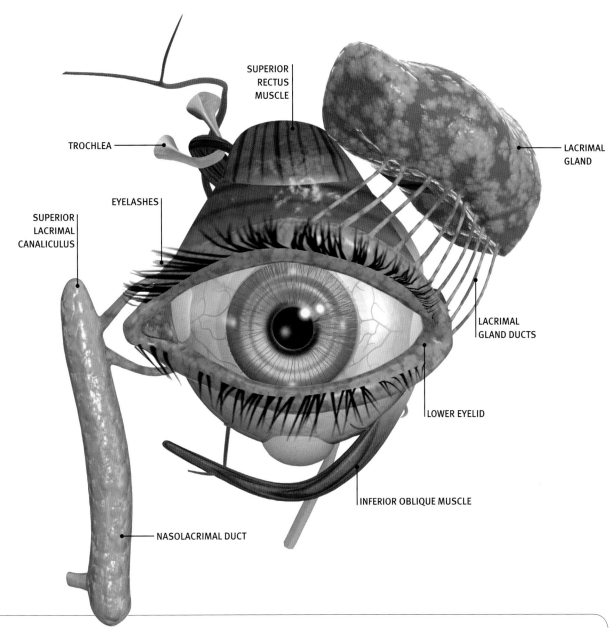

SUPERIOR
RECTUS
MUSCLE

TROCHLEA

LACRIMAL
GLAND

EYELASHES

SUPERIOR
LACRIMAL
CANALICULUS

LACRIMAL
GLAND DUCTS

LOWER EYELID

INFERIOR OBLIQUE MUSCLE

NASOLACRIMAL DUCT

Lacrimal gland

The lacrimal gland (tear gland) is about the size and shape of an almond, and nestles in a dip in the frontal bone just above and to the side of the eyeball. The cells of the lacrimal gland secrete a watery alkaline liquid that supplies nutrients and oxygen to the corneal cells. The fluid collects into droplets that are squeezed out of the gland.

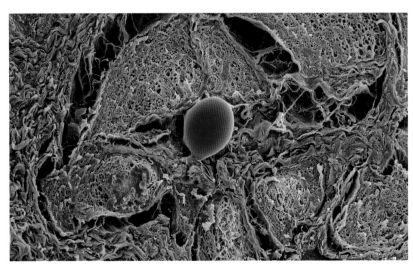

Touch

Your skin contains a number of nerve endings that can detect light touch, sustained pressure, cold, warmth or pain. Some sense receptors are simple, bare nerve endings, such as those that detect the movement of fine hairs, while others have a more complex structure.

SENSATION AND THE CENTRAL NERVOUS SYSTEM

Sensory receptors are the conduit for information from the environment to be transmitted to the central nervous system. Each receptor has its own sensitivity that is characteristic (touch, pain, heat etc.). An arriving stimulus can take many forms – physical force, dissolved chemical, sound and light, for example.

The ultimate destination of the information depends on its location and nature. Some sensations are dealt with at the level of the spinal cord, and some travel all the way

to the brain where they are 'translated' within the sensory cortex. Only about one per cent of information received by receptors actually reaches our conscious awareness.

HOT AND COLD SENSATION

Temperature receptors are free nerve endings found in the skin, skeletal muscles and the liver. There are three times as many cold receptors as warm; cold temperature sensation travels along the same pathways as pain. Receptors pick up temperature change quickly, then adapt quickly (in other words stop firing) when stable levels are reached. So for example, when you enter an air conditioned room it feels cold initially, but then you become comfortable.

TICKLE AND ITCH

These sensations are very similar to touch and pain. Tickle sensation is produced by a light touch moving across the skin. Psychological factors are involved too, and the sensitivity differs greatly from one person to another. Itch is probably produced by the same receptors and can be extremely unpleasant.

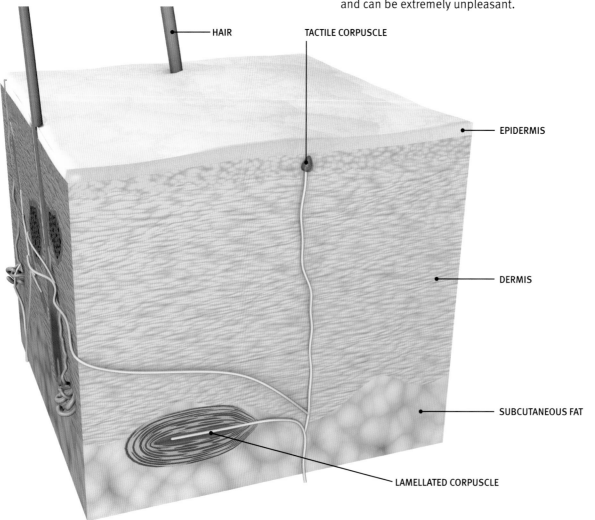

HAIR — TACTILE CORPUSCLE — EPIDERMIS — DERMIS — SUBCUTANEOUS FAT — LAMELLATED CORPUSCLE

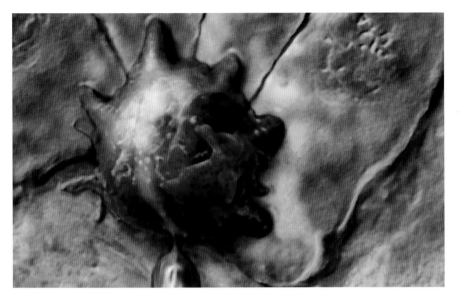

MERKEL'S DISCS
These are a type of touch receptor that detect light touch on non-hairy skin. A similar touch receptor, Ruffini's corpuscles – flattened spindle-shaped nerve endings – detect stretching of the skin and joint movements.

MEISSNER'S TACTILE CORPUSCLES
These lie just beneath the epidermis. They are non-insulated (unmyelinated) nerve endings surrounded by a fibrous capsule. Relatively light pressure changes the shape of the capsule, allowing these nerve endings to detect gentle touches and hair movements. They are found in large numbers on sensitive areas of the skin, such as the fingertips, palms, soles, lips, tongue, eyelids, nipples and genitals. With repeated stimulation, they stop sending signals to the brain, so after putting on gloves, for example, you soon stop feeling them on your skin.

PACINIAN LAMELLATED CORPUSCLES
These lie beneath the dermis in the subcutaneous layer of fat. They are non-insulated (unmyelinated) nerve endings surrounded by an oval, fluid-filled inner bulb. The 20–60 layers of the bulb are made up of modified Schwann neuroglia cells (see page 71). Strong pressure changes the shape of the bulb, allowing the nerve endings to detect firm or rapid touch and vibrations. These corpuscles are found in greatest numbers in the intestinal tract, near the joints and muscles as well as in the bladder wall.

Pain

This is an unpleasant sensory and emotional experience associated with actual or potential tissue damage. It is subjective, and the severity of pain felt does not always correspond to the degree of tissue damage present.

Pain sensation is triggered by stimulation of peripheral nerve endings in the body tissues known as nociceptors. Such stimulation may take the form of an injury, inflammation, infection or other disease. Some nociceptors detect temperature, some detect pressure or damage and some detect the presence of certain chemicals such as capsaicin from chilli peppers. While some nociceptors are very sensitive and give warning pains with minimal stimulation, others are less sensitive and are activated only by severe stimulation, such as cutting, pricking or burning.

When a nociceptor is stimulated, it triggers an electrical message (action potential, see page 72), which is sent up to the spinal cord and relayed on to the brain. Nociceptors with myelinated axons (delta fibres) send pain messages at a speed of 20m (66ft) per second, while those with non-myelinated axons (C fibres) transmit the message at a speed of 2m (6ft 6in) per second. The sensation of pain therefore has two phases: an initial sharp pain, which may trigger a reflex reaction via the spinal nerves (see page 92), and a slower, less intense sensation that quickly follows.

Sensory homunculus

Some parts of the body are connected to more sensory neurons than other parts. A homunculus can represent the relative space these neurons occupy within the brain and demonstrates that the lips, hands, feet and genitals are the most richly supplied with sensory neurons. The sensory neurons are found in the postcentral gyrus in the cerebral cortex (shown below). The cross-section of cerebral cortex (shown right) is coloured to show where the various sensations are picked up.

Handedness is also controlled by the cerebral cortex. In most right-handed people, the left hemisphere is dominant and controls logic and speech, while the right hemisphere produces imaginative and creative thoughts, and deals with the perception of shape and feelings.

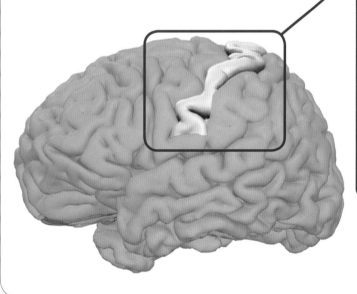

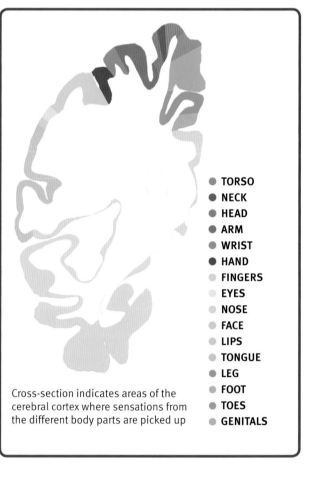

- TORSO
- NECK
- HEAD
- ARM
- WRIST
- HAND
- FINGERS
- EYES
- NOSE
- FACE
- LIPS
- TONGUE
- LEG
- FOOT
- TOES
- GENITALS

Cross-section indicates areas of the cerebral cortex where sensations from the different body parts are picked up

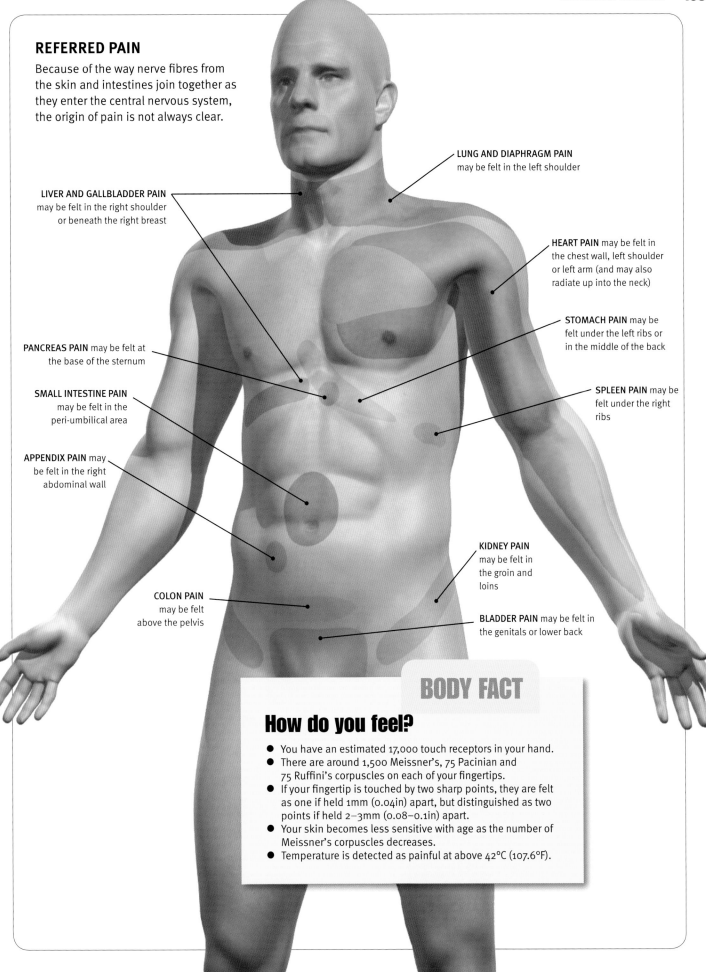

REFERRED PAIN

Because of the way nerve fibres from the skin and intestines join together as they enter the central nervous system, the origin of pain is not always clear.

LUNG AND DIAPHRAGM PAIN may be felt in the left shoulder

LIVER AND GALLBLADDER PAIN may be felt in the right shoulder or beneath the right breast

HEART PAIN may be felt in the chest wall, left shoulder or left arm (and may also radiate up into the neck)

PANCREAS PAIN may be felt at the base of the sternum

STOMACH PAIN may be felt under the left ribs or in the middle of the back

SMALL INTESTINE PAIN may be felt in the peri-umbilical area

SPLEEN PAIN may be felt under the right ribs

APPENDIX PAIN may be felt in the right abdominal wall

KIDNEY PAIN may be felt in the groin and loins

COLON PAIN may be felt above the pelvis

BLADDER PAIN may be felt in the genitals or lower back

BODY FACT

How do you feel?

- You have an estimated 17,000 touch receptors in your hand.
- There are around 1,500 Meissner's, 75 Pacinian and 75 Ruffini's corpuscles on each of your fingertips.
- If your fingertip is touched by two sharp points, they are felt as one if held 1mm (0.04in) apart, but distinguished as two points if held 2–3mm (0.08–0.1in) apart.
- Your skin becomes less sensitive with age as the number of Meissner's corpuscles decreases.
- Temperature is detected as painful at above 42°C (107.6°F).

Nose and smelling

Your sense of smell (also known as olfaction) is provided by chemoreceptors in paired olfactory organs in the nasal cavity on either side of the nasal septum.

Chemoreceptors (sensory receptor cells that sample odour molecules) trigger nerve signals to the brain via the olfactory nerve, to reach the olfactory bulbs situated beneath the frontal cortex on each side. Messages are then relayed to the olfactory cortex of the brain, in the limbic system, where smells are interpreted.

NOSE

As air enters the lower part of the nasal cavity the inferior nasal conchae create turbulence in the air, which increases the surface area and promotes warming of the odorant molecules.

Further warming and turbulence occurs as air continues and passes up and back over the middle and superior nasal conchae (part of the ethmoid bone).

Smell receptors are located in the epithelium that covers the lower surfaces of the cribiform plate and the medial (middle) surfaces of the superior nasal concha.

CILIA OF THE OLFACTORY RECEPTOR CELLS

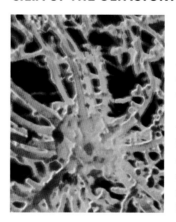

Dissolved chemicals interact with receptors (odorant binding proteins) to spark a nerve impulse down the olfactory nerve. Cilia are whip-like filaments that increase the surface area to which odour molecules bind. Humans have 10–20 million olfactory receptors in an area of 5 squared cm. A drug-sniffing German Shepherd dog, however, has an olfactory receptor surface 72 times greater than that of a human's.

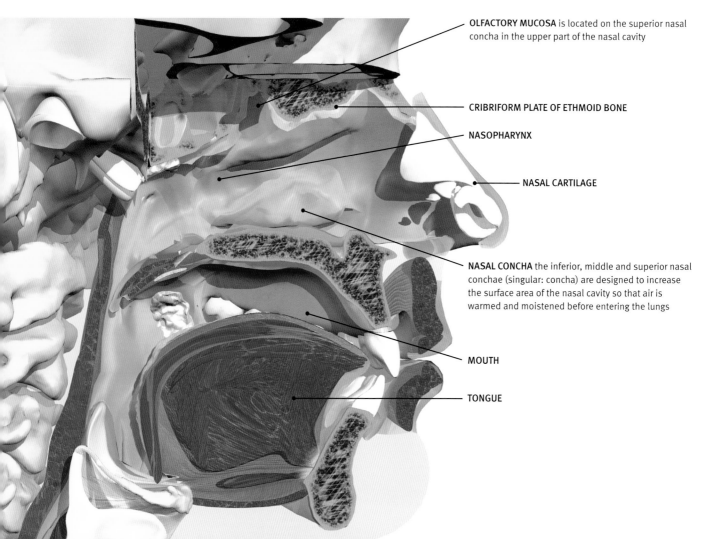

OLFACTORY MUCOSA is located on the superior nasal concha in the upper part of the nasal cavity

CRIBRIFORM PLATE OF ETHMOID BONE

NASOPHARYNX

NASAL CARTILAGE

NASAL CONCHA the inferior, middle and superior nasal conchae (singular: concha) are designed to increase the surface area of the nasal cavity so that air is warmed and moistened before entering the lungs

MOUTH

TONGUE

SMELLING

Breathing draws airborne particles and gases up to the superior concha – a process that is helped by the action of sniffing to detect faint smells. Aromatic molecules, known as odorants, dissolve in mucus on the olfactory epithelium. These are detected by tiny, hair-like sensory nerve endings (cilia) that project from the dendrites of the olfactory receptor cells into the mucus. Odorants bind to specific receptors on the cilia, each of which detects only one particular smell. You have an estimated 12 million olfactory receptor cells, which are divided into around 1,000 different odorant receptor types. Each type responds to a specific group of odorant molecules only.

OLFACTORY NERVES

The axons of the sensory neurones form 15–20 olfactory nerves that are together known as cranial nerve I. These olfactory nerves pass up through the cribriform plate – a series of holes in the ethmoid bone – to reach the olfactory bulbs beneath the frontal cortex on each side (see page 80). Messages are then relayed on to the olfactory cortex of the brain, which is in the limbic system (see page 85).

BODY FACT

Know your nose

- Between 10 and 30 cilia project from each of your olfactory receptor cells.
- Unlike other neurons, olfactory receptor neurons continue to form throughout your life, extending new axons to the olfactory bulb.
- Different combinations of electrical activity enable you to detect between 4,000 and 10,000 different smells, although you have only 1,000 different olfactory receptor types.
- Around 80 per cent of the flavour of food is contributed by the sense of smell.
- Hunger heightens your sense of smell.
- Women have a more sensitive sense of smell than men, and it is strongest around the time of ovulation.
- Your brain quickly becomes used to persistent smells and stops detecting them.

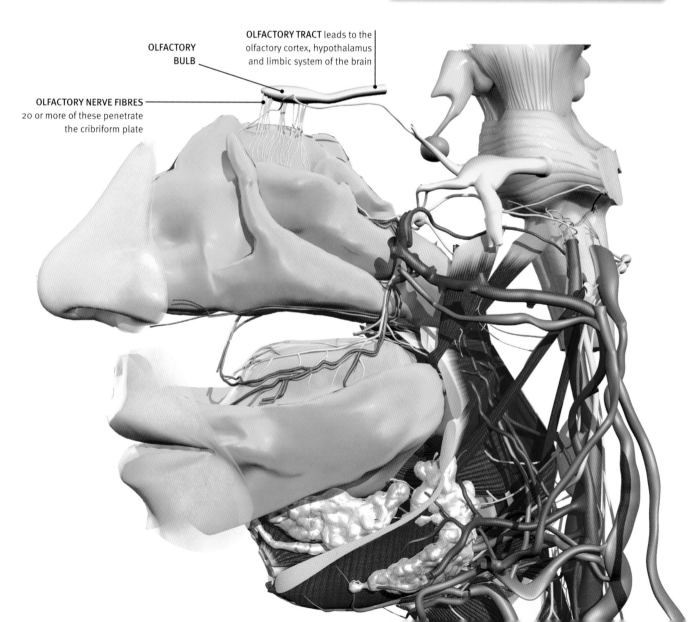

OLFACTORY BULB

OLFACTORY TRACT leads to the olfactory cortex, hypothalamus and limbic system of the brain

OLFACTORY NERVE FIBRES
20 or more of these penetrate the cribriform plate

Ears and hearing

Your ears are divided into three parts: the outer visible part of the ear, the middle ear and the inner ear. The outer ears collect sound vibrations and funnel them through the auditory canal to the tympanic membrane (or eardrum). Movement of the tympanic membrane triggers a chain of movement in three tiny bones within the middle ear. These hinged bones, called ossicles, amplify the vibrations and pass them on to the inner ear to be converted into electrical impulses, which are sent to the brain, where they are perceived as sounds. The delicate middle and inner ear are protected by the bones of the skull.

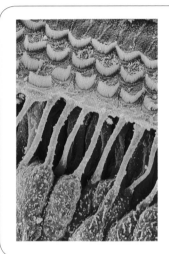

SENSORY HAIR CELLS OF THE INNER EAR
The ear converts sound waves into nerve impulses by stimulating the stereocilia projections at the end of the hair cells (the pink and brown). Sound waves displace the fluid in the ear causing the hairs to bend, generating nerve impulses that travel to the brain via the auditory nerve.

Outer ear

Also known as the pinna, this flap of cartilage and flesh provides a physical barrier to foreign objects that might get into the ear; its primary function. however, is to collect sound. It functions in a similar way to a satellite dish, collecting sounds and directing them towards the auditory canal. The folds and grooves of the pinna modify the transmission of sound waves to the middle and inner ear helping the brain determine the location of the source of the sound.

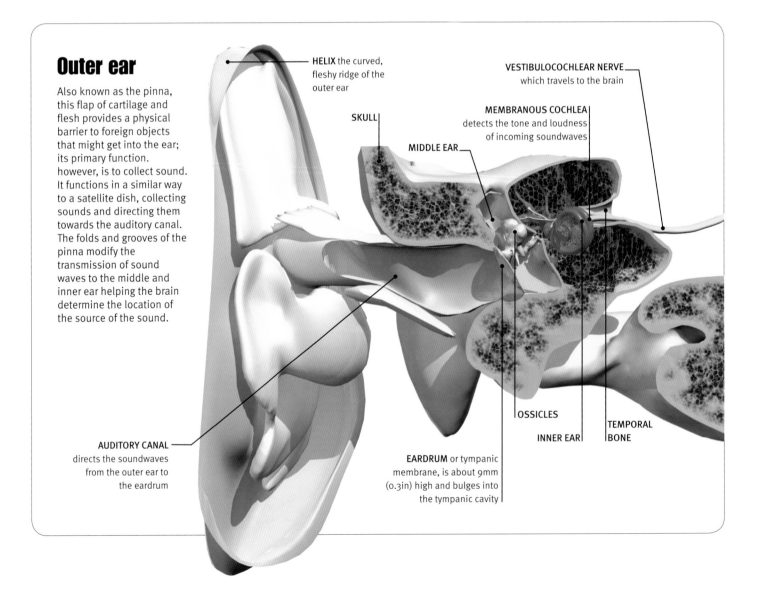

HELIX the curved, fleshy ridge of the outer ear

SKULL

MIDDLE EAR

VESTIBULOCOCHLEAR NERVE which travels to the brain

MEMBRANOUS COCHLEA detects the tone and loudness of incoming soundwaves

OSSICLES

INNER EAR

TEMPORAL BONE

AUDITORY CANAL directs the soundwaves from the outer ear to the eardrum

EARDRUM or tympanic membrane, is about 9mm (0.3in) high and bulges into the tympanic cavity

Middle ear

The middle ear contains three ossicles (bones): the malleus (hammer), incus (anvil) and stapes (stirrup), which are named after their shape. They are the three tiniest bones in the body and their role is to transmit sound from the eardrum to the inner ear. The sensory structures of the inner ear are surrounded with fluid, which is more difficult for the soundwaves to move through than air. The ossicles amplify the sound vibrations as they pass from the eardrum through to a membrane-covered opening called the oval window, located behind the stapes.

The tensor tympani muscle stabilizes the malleus to damp down vibrations caused by chewing. The stapedius muscle reduces excessive movement in the stapes to control the amplitude of sound waves transmitted to the inner ear.

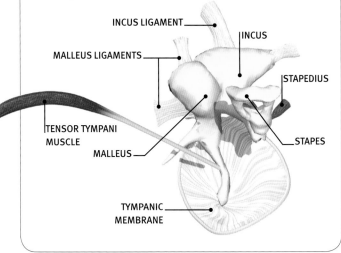

INCUS LIGAMENT
INCUS
MALLEUS LIGAMENTS
STAPEDIUS
TENSOR TYMPANI MUSCLE
MALLEUS
STAPES
TYMPANIC MEMBRANE

Inner ear

The inner ear consists of the coiled cochlea, which detects sounds, plus the vestibular apparatus, which detects movement.

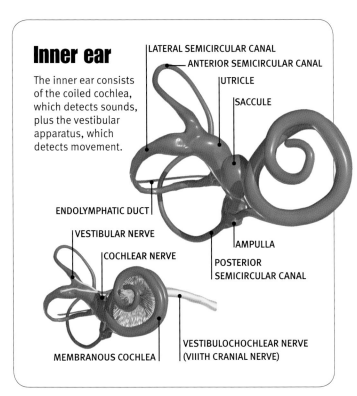

LATERAL SEMICIRCULAR CANAL
ANTERIOR SEMICIRCULAR CANAL
UTRICLE
SACCULE
ENDOLYMPHATIC DUCT
VESTIBULAR NERVE
COCHLEAR NERVE
AMPULLA
POSTERIOR SEMICIRCULAR CANAL
MEMBRANOUS COCHLEA
VESTIBULOCHOCHLEAR NERVE (VIIITH CRANIAL NERVE)

SOUND TRANSMISSION

The cochlea is divided lengthwise by a fluid-filled tube known as the cochlear duct. This contains the organ of Corti, which is made up of sensitive sound receptors attached to a basilar membrane. The sound receptor cells have hair-like projections on their surface known as stereocilia, which are in contact with an overhanging tectorial membrane (far left). Sounds transmitted to the inner ear cause the basilar membrane of the cochlear duct to vibrate. This causes the hair cells to brush against the overhanging tectorial membrane, which bends the stereocilia. The receptors then send a signal to the brain, via the vestibulocochlear nerve and this is interpreted as a sound. The frequency of the sound waves determines how far along the membrane the vibrations travel and this determines which sound receptors are stimulated. Because of their position on the basilar membrane, each hair cell responds best to a single frequency.

MOTION

The organs of balance are found in the inner ear and are made up of the utricle, which detects horizontal movements; the saccule, which detects vertical movements; and three semicircular canals, which detect rotational movement. They all contain endolymph fluid.

The semicircular canals are perpendicular to each other. One end of each canal carries a swelling (the ampulla) containing a cluster of hair cells. Each hair cell has 30–150 hair-like projections (the stereocilia) on its surface. One end of each hair cell is embedded in a gelatinous structure (the cupula), while the other end connects to the vestibulocochlear nerve (cranial nerve VIII).

The utricle and saccule both contain hair cells, over which lies a membrane embedded with microscopic crystals of calcium carbonate. These are known as otoconia (ear dust) and are displaced by movement in any direction. As the otoconia brush against the hair cells and displace the stereocilia, movement is detected. The otoconia are also sensitive to the pull of gravity, helping with reflex righting of the head and orientation in space.

The act of turning round and round (rotational acceleration) causes swirling movements in the endolymph inside the ampulla, in the opposite direction of rotation. This deforms the cupula, bending the hair cells, which send messages to the cerebellum in the brain, where they are interpreted as rotational motion.

Tongue and tasting

Your sense of taste is known as gustation, and your taste buds are the chemoreceptors (chemical receptors) located inside your mouth, mainly on your tongue. These detect five basic taste perceptions: bitter, sweet, salty, sour and savoury – a recently recognized taste sensation known by the Japanese term 'umami'. Umami is triggered by certain amino acids such as glutamate and aspartate. A sixth taste perception, known as 'fatness', may be added to this classification; this is triggered by certain dietary fatty acids, for example, linoleic acid.

HOW TASTE WORKS

Researchers increasingly believe that taste is not made up of these individual primary 'building blocks' at all, but involves a continuum of flavour perception similar to that of colour vision. Other nuances of flavour come from your sense of smell, texture, temperature, astringency, spiciness, coolness (for example, menthol), numbness, fizziness, a metallic taste and mouth 'feel' (known by the Japanese term 'kokumi'), with input from your visual and auditory stimuli.

Taste bud information is taken to the brain by several of the cranial nerves (see page 89). Here, it is added to and translated with data regarding food texture, smell and peppery hot sensations in the frontal cortex.

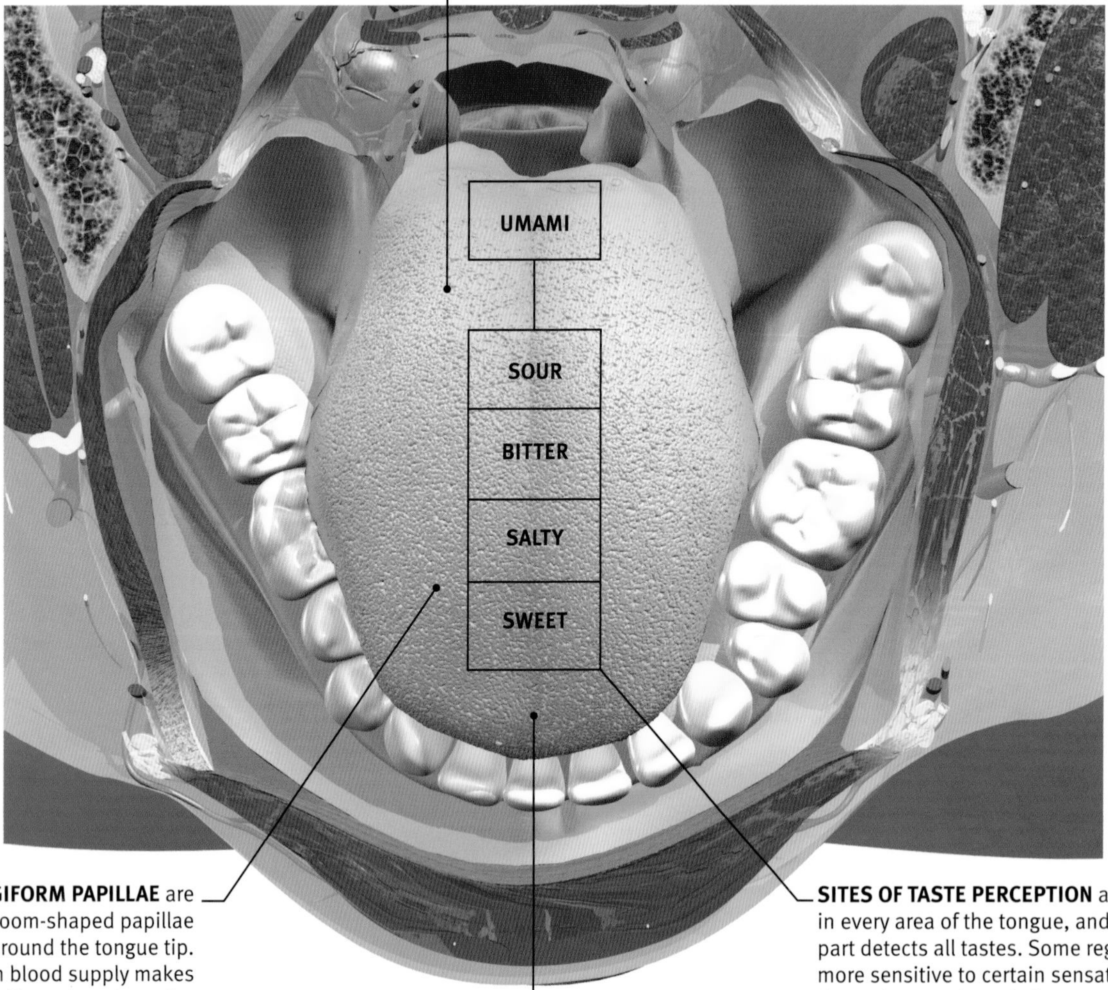

CIRCUMVALLATE PAPILLAE sensitive to sour and bitter taste

UMAMI

SOUR

BITTER

SALTY

SWEET

FUNGIFORM PAPILLAE are mushroom-shaped papillae clustered around the tongue tip. Their rich blood supply makes them look like red spots on the tongue. They are sensitive to the full range of taste perception

FILIFORM PAPILLAE

SITES OF TASTE PERCEPTION are found in every area of the tongue, and every part detects all tastes. Some regions are more sensitive to certain sensations than others and one in four people have a heightened sense of taste perception. Known as supertasters, they have more fungiform papillae on their tongues.

Tongue muscles

The intrinsic muscles of the tongue have fibres that run vertically and longitudinally as well as transversely.

The extrinsic muscles of the tongue (the hyoglossus, styloglossus, genioglossus and geniohyoid) assist movements of the tongue during talking, chewing and swallowing.

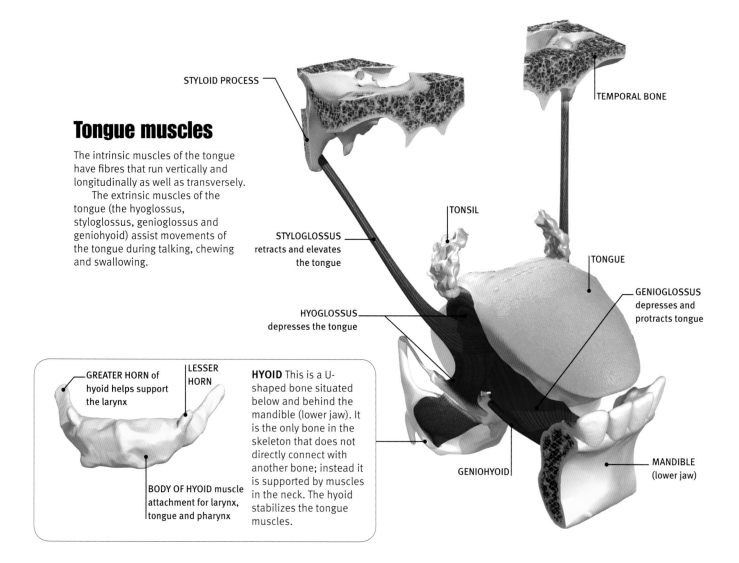

STYLOID PROCESS

TEMPORAL BONE

TONSIL

STYLOGLOSSUS retracts and elevates the tongue

TONGUE

HYOGLOSSUS depresses the tongue

GENIOGLOSSUS depresses and protracts tongue

GENIOHYOID

MANDIBLE (lower jaw)

GREATER HORN of hyoid helps support the larynx

LESSER HORN

HYOID This is a U-shaped bone situated below and behind the mandible (lower jaw). It is the only bone in the skeleton that does not directly connect with another bone; instead it is supported by muscles in the neck. The hyoid stabilizes the tongue muscles.

BODY OF HYOID muscle attachment for larynx, tongue and pharynx

Taste buds

Located on small bumps on the tongue surface (papillae), taste buds consist of a central pore filled with saliva and many spindle shaped receptor cells (taste hairs) that dip into the pool to detect dissolved chemicals. Messages are sent to the gustatory region of the brain cortex for translation. Each gustatory cell has a lifespan of about only 10 days, after which it is replaced.

TASTE PORE filled with saliva

TASTE HAIR

Taste-based statistics

- There are over 10,000 taste buds on your tongue.
- You have an estimated 200 fungiform papillae, containing 1,100 taste buds in total.
- You have around ten foliate papillae, containing 1,200 taste buds in total.
- You also have around three to 13 circumvallate papillae, containing 2,200 taste buds in total.
- There are another 2,500 or so taste buds on the soft tissues of your pharynx.
- Taste bud cells survive for a week only before being renewed.
- There is a wide genetic variation in the ability to taste different flavours, especially bitterness.

RESPIRATORY SYSTEM

BREATH OF LIFE
These coloured X-rays show the process of breathing in and
out. During inhalation the ribs move up and outwards
allowing the lungs to expand. Here, the ribs move down and
in, forcing air out of the lungs during exhalation.

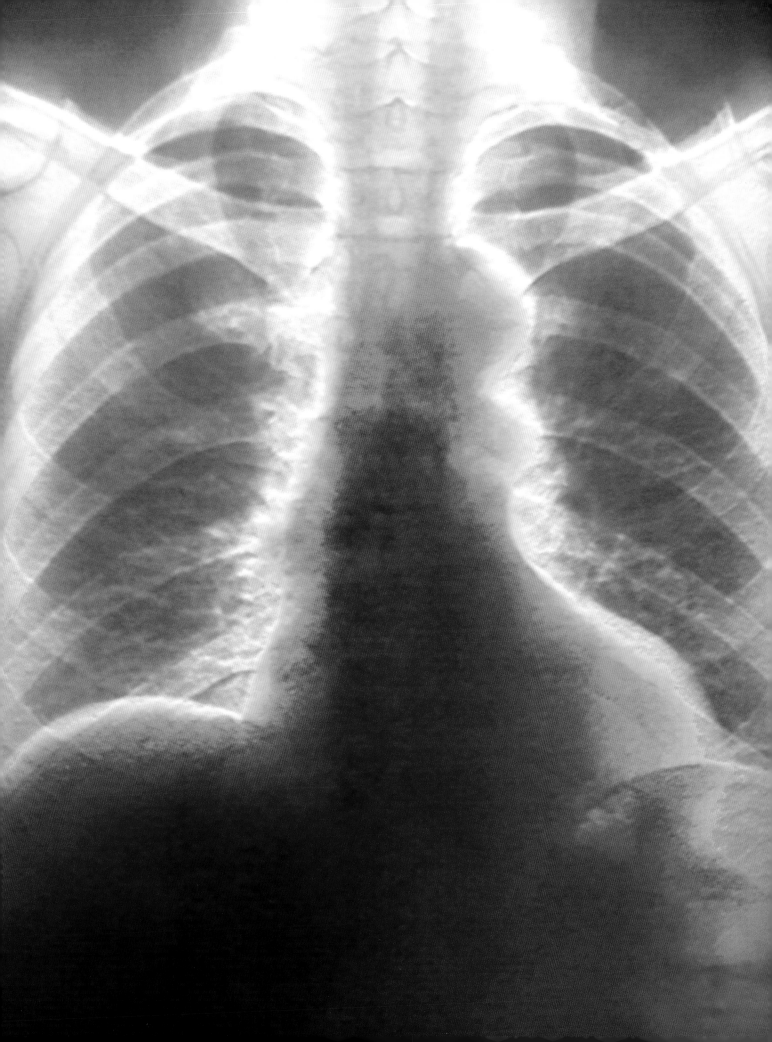

Upper respiratory system

Air is drawn into your body through your nose and, sometimes, your mouth during breathing. Your nose has two entrances, the left and right nostrils (nares), which are separated by the nasal septum.

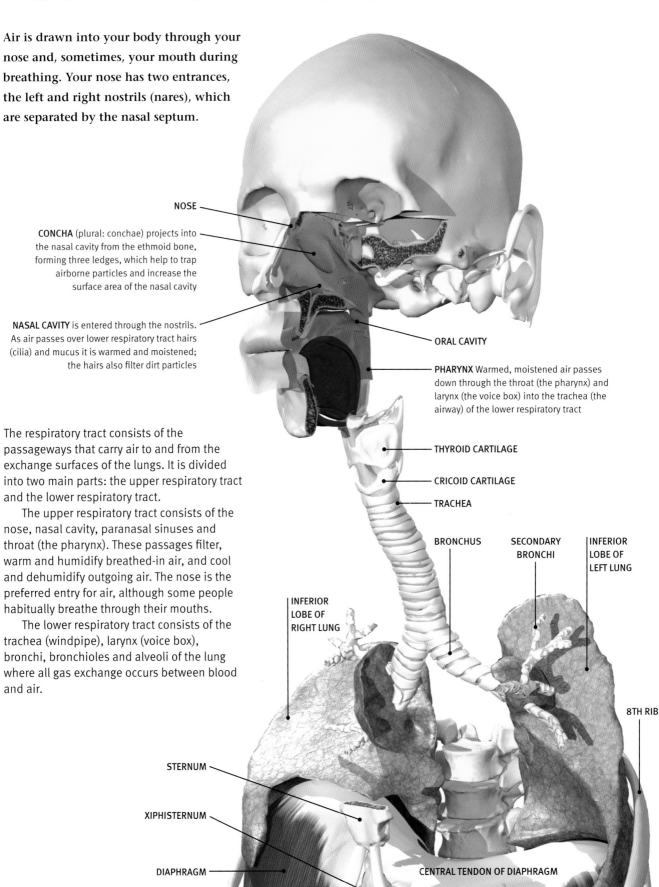

NOSE

CONCHA (plural: conchae) projects into the nasal cavity from the ethmoid bone, forming three ledges, which help to trap airborne particles and increase the surface area of the nasal cavity

NASAL CAVITY is entered through the nostrils. As air passes over lower respiratory tract hairs (cilia) and mucus it is warmed and moistened; the hairs also filter dirt particles

ORAL CAVITY

PHARYNX Warmed, moistened air passes down through the throat (the pharynx) and larynx (the voice box) into the trachea (the airway) of the lower respiratory tract

THYROID CARTILAGE

CRICOID CARTILAGE

TRACHEA

BRONCHUS

SECONDARY BRONCHI

INFERIOR LOBE OF LEFT LUNG

INFERIOR LOBE OF RIGHT LUNG

8TH RIB

STERNUM

XIPHISTERNUM

DIAPHRAGM

CENTRAL TENDON OF DIAPHRAGM

The respiratory tract consists of the passageways that carry air to and from the exchange surfaces of the lungs. It is divided into two main parts: the upper respiratory tract and the lower respiratory tract.

The upper respiratory tract consists of the nose, nasal cavity, paranasal sinuses and throat (the pharynx). These passages filter, warm and humidify breathed-in air, and cool and dehumidify outgoing air. The nose is the preferred entry for air, although some people habitually breathe through their mouths.

The lower respiratory tract consists of the trachea (windpipe), larynx (voice box), bronchi, bronchioles and alveoli of the lung where all gas exchange occurs between blood and air.

Larynx

The larynx protects the entrance to the trachea and houses the vocal cords. It is made up of nine pieces of cartilage: the thyroid cartilage, cricoid cartilage, epiglottis, two arytenoid cartilages, two corniculate cartilages and two cuneiform cartilages. The image below is a frontal section of the larynx showing a vocal cord.

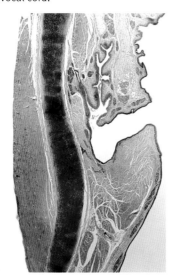

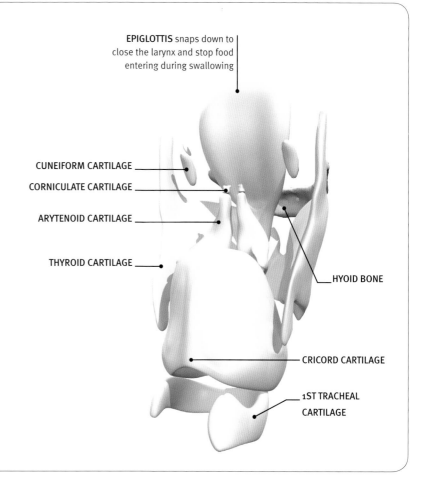

EPIGLOTTIS snaps down to close the larynx and stop food entering during swallowing

CUNEIFORM CARTILAGE

CORNICULATE CARTILAGE

ARYTENOID CARTILAGE

THYROID CARTILAGE

HYOID BONE

CRICORD CARTILAGE

1ST TRACHEAL CARTILAGE

Phonation

The vocal cords are formed from two folds of mucous membrane stretched horizontally across the larynx. They are attached to the thyroid cartilage at the front, and to the arytenoid cartilages at the back. The vocal cords lie open when at rest to allow inhalation and exhalation of air. When the cords close, air passing through them during exhalation causes them to vibrate, producing sound.

ARYEPIGLOTTIC FOLD

VOCAL FOLD (CORD)

UPPER TRACHEA

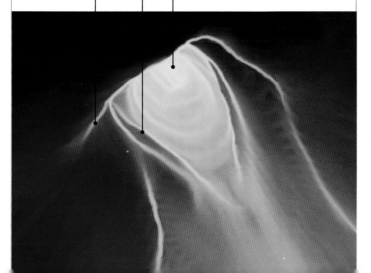

BODY FACT

Achoo!

- During cold weather, the respiratory cilia that sweep mucus away from your nostrils towards the throat work more slowly so that your nose starts to drip.
- Inflammation of the mucosa lining the upper respiratory system (caused by, for example, virus infections or allergies) causes congestion and increased production of mucus.
- Your vocal cords and the space between them are together known as your glottis.
- Hiccups are caused by a rapidly contracting diaphragm involuntarily forcing air through the vocal cords.
- Half a litre (one pint) of water is lost from the body through the lungs each day.

Respiratory reflexes

Respiration is controlled by the respiratory centres in the brain. Sensory information is delivered by receptors sensitive to oxygen, carbon dioxide and acidity levels in the blood and cerebrospinal fluid, blood pressure receptors, stretch receptors in the lungs and other sensations such as pain and nasal irritation. This information alters the breathing pattern to increase and decrease the rate and depth of respiration. Certain reflexes prevent the lungs over-inflating, or reduce exposure to irritant chemicals. Most breathing is subconscious, but thought processes and emotions can also affect it.

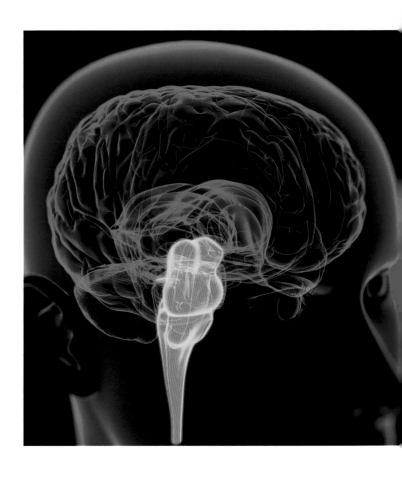

MEDULLA OBLONGATA

The medulla oblongata – often simply referred to as the medulla – is the lower half of the brainstem which connects the brain to the spinal cord. It controls the cardiac, respiratory and vasomotor centres and deals with autonomic, involuntary functions, such as breathing, heart rate and blood pressure, as well as the respiratory reflexes.

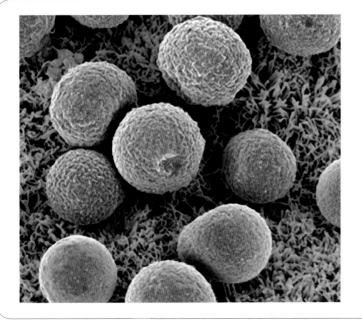

Coughing

This is the forceful release of air from the lungs. It helps to clear the airways (trachea and bronchi) when cough receptors are irritated by inhaled particles or excessive mucus. A cough starts with a deep breath in, then the glottis (the vocal cords and the space between them) snaps shut, trapping air in the lungs. The diaphragm and other breathing muscles then forcefully contract. The pressure causes the glottis to snap open, producing an explosive outflow of air. Mucus droplets (right) are expelled during coughing, which expels bacteria and dust particles.

Sneezing

This helps to clear the upper respiratory passages when the nasal lining (the mucosa) is irritated by inhaled particles, strong odours or infection. Sneezing starts with one or more large inhalations of air (ah ... ah .... ah ...). The reflex closes the glottis and the eyes, and forceful contraction of the respiratory muscles opens the glottis and forces air out through the nose and mouth (ah... chooo). The tongue may block the back of the mouth, so the force of the sneeze is directed out through the nose. Sneezing is triggered in around one in three people by the sudden exposure to bright light (photic sneeze response). This occurs when overstimulation of the optic nerve (cranial nerve II) produces a response in the trigeminal nerve (cranial nerve V), and is an inherited genetic trait.

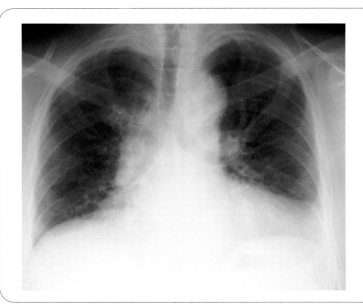

Yawning

This is an involuntary action that is learned during embryonic development. All vertebrate animals yawn, and the mechanism persists even in those who have brain damage. It is thought to be an involuntary inspiration triggered by raised blood levels of carbon dioxide, to draw more oxygen into the lungs and raise blood oxygen levels. Researchers have shown that it also cools blood as it passes through the brain.

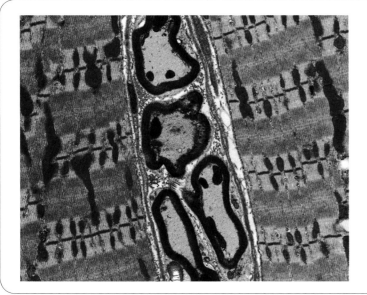

Hiccups

These are sudden involuntary contractions of the diaphragm. Scientists suspect this is a throwback to when our ancestors were amphibious, living partly in water and partly on land. Hiccuping closes the glottis and would have stopped water entering the primitive lungs as it was pushed across the gills. A fetus hiccups within the amniotic fluid of the womb, and this reflex may have become adapted to help newborn babies close their glottis while suckling, so that milk doesn't enter the lungs. Hiccups are activated by nerves in the diaphragm controlling muscle activity.

Lower respiratory system

Your lower respiratory system consists of the trachea (airway), the left and right bronchi (singular: bronchus) and their subdivisions and the left and right lung tissues, where gaseous exchange takes place.

AIRWAYS

The largest airway in your lower respiratory tract is the trachea. It extends from the larynx into the upper chest, where it divides to form the left and right main bronchi (singular: bronchus) – one for each lung. This division is about level with the fourth or fifth thoracic vertebrae. The right bronchus is wider, shorter and more vertical than the left one.

Each bronchus further subdivides into smaller bronchi, then smaller tubes called bronchioles within the lungs. At the end of the tubes are air sacs (alveoli, singular: alveolus) where oxygen is picked up by the blood and carbon dioxide is given up.

LUNGS

There are two lungs. Each is shaped like a cone, with a narrow apex and a wide base. The right lung has three lobes, while the left has only two to make room for the heart. The lobes are further divided into segments, separated from each other by connective tissue. These segments are further divided into lobules.

PLEURAL SACS

Each lung is enclosed in a pleural sac that has two layers. The outer, or parietal, wall of each sac is attached to the chest wall while the inner, or visceral, wall is attached to the lung beneath it. The pleura are separated by a thin layer of lubricating fluid that allows the lungs to slide over the chest wall when they expand (inflate) and relax (deflate) during breathing.

LOWER RESPIRATORY TRACT LINING

The lower respiratory tract passages (like the upper tract passages) are lined by a moist mucous membrane (mucosa). The bronchi are lined by ciliated columnar epithelium, which secretes mucus. Tiny, hair-like projections on their cell surface (cilia) beat in a co-ordinated fashion to move mucus and trapped particles up out of the lungs on the so-called mucociliary escalator.

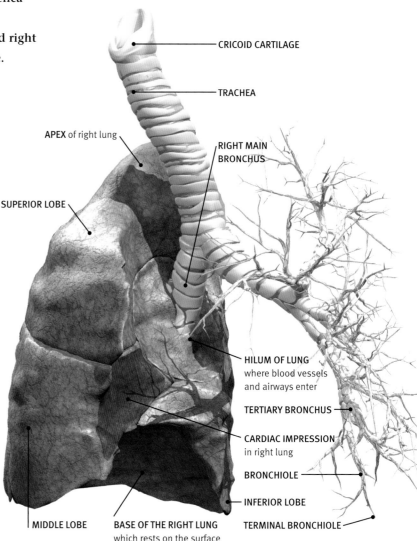

RIGHT LUNG

CRICOID CARTILAGE

TRACHEA

APEX of right lung

RIGHT MAIN BRONCHUS

SUPERIOR LOBE

HILUM OF LUNG where blood vessels and airways enter

TERTIARY BRONCHUS

CARDIAC IMPRESSION in right lung

BRONCHIOLE

INFERIOR LOBE

MIDDLE LOBE

BASE OF THE RIGHT LUNG which rests on the surface of the diaphragm

TERMINAL BRONCHIOLE

Composition of air and gas exchange

The air you inhale and exhale consists mostly of the inert gas, nitrogen. Atmospheric air is around 21 per cent oxygen, and your body extracts a small percentage of this – the air you exhale is around 16 per cent oxygen (enough to provide oxygen during mouth-to-mouth ventilation).

Inhaled air contains a tiny amount of carbon dioxide (0.038 per cent), but exhaled air contains much more (four per cent). This is because the processes of metabolism generate carbon dioxide, which must be disposed of before it builds up to toxic levels. Oxygen is taken into your body and the carbon dioxide disposed of during gas exchange within your lungs.

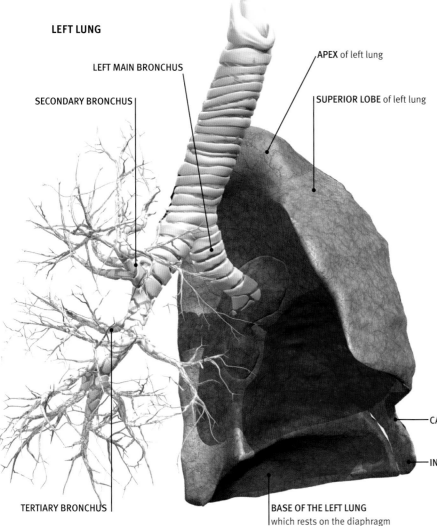

LEFT LUNG

LEFT MAIN BRONCHUS

SECONDARY BRONCHUS

APEX of left lung

SUPERIOR LOBE of left lung

CARDIAC NOTCH

INFERIOR LOBE of left lung

TERTIARY BRONCHUS

BASE OF THE LEFT LUNG
which rests on the diaphragm

Bronchioles and air sacs

The two main left and right bronchi each further subdivide within the lungs. The right main bronchus divides to form three secondary bronchi, while the left main bronchus divides to form two. These divide into smaller and smaller tubes called bronchioles. At the end, or terminal point, of each tube is a network of tiny air sacs where the gaseous exchange takes place.

In the centre of this electron micrograph of a section of human lung is the top of one of the many bronchioles as it branches from a bronchus. Unlike the main air passages of the respiratory system, the walls of the bronchioles do not contain cartilage, and are not lined with mucous cells.

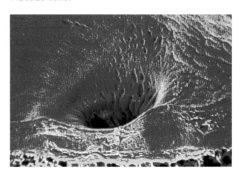

DIAPHRAGM

Below the lungs is a sheet of muscle called the diaphragm (see page 112). During breathing, this muscle contracts and flattens. This reduces pressure in the thoracic cavity, which allows the lungs to expand downwards. The diaphragm then returns to its previous position and the lungs return to their previous shape, pushing the air out.

Protecting the airways

The walls of the trachea and main bronchi are kept open by rings of tracheal cartilage. The bronchi and bronchioles contain smooth (involuntary) muscles that constrict or dilate to vary their diameter. The pleural membranes surround each lung.

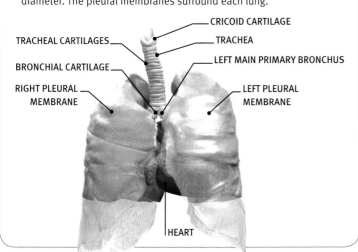

CRICOID CARTILAGE

TRACHEAL CARTILAGES

TRACHEA

BRONCHIAL CARTILAGE

LEFT MAIN PRIMARY BRONCHUS

RIGHT PLEURAL
MEMBRANE

LEFT PLEURAL
MEMBRANE

HEART

BODY FACT

All about breathing

● You breathe 12–15 times per minute at rest increasing to 20 times a minute or more during physical exertion. This adds up to over ten million breaths taken per year and over 750 million breaths during an average life span. Most of the time, breathing is an involuntary action.
● A newborn baby breathes around 44 times per minute.

CARDIOVASCULAR
SYSTEM

PROLIFIC RED BLOOD CELLS
Coloured scanning electron micrograph of red blood cells in an arteriole in the lungs. These biconcave, disc-shaped cells transport oxygen from the lungs to other cells, circulating around the body in the bloodstream. They also transport some of the waste gas, carbon dioxide, back to the lungs for exhalation. They are the most abundant cell in the blood; their red colour is produced by the oxygen-carrying protein, haemoglobin.

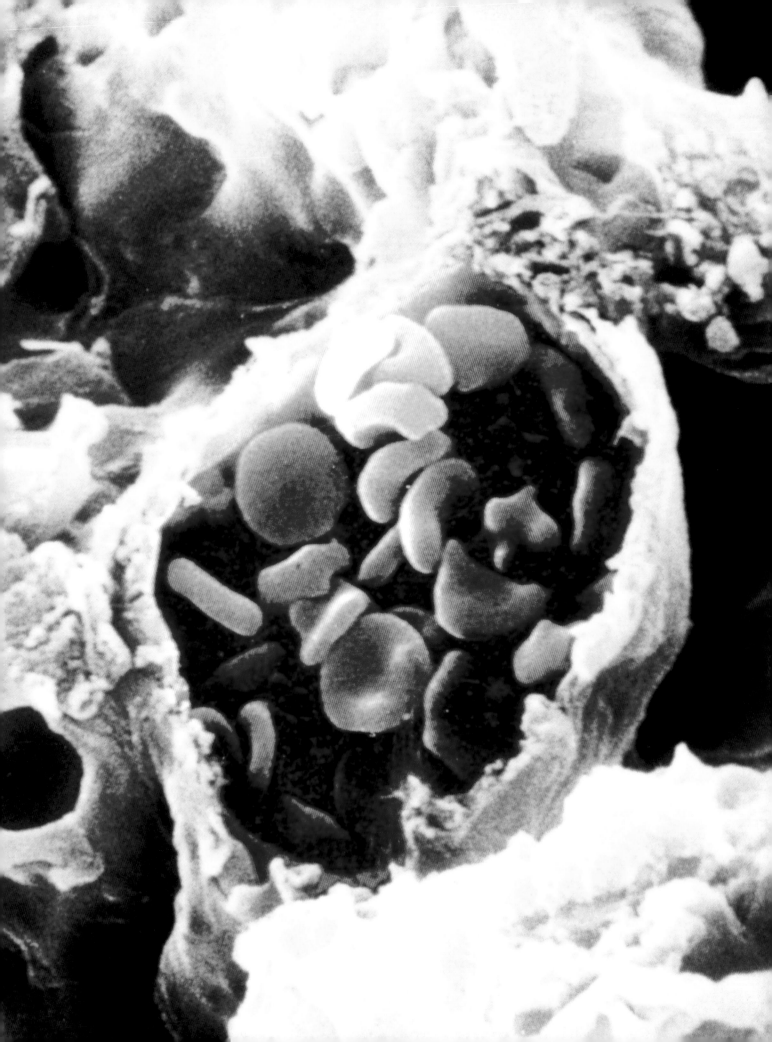

Cardiovascular system

Your cardiovascular system comprises the heart, arteries, capillaries and veins. It transports blood around your body, carrying oxygen, glucose and nutrients to the tissues, and removing waste products such as carbon dioxide, lactic acid, urea and excess fluid for excretion.

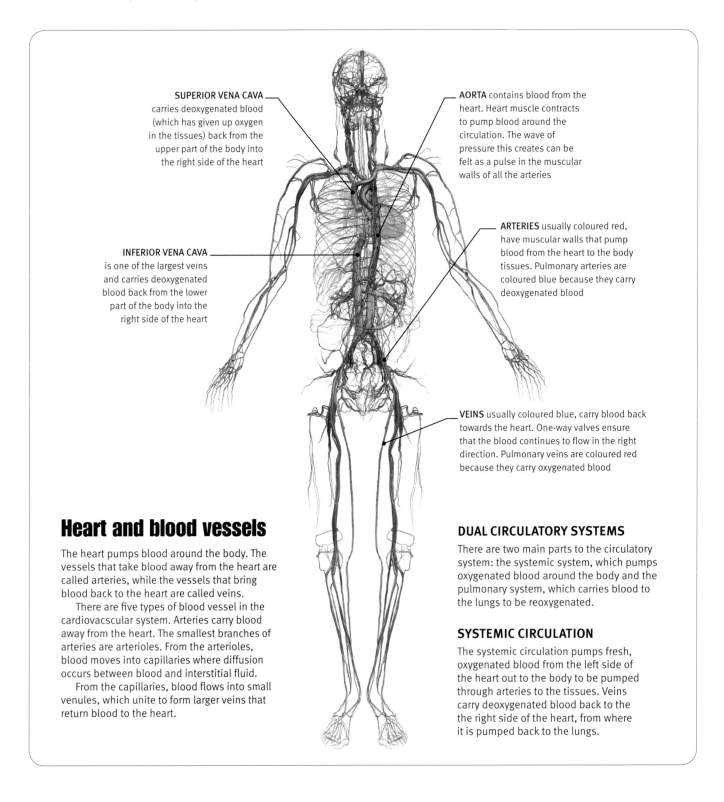

SUPERIOR VENA CAVA carries deoxygenated blood (which has given up oxygen in the tissues) back from the upper part of the body into the right side of the heart

AORTA contains blood from the heart. Heart muscle contracts to pump blood around the circulation. The wave of pressure this creates can be felt as a pulse in the muscular walls of all the arteries

INFERIOR VENA CAVA is one of the largest veins and carries deoxygenated blood back from the lower part of the body into the right side of the heart

ARTERIES usually coloured red, have muscular walls that pump blood from the heart to the body tissues. Pulmonary arteries are coloured blue because they carry deoxygenated blood

VEINS usually coloured blue, carry blood back towards the heart. One-way valves ensure that the blood continues to flow in the right direction. Pulmonary veins are coloured red because they carry oxygenated blood

Heart and blood vessels

The heart pumps blood around the body. The vessels that take blood away from the heart are called arteries, while the vessels that bring blood back to the heart are called veins.

There are five types of blood vessel in the cardiovascsular system. Arteries carry blood away from the heart. The smallest branches of arteries are arterioles. From the arterioles, blood moves into capillaries where diffusion occurs between blood and interstitial fluid.

From the capillaries, blood flows into small venules, which unite to form larger veins that return blood to the heart.

DUAL CIRCULATORY SYSTEMS

There are two main parts to the circulatory system: the systemic system, which pumps oxygenated blood around the body and the pulmonary system, which carries blood to the lungs to be reoxygenated.

SYSTEMIC CIRCULATION

The systemic circulation pumps fresh, oxygenated blood from the left side of the heart out to the body to be pumped through arteries to the tissues. Veins carry deoxygenated blood back to the the right side of the heart, from where it is pumped back to the lungs.

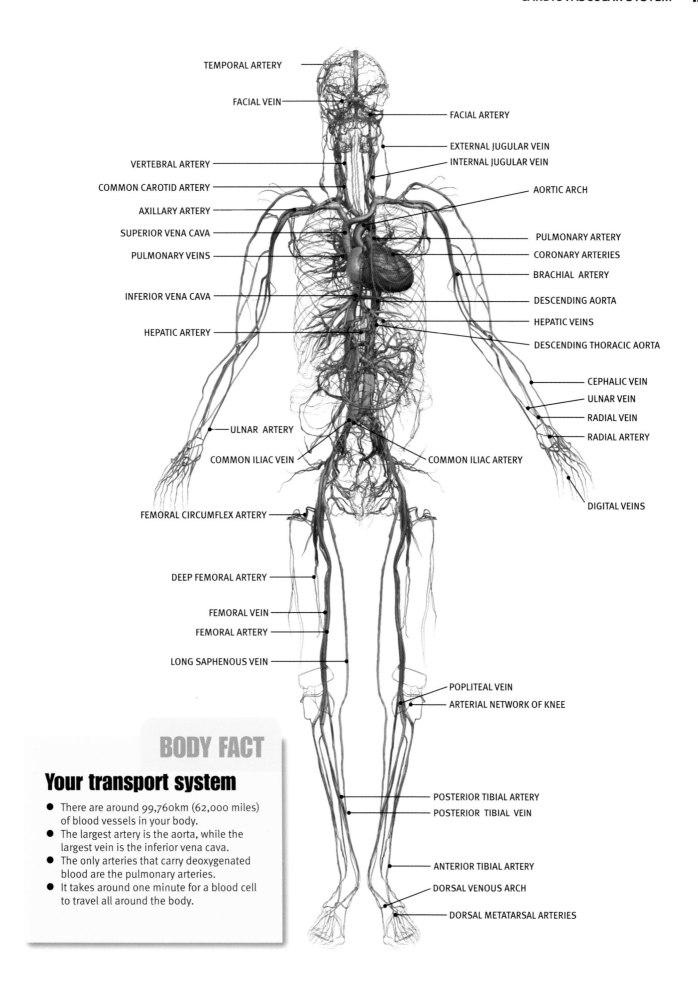

TEMPORAL ARTERY

FACIAL VEIN

FACIAL ARTERY

EXTERNAL JUGULAR VEIN

INTERNAL JUGULAR VEIN

VERTEBRAL ARTERY

COMMON CAROTID ARTERY

AORTIC ARCH

AXILLARY ARTERY

SUPERIOR VENA CAVA

PULMONARY ARTERY

PULMONARY VEINS

CORONARY ARTERIES

BRACHIAL ARTERY

INFERIOR VENA CAVA

DESCENDING AORTA

HEPATIC VEINS

HEPATIC ARTERY

DESCENDING THORACIC AORTA

CEPHALIC VEIN

ULNAR VEIN

RADIAL VEIN

RADIAL ARTERY

ULNAR ARTERY

COMMON ILIAC VEIN

COMMON ILIAC ARTERY

DIGITAL VEINS

FEMORAL CIRCUMFLEX ARTERY

DEEP FEMORAL ARTERY

FEMORAL VEIN

FEMORAL ARTERY

LONG SAPHENOUS VEIN

POPLITEAL VEIN

ARTERIAL NETWORK OF KNEE

BODY FACT

Your transport system

- There are around 99,760km (62,000 miles) of blood vessels in your body.
- The largest artery is the aorta, while the largest vein is the inferior vena cava.
- The only arteries that carry deoxygenated blood are the pulmonary arteries.
- It takes around one minute for a blood cell to travel all around the body.

POSTERIOR TIBIAL ARTERY

POSTERIOR TIBIAL VEIN

ANTERIOR TIBIAL ARTERY

DORSAL VENOUS ARCH

DORSAL METATARSAL ARTERIES

Pulmonary system

This is where deoxygenated blood that has circulated around the body is reoxygenated. Pulmonary arteries carry blood from the heart to the lungs (see page 116) where waste carbon dioxide is given up and the blood is replenished with oxygen. This is the only part of the circulatory system in which arteries contain deoxygenated blood and the veins carry oxygenated blood.

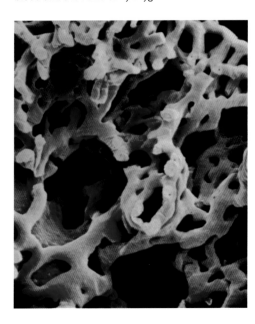

BLOOD SUPPLY IN THE ALVEOLI These are the smallest sacs in the lungs (shown below in blue) where gas exchange occurs. Each alveolus is surrounded by a network of capillaries (the areas in pale pink) supported by elastic fibres. The capillaries are the end branches of the pulmonary arteries, which bring in blood that is low in oxygen. The red blood cells are the areas shown in red below.

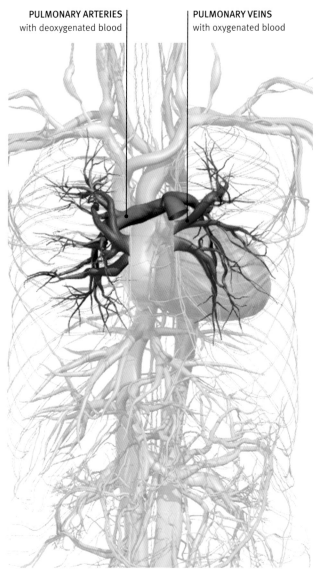

PULMONARY ARTERIES
with deoxygenated blood

PULMONARY VEINS
with oxygenated blood

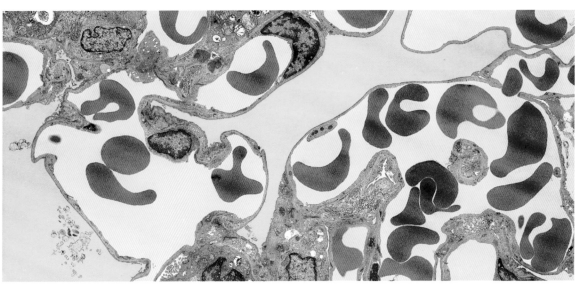

Heart

Your heart is a powerful muscular pump that is divided into two distinct halves, separated by a thick muscular wall known as the septum. Each half of the heart is further divided into two communicating chambers: an upper atrium and a lower ventricle through which blood is pumped.

Your unbeatable pump

- Your heart beats on average 70 times per minute, which is 100,800 times per day, 36,792,000 times per year and over 2,760 million times during the average lifespan.
- Your heart pumps 80ml (2¾ fl oz) of blood with each beat, that is over 8,000 litres (about 14,000 pints) of blood per day, 3,000,000 litres (5,300,000 pints) per year, and over 225,000,000 litres (375,000,000 pints) during an average life span.
- The sound of the heart valves opening and closing produces the familiar 'lub-dub' sounds.
- The lowest blood pressure in the circulation occurs when the heart rests between contractions (diastole).
- The highest blood pressure in the circulation occurs when the ventricles contract (ventricular systole).

Coronary circulation

The muscular walls of the heart need more oxygen and energy than any other muscles in your body. To facilitate this, the heart has its own supply of blood vessels, the coronary blood vessels. There are two main arteries, the right and left coronary arteries, which branch out of the aorta. These further subdivide into a complex network of smaller and smaller blood vessels that supply the heart muscle with its oxygen. As in the rest of the body, blood that has given up its oxygen is carried back to the heart through veins. Most of the blood collects into one vein, the coronary sinus, which empties into the right side of the heart.

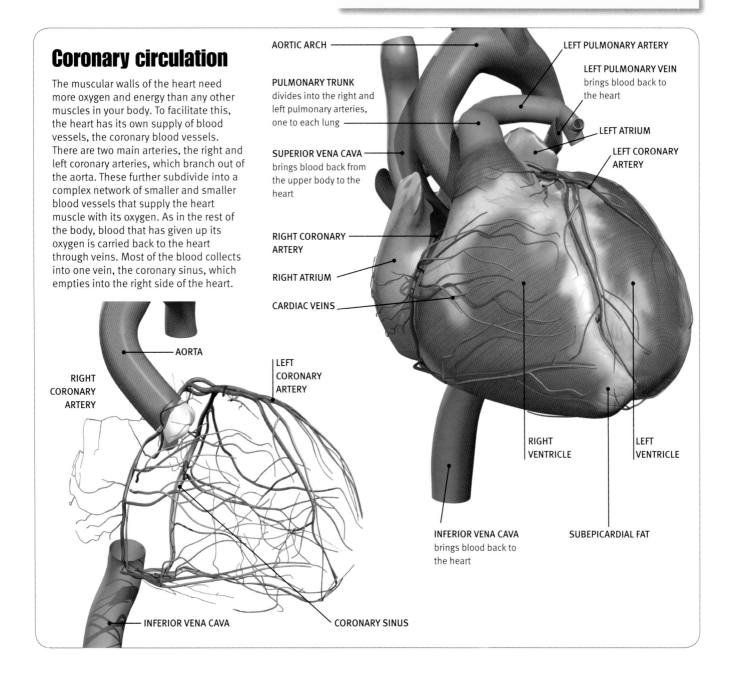

AORTIC ARCH

LEFT PULMONARY ARTERY

PULMONARY TRUNK
divides into the right and left pulmonary arteries, one to each lung

LEFT PULMONARY VEIN
brings blood back to the heart

SUPERIOR VENA CAVA
brings blood back from the upper body to the heart

LEFT ATRIUM

LEFT CORONARY ARTERY

RIGHT CORONARY ARTERY

RIGHT ATRIUM

CARDIAC VEINS

AORTA

RIGHT CORONARY ARTERY

LEFT CORONARY ARTERY

RIGHT VENTRICLE

LEFT VENTRICLE

INFERIOR VENA CAVA
brings blood back to the heart

SUBEPICARDIAL FAT

INFERIOR VENA CAVA

CORONARY SINUS

Phases of the heartbeat

Each heartbeat consists of three phases: resting, atrial contraction, then ventricular contraction. During the resting phase (diastole), the right side of the heart fills with deoxygenated blood (from the body) and the left side of the heart fills with oxygenated blood (from the lungs). Some blood passively trickles through the atria into the ventricles through the open, non-return valves. During the second phase (atrial systole), the two atria contract simultaneously to squeeze more blood into the two ventricles. During the third phase (ventricular systole), both ventricles contract and snap closed – see below, coloured green – and blood is pumped out into the lungs (from the right ventricle) and body (from the left ventricle). When the ventricles are empty, the heart relaxes (diastole) and the cycle begins again.

DIASTOLE PHASE is the stage when the heart muscle relaxes and upper chambers of both sides of the heart fill with blood

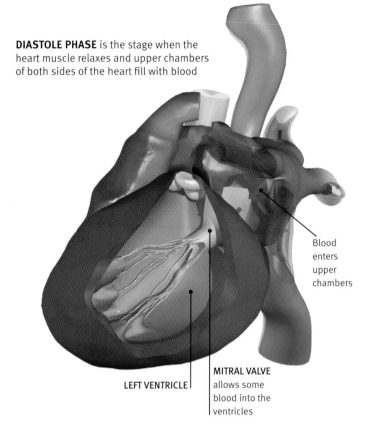

Blood enters upper chambers

LEFT VENTRICLE

MITRAL VALVE allows some blood into the ventricles

ATRIAL SYSTOLE causes the atria to contract pushing blood into the lower chambers of the heart – the ventricles – forcing the mitral valve to open.

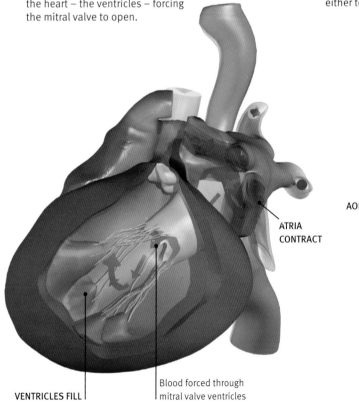

ATRIA CONTRACT

VENTRICLES FILL

Blood forced through mitral valve ventricles

VENTRICULAR SYSTOLE causes the ventricles to contract and push blood back out into the arteries, either to the puilmonary arteries or into the aorta.

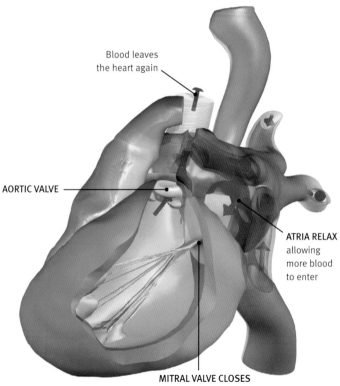

Blood leaves the heart again

AORTIC VALVE

ATRIA RELAX allowing more blood to enter

MITRAL VALVE CLOSES

NON-RETURN VALVES

The heart is a double pump made up of four chambers: a left atrium, a right atrium, a left ventricle and a right ventricle. Each chamber holds the same volume of blood (around 80ml/2.7fl oz). The atria only pump blood into the ventricles, so their walls are relatively thin. The ventricles, however, have to pump blood to the lungs or out into the body against considerable pressure, and therefore they have thicker, more muscular walls.

The chambers of the heart each have a one-way valve that ensures that blood flows in only one direction when the muscles contract. This prevents unwanted back flow.

The right ventricle is separated from the right atrium by three flaps of tissue called the tricuspid valve. The left atrium is separated from the left ventricle by the mitral, or bicuspid, valve which contains two flaps of tissue.

The pulmonary valve protects the entrance to the pulmonary trunk, which takes blood from the heart to the lungs. The aortic valve protects the entrance to the aorta, which takes oxygenated blood from the heart to the rest of the body.

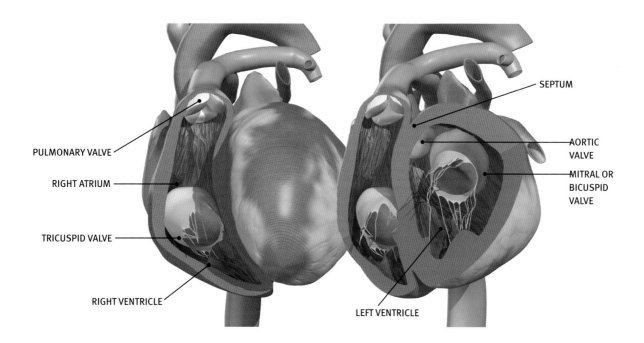

PULMONARY VALVE

RIGHT ATRIUM

TRICUSPID VALVE

RIGHT VENTRICLE

SEPTUM

AORTIC VALVE

MITRAL OR BICUSPID VALVE

LEFT VENTRICLE

Electrical impulses

Your heart contains specialized cardiac muscle cells (see page 24). A natural pacemaker, called the sinoatrial node, generates regular electrical impulses that cause the heart muscle to contract in a controlled sequence. The heart rate is further regulated by sympathetic and parasympathetic nerves, which speed it up or slow it down as necessary.

An electrical impulse is conducted through the heart muscle via specialized nerve fibres. As the message spreads throughout the heart, it triggers an orderly contraction of all of the muscle fibres. There are three stages to each 'beat'. First, the electrical stimulus triggers the muscles of the atria at the top of the heart to contract, then, in stage two, it stimulates the muscles of the ventricles to contract; finally the muscles relax.

The electrical impulses flowing through the heart can be recorded to produce a tracing called an electrocardiogram (ECG).

CONDUCTING PATHWAYS direct the electrical impulse throughout the atria, then down the septum to the ventricles, causing them to contract.

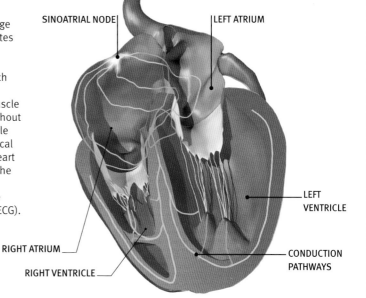

SINOATRIAL NODE

LEFT ATRIUM

LEFT VENTRICLE

RIGHT ATRIUM

RIGHT VENTRICLE

CONDUCTION PATHWAYS

Blood circulation

The circulatory system connects all of your body systems. Blood supplies every tissue with oxygen and nutrients, while also picking up and flushing away the waste products of metabolism. It transports the chemicals needed for regulation of body systems, such as hormones, as well as those synthesized by different cells, including cholesterol and triglycerides. The blood also carries nutrients absorbed from your digestive tract directly to your liver for processing.

HOW BLOOD CIRCULATES

Oxygenated blood pumped out of the left ventricle of the heart passes through smaller and smaller arteries to reach the smallest branches known as arterioles. From here, blood passes into the capillary network. Within the capillaries, oxygen and nutrients diffuse into the tissues in exchange for carbon dioxide gas and other waste products. Deoxygenated blood passes from the capillaries into tiny veins (the venules), where some gaseous exchange continues, and then into larger veins until it reaches the venae cavae that empty into the right side of the heart. Deoxygenated blood is then pumped out into the pulmonary system for reoxygenation, before returning to the left side of the heart again.

ARTERIES AND VEINS

Typically these blood vessels lie side by side in the region they service, and commonly travel together with their nerves in a neurovascular bundle. Arteries carry blood at high pressure. The pressure in veins and venules is so low that it cannot overcome gravity, so the long leg veins contain valves that prevent back flow.

CAPILLARIES

The real work of the cardiovascular system is done in the capillaries. They form intricate networks around muscle fibres, through connective tissue and beneath the basal layers of epithelial membranes. The capillary walls are very thin and allow oxygen and nutrients to pass into the tissues, and excess fluid, waste and other products to be picked up. Some capillaries are so fine that red blood cells have to pass through them in single file. Their diameter is controlled by contraction and relaxation of the muscle in the walls of the arterioles and venules. The entrance to some capillaries is protected by rings of muscle (precapillary sphincters), which can shut that part of the network down so that blood cannot flow through. Blood in the capillaries is at very low pressure.

Structure of veins

Large veins (including the superior and inferior venae cavae), have the three tunica layers, with a particularly thick tunica externa. Folds of the tunica intima, pointing in the direction of blood flow, project into the leg veins. These 'valves' permit blood to travel in one direction and against gravity, preventing back flow.

Medium-sized veins range from 2–9mm in internal diameter, and are comparable in size to the muscular arteries. However, the tunica media is thin, containing relatively few muscle cells.

Venules are the smallest veins, collecting blood from capillary beds. They have no tunica media.

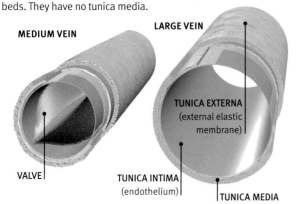

MEDIUM VEIN

LARGE VEIN

TUNICA EXTERNA (external elastic membrane)

TUNICA INTIMA (endothelium)

TUNICA MEDIA

VALVE

Structure of arteries

The walls of blood vessels contain three distinct layers: the tunica intima (innermost layer), which in arteries includes a thick elastic fibre layer; the tunica media (middle layer), a layer of muscle fibres; and the tunica externa (outermost layer), a sheath of connective tissue.

The arterial walls are relatively thick and strong. The diameter varies slightly as blood pressure or volume changes. The walls of arteries are thicker than veins. The tunica media contains more smooth muscle and elastic tissue than veins, which enables it to resist the pressure generated by the heartbeat.

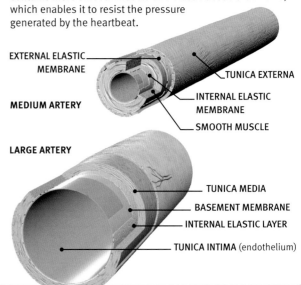

EXTERNAL ELASTIC MEMBRANE

MEDIUM ARTERY

TUNICA EXTERNA

INTERNAL ELASTIC MEMBRANE

SMOOTH MUSCLE

LARGE ARTERY

TUNICA MEDIA

BASEMENT MEMBRANE

INTERNAL ELASTIC LAYER

TUNICA INTIMA (endothelium)

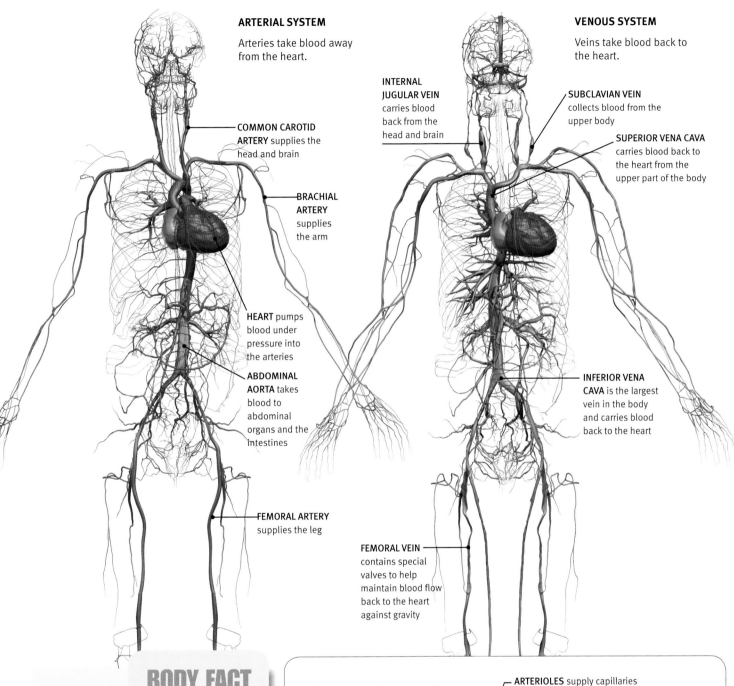

ARTERIAL SYSTEM

Arteries take blood away from the heart.

COMMON CAROTID ARTERY supplies the head and brain

BRACHIAL ARTERY supplies the arm

HEART pumps blood under pressure into the arteries

ABDOMINAL AORTA takes blood to abdominal organs and the intestines

FEMORAL ARTERY supplies the leg

VENOUS SYSTEM

Veins take blood back to the heart.

INTERNAL JUGULAR VEIN carries blood back from the head and brain

SUBCLAVIAN VEIN collects blood from the upper body

SUPERIOR VENA CAVA carries blood back to the heart from the upper part of the body

INFERIOR VENA CAVA is the largest vein in the body and carries blood back to the heart

FEMORAL VEIN contains special valves to help maintain blood flow back to the heart against gravity

BODY FACT

Your circulation

- The circulation contains around 5 litres (8.3 pints) of blood.
- The capillaries have a diameter that is just a 30th of a human hair.
- Your capillaries form a network that, laid end to end, would measure 96,000km (around 60,000 miles).
- The slowest blood flow in your body is through the capillaries.
- The greatest resistance against which the heart has to pump blood comes from the arterioles.

Gas exchange in the capillaries

The capillary walls are very thin and contain only a single layer of epithelial cells. This allows oxygen and nutrients to pass readily into the tissues, while excess fluid, wastes and other products can pass from the tissues into the blood.

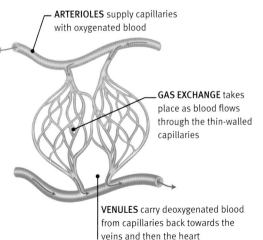

ARTERIOLES supply capillaries with oxygenated blood

GAS EXCHANGE takes place as blood flows through the thin-walled capillaries

VENULES carry deoxygenated blood from capillaries back towards the veins and then the heart

Blood

Blood is made up of a straw-coloured fluid called plasma in which float billions of red blood cells (erythrocytes), white blood cells (leucocytes – see immune system, pages 130–141) and cell fragments (platelets). Plasma also contains dissolved salts, hormones, fats, sugars and proteins.

Mature erythrocytes or red blood cells, do not contain a nucleus and have few organelles (see pages 16–17). Their main function is to carry oxygen from the lungs to the tissues. They are flexible, concave discs with a doughnut-shaped outline, and can squeeze through even the narrowest capillary walls. Red blood cells contain the red pigment, haemoglobin. Most oxygen carried in the blood is chemically bound to haemoglobin.

TRANSPORTING OXYGEN AND CARBON DIOXIDE

Each red blood cell contains millions of molecules of haemoglobin. Every one molecule consists of four ring-like haem groups, each of which contains an atom of iron and a protein chain called a globin. Oxygen binds weakly to the iron atoms to form bright red oxyhaemoglobin. Deoxyhaemoglobin, from which the oxygen has been removed, is dark blue-red. Carbon dioxide is around 20 times more soluble than oxygen, so it dissolves readily in plasma. Only around 15 per cent of the carbon dioxide carried in blood is bound to haemoglobin, however. The rest is dissolved in the plasma and erythrocytes in the form of dissolved carbon dioxide gas, carbonic acid and bicarbonate ions. Within the haemoglobin, carbon dioxide binds to the amino acids of the globin chains, not the haem groups.

Blood types

Erythrocytes and many other body cells carry tissue types that you inherit from your parents and which collectively form the blood group system. Over 30 different antigens are now recognized, of which the most well-known are the ABO and Rhesus blood group antigens. All blood samples can be classified as A, B, AB or O and can be further divided into Rhesus positive or Rhesus negative. Each blood group is associated with the presence of certain antibodies (see page 136) – immune proteins that determine whether or not your body will accept or reject a blood transfusion or transplanted organ.

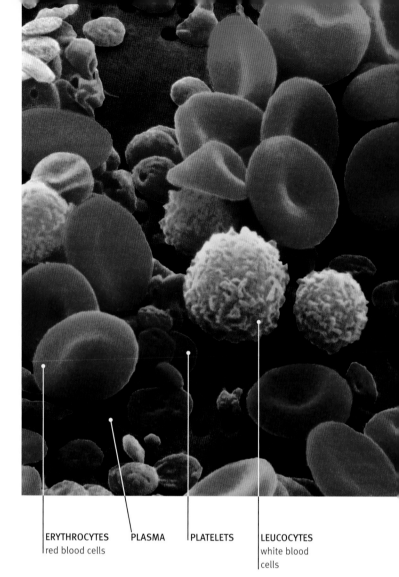

ERYTHROCYTES red blood cells   PLASMA   PLATELETS   LEUCOCYTES white blood cells

FORMATION OF BLOOD CELLS

The production of blood cells, a process known as haematopoiesis, occurs in the body's red marrow, which is found inside the flat bones (such as the pelvis, sternum and scapulae) and in the cancellous (spongy) ends of the long bones (such as the femur and humerus).

All types of blood cell arise from stem cells called haemocytoblasts. The production of red blood cells, known as erythropoiesis, involves the development of immature erythrocytes whose nucleus and ribosomes (see page 21) direct the synthesis of haemoglobin molecules (that is, the DNA provides the template for the gene that codes for haemoglobin, and the ribosomes put the necessary amino acids in the right order to make it). Once the red blood cell is full of haemoglobin, the cell nucleus and most of the organelles are ejected, and the mature red blood cell enters the circulation.

The rate at which red blood cells are produced is regulated by a hormone, erythropoietin, which is produced in the kidneys. Kidney cells produce more erythropoietin if they are lacking in oxygen.

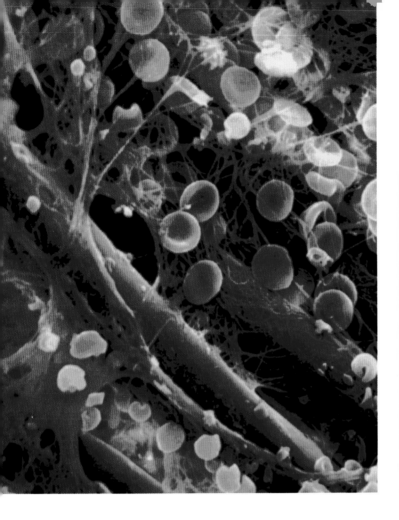

Red blood cells

- There are around 28,000 billion red blood cells (erythrocytes) in your circulation.
- You also have around 1,680 billion platelets in your circulation at any one time.
- Each red cell lives for between 100 and 120 days before being filtered out and destroyed by cells in your liver and spleen.
- You produce around 2 million new red blood cells per second.
- Recycled haemoglobin is broken down to form bilirubin – a yellow pigment secreted by the liver into the bile.
- Each red blood cell contains an estimated 250 million molecules of haemoglobin. Each haemoglobin molecule can transport four molecules of oxygen. Each erythrocyte can therefore carry 1 billion molecules of oxygen.
- Blood normally contains 150,000–400,000 platelets per microlitre.

BLOOD CLOTTING

If a tissue is damaged, this triggers coagulation, whereby the wound is plugged with a clot before too much blood leaks from the circulation.

Proteins such as collagen are exposed when the endothelial lining of blood vessels is damaged. This attracts platelets (circulating cell fragments called thrombocytes), which stick to the exposed tissues and release stored chemicals into the plasma. These chemicals activate other platelets and trigger a cascade of reactions within the circulating proteins. This, the so-called coagulation cascade, results in the formation of a sticky web of insoluble fibrin molecules (see above). Red blood cells become trapped in the fibrin web to form a clot. On the surface of the body, the clot dries out to form a scab, and this protects the wound while it heals.

HOMEOSTASIS

The level of each constituent within your blood is kept within a narrow range to ensure your cells have a constant environment. This is important because blood fluid (plasma) and chemicals seep out of the circulation to bathe your cells. Known as interstitial fluid, this supplies your cells with oxygen and nutrients, flushes away cell products and wastes, and helps to maintain a constant cell environment. If the composition of blood and interstitial fluids moves outside of a narrow range of acceptability, your cells are unable to function properly and may die. Your cells especially need a constant level of acidity, salt concentrations and temperature.

The regulation and maintenance of your body's blood and internal environment is known as homeostasis. Homeostatic control mechanisms involve all your internal organs (especially your lungs, liver and kidneys), endocrine glands and your sympathetic and parasympathetic nervous systems.

FEEDBACK MECHANISMS

There are two main ways in which homeostasis is regulated. The most common is a process called negative feedback. When a change is detected, the body responds with hormones and nervous system responses that neutralize the change and return the situation to normal.

Less common is positive feedback, in which the body responds to a detected change by strengthening the stimulus, so the situation escalates. This occurs when a rapid response is needed, in a potentially life-threatening situation. Platelets and blood clotting factors involved in blood coagulation (see left) are activated to prevent the non-stop haemorrhaging of blood. Eventually, negative feedback will take over to limit the extent of the changes.

IMMUNE SYSTEM

DESTROYING INVADERS
Immune cells called macrophages are shown here engulfing and
destroying a foreign particle to prevent infection in the body.

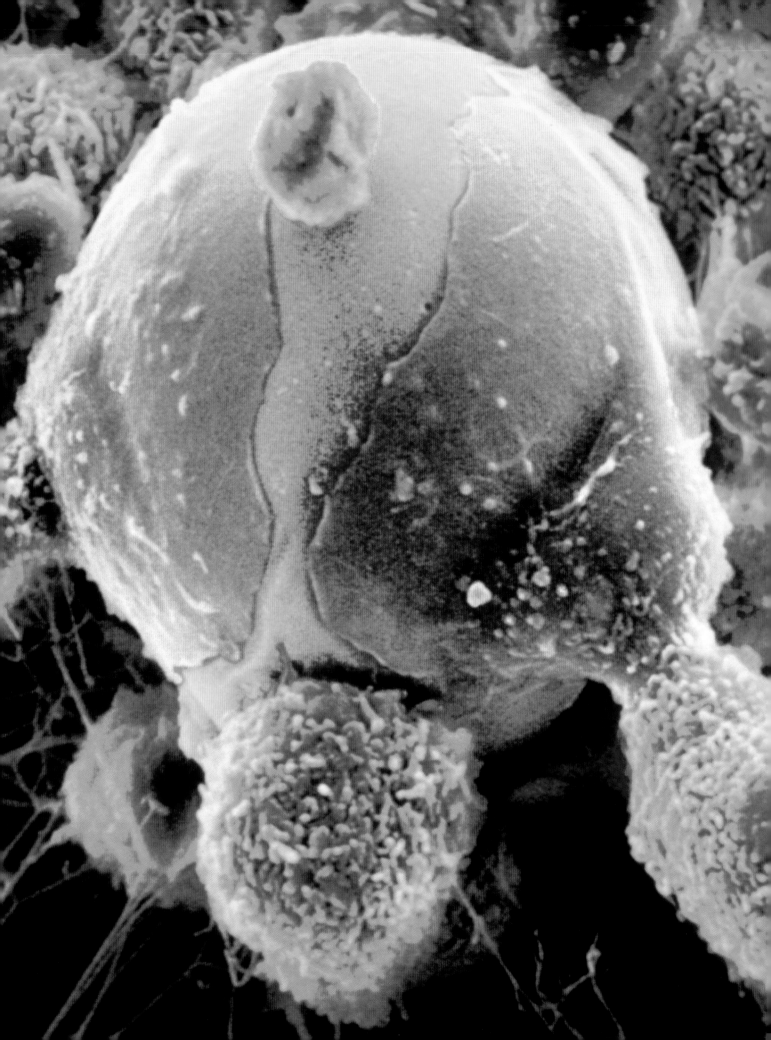

Immune system

Your body has a number of general defences it uses to fight infection. These include: skin, which acts as an external barrier to disease; your stomach acids and enzymes, which kill bacteria you take in via your mouth; and substances in your saliva, tears and the fluids that line your respiratory, urinary, reproductive and gastrointestinal tracts. Your most important defence against infection, however, is your immune system, which incorporates the lymphatic system.

LYMPHATIC SYSTEM

The organs and vessels of the lymphatic system play a vital role in your defence mechanisms. The active part of the system is a fluid called lymph, which is carried around the body through a series of vessels. The larger vessels are called lymphatics, which drain into networks of tiny capillaries. Throughout the system there are special filters and storage areas – lymph nodes, or glands. The lymph carries cells that help fight infection around the body. Several organs in the body play an active role in the lymphatic system, such as the adenoids, tonsils, thymus, spleen and parts of the intestine. White cells are also made in the bone marrow.

HOW THE IMMUNE SYSTEM PROTECTS THE BODY

Your body's immune system is made up of millions of 'armed' cells that patrol your body to protect against disease. In particular, they are primed to recognize and destroy substances that are not usually found within your body. These include:

- Foreign invaders (such as bacteria, fungi and viruses).
- Poisonous proteins (toxins).
- Infected or diseased cells, which tend to make abnormal proteins.
- Transplanted tissues, for example, unmatched blood.
- Foreign bodies (for example, splinters and shrapnel).

There are two main lines of defence: a first-line or 'non-specific' immune response, which is programmed into everyone at birth, and a second-line, or acquired immunity, which develops as your body encounters each infection or invader.

ACQUIRED IMMUNITY

The acquired immune responses develop after the body has been exposed to a foreign protein. Memory cells form that are primed to recognize specific foreign proteins. Dormant memory cells patrol your body and are activated only if they encounter the protein again. Specific immunity involves interactions between two types of cell: B-lymphocytes, which produce antibodies, and T-lymphocytes, which regulate antibody production, see page 135.

DIFFERENTIATING BETWEEN SELF AND NON-SELF

As well as recognizing foreign proteins, immune cells must learn to identify normal components of your body and leave them alone. To add to the complexity of this task, they must also detect body cells that have changed in some way, as a result of infection or disease.

Every cell carries a set of identity tags on its surface that brand it as part of the self ('self-markers'). These tags, known as human leucocyte antigens (HLAs), are coded by a set of genes known as the major histocompatibility complex (MHC). The immune cells learn to recognize HLA self-markers during embryonic development.

Body cells continually process and break down internal proteins, fragments of which are transported to the cell membrane and displayed on its surface, along with the HLA proteins. This allows each cell to communicate information about its internal conditions to immune cells. If they encounter an infected or diseased cell with both a self hallmark and a foreign protein (for example, a viral protein) the cell is usually recognized as undesirable and destroyed.

Peyer's Patches

The gastrointestinal tract is one of the main areas where foreign antigens enter the body, in the form of food. The gut is therefore lined with lymphoid tissue, clustered in the tonsils, adenoids, appendix and intestinal walls. The small intestines contain numerous areas of lymphoid tissue known as Peyer's patches.

Peyer's patches only have outgoing lymphatics. They are capped by flattened, folded epithelial cells known as M (microfold) cells. These take samples of antigens present in the intestines, enclose them in vesicles (little sacs), and transport them into the centre of the Peyer's patch. Here, both T- and B-lymphocytes are presented with the antigens and will mount an immune response if infection is detected, to generate antigen-specific IgM and IgA antibodies (see page 136).

M cells are selective about the antigens they transport. They don't just take random 'sips' from the gut. Instead, they transport only antigens that bind to molecules on their surface. This helps to avoid activating the immune system against innocuous food antigens.

THYMUS

This major organ of the lymphatic system is located above the heart just behind the sternum. It is large at birth and continues to grow slightly until puberty after which it does not change markedly in size, but the lymphoid tissue is gradually replaced by fat. T-lymphocyte precursor cells develop, differentiate and multiply in the thymus, gaining their antigen specificity and immune tolerance to the body's own tissues. The inner core is mostly composed of connective tissue, with only a small amount of lymphoid tissue. The fibrous outer layer is partitioned into lobules.

LYMPH VESSELS

The lymph vessels have a similar structure to blood vessels, but the lymph capillaries are closed at one end with a special valve-like junction. This allows lymph to enter the nodes but not leak back into the interstitial fluid. Lymph capillaries drain lymph fluid into larger collecting lymph vessels where half-moon-shaped semilunar valves reduce any back flow. Lymph fluid is 'massaged' through the lymph capillaries by the contraction of the skeletal muscles during body movements. Rhythmic contraction of the smooth muscle cells in the walls of the larger lymph vessels also draws fluid along.

LYMPH NODES

Collecting lymph vessels divide to form incoming (afferent) lymph vessels that lead into a lymph node. Each lymph node varies from 1–20mm (up to 0.8in) in diameter and contains a series of channels packed full of macrophages and lymphocytes. Any debris or infection present in the fluid is filtered out by the sieve-like action of the lymph nodes and promptly attacked and destroyed by the immune cells. Filtered lymph leaves the node via an outgoing (efferent) lymph vessel and flows into either the right lymphatic duct (which drains into the right subclavian vein), or into the thoracic duct, which drains into the left subclavian vein.

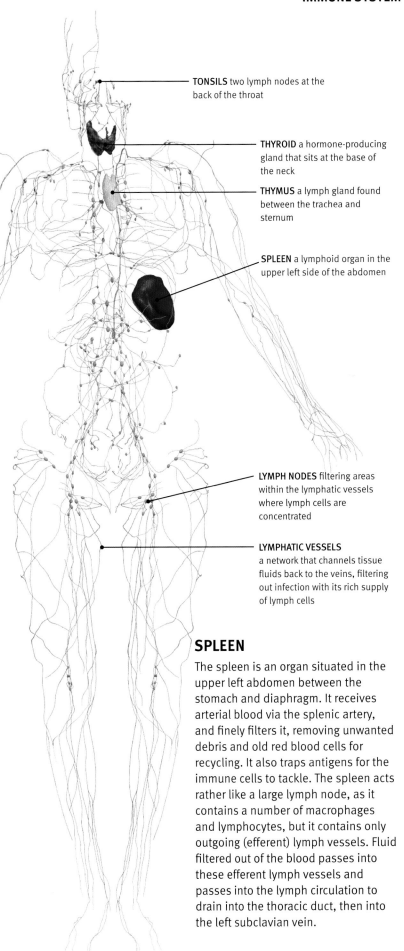

TONSILS two lymph nodes at the back of the throat

THYROID a hormone-producing gland that sits at the base of the neck

THYMUS a lymph gland found between the trachea and sternum

SPLEEN a lymphoid organ in the upper left side of the abdomen

LYMPH NODES filtering areas within the lymphatic vessels where lymph cells are concentrated

LYMPHATIC VESSELS a network that channels tissue fluids back to the veins, filtering out infection with its rich supply of lymph cells

SPLEEN

The spleen is an organ situated in the upper left abdomen between the stomach and diaphragm. It receives arterial blood via the splenic artery, and finely filters it, removing unwanted debris and old red blood cells for recycling. It also traps antigens for the immune cells to tackle. The spleen acts rather like a large lymph node, as it contains a number of macrophages and lymphocytes, but it contains only outgoing (efferent) lymph vessels. Fluid filtered out of the blood passes into these efferent lymph vessels and passes into the lymph circulation to drain into the thoracic duct, then into the left subclavian vein.

Immune cells

Immune cells are the white blood cells known as leucocytes. All of your leucocytes are derived from common stem cells that develop within your bone marrow. One type of immature cell travels to the thymus. Here they are reprogrammed to form T-lymphocytes as they mature. The thymus is a two-lobed gland found in the upper part of your chest. It is relatively large in infancy and childhood, when the body is building its acquired immunity, but starts to shrink at puberty, and has virtually disappeared by adulthood.

IMMUNE CELL FUNCTION

Immune cells can be divided into two groups. Those of the first-line defence system (non-specific immune response) are the macrophages, neutrophils and some natural killer cells. Also part of this system are the immune proteins, complement and interferon (see page 139). The lymphocytes are an important part of the acquired immune system. Neutrophils, monocytes and macrophages all engulf foreign proteins, bacteria or viruses (antigens) and destroy them with powerful digestive enzymes. This process is called phagocytosis.

TYPES OF IMMUNE CELL

Immune cells circulate within your blood and lymphatic systems. They communicate with each other through chemical signals called cytokines. Cytokines are soluble elements that attract other patrolling immune cells into a specific area where they super-stimulate them to create a swift immune response. When circulating immune cells encounter cytokines, they squeeze through capillary and lymph vessel walls to enter the tissues, putting out cell elongations known as pseudopodia, or 'false feet'.

LYMPHOCYTES

These make up 40 per cent of circulating white blood cells. The image, right, shows a typical lymphocyte; it is round, with long microvilli projecting from the surface. There are three main types, each with different surface proteins and different patterns of activity:
- Natural killer (NK) cells (10 per cent of total lymphocytes),
- B-lymphocytes (20 per cent of total; formed in the bone marrow),
- T-lymphocytes (70 per cent of total; formed in the thymus).

NATURAL KILLER (NK) CELLS

Abnormal body cells are destroyed by the natural killer cells. They are super-stimulated by tissue macrophages (see opposite) and provide a rapid response while the more specific T- and B-lymphocytes are activated. NK cells usually die during their attack.

B-LYMPHOCYTES

These cells make antibodies. You inherit many different B-cell lines, each of which makes only one specific antibody against a particular foreign protein (antigen). Examples of the antibody made by each B-lymphocyte stick out from its surface, ready to detect an antigen. Until activated, B-lymphocytes patrol the body in low numbers as B-memory cells. When a B-memory cell encounters the foreign protein against which its antibody reacts, it powers up and produces large numbers of its single, specific antibody. These activated lymphocytes are known as B-plasma cells. During activation, B-plasma cells divide repeatedly to build up a large sub-population of cells that produce identical antibodies. Once the infection is over, larger numbers of those particular B-lymphocytes continue to patrol your body as B-memory cells. If the same infection is encountered again, the immune response is quicker and more overwhelming. In most cases, this means your immune system will neutralize the infection before you start to feel unwell – you are now immune to a second attack.

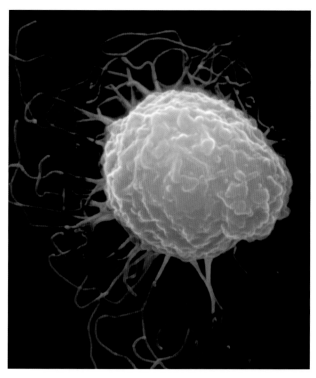

T-LYMPHOCYTES

These are lymph cells that mature within the thymus gland. Here, they acquire a surface protein called the T-cell receptor, which is produced by random genetic rearrangements, so that each T-cell recognizes a distinct, and limited, set of foreign proteins. T-lymphocytes undergo a rigorous process of selection, so that only those carrying T-cell receptors capable of recognizing foreign proteins are allowed to develop. T-lymphocytes whose T-cell receptors recognize only self-antigens (major histocompatibility complex/MHC proteins) are usually destroyed to prevent autoimmune attack on parts of the body. T-lymphocytes exist in several different forms:

- T-helper cells super-stimulate B-memory cells to produce antibodies.
- T-suppressor cells bring antibody production to a halt once an infection is beaten.
- T-cytotoxic (killer) cells are more sophisticated versions of the natural killer cell, which tend to survive their attacks and go on to assassinate other targets.
- T-delayed-hypersensitivity cells are involved in some hypersensitivity (allergic) reactions.

GRANULOCYTES

These are leucocytes that contain granules. There are three main types, identified in a laboratory by how they respond to artificial tissue dyes: neutrophils (neutral staining), basophils (purple staining) and eosinophils (red staining).

NEUTROPHILS

These make up 60 per cent of the circulating white blood cells (see above right). These cells 'phagocytose' bacteria and viruses, a process in which bacteria and viruses are engulfed and absorbed into the cell. Neutrophils also interact with antibodies and immune proteins called

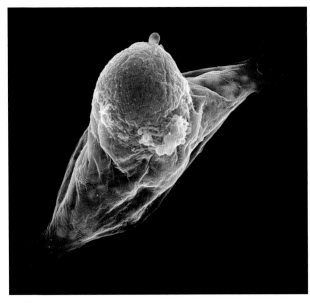

complement proteins (see page 138). Neutrophil granules contain glycogen energy stores, which allows these cells to survive within inhospitable areas, such as an abscess, despite a lack of other nutrients or oxygen.

BASOPHILS

Less than one per cent of circulating leucocytes are basophils. Their granules contain histamine, a chemical involved in allergic reactions.

EOSINOPHILS

Between one and six per cent of circulating leucocytes are eosinophils. Their granules contain chemicals such as peroxidase and major basic protein, which are involved in fighting parasites (for example, worms) and in allergic responses. They are especially concentrated in the lower gastrointestinal tract, reproductive organs, spleen and lymph nodes.

Macrophages

Round monocytes circulate in the bloodstream; once they enter the tissues, they are known as macrophages. These long-lived scavengers engulf bacteria, viruses and general debris, and are particularly concentrated in the liver, spleen and lymph nodes. The two macrophages right are engulfing the bacteria *Escheria coli* (the small red rods). Macrophages present recycled foreign proteins, from material they have ingested, on their surface to super-stimulate other immune cells.

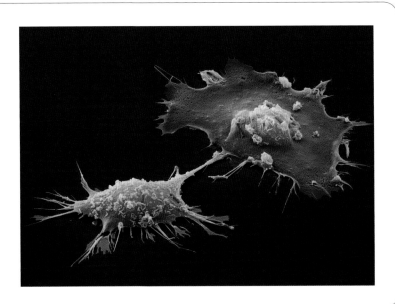

Inflammatory and immune responses

Your immune cells also make substances called antibodies, as well as complement proteins and interferons. All the different elements of the system work together in response to infection.

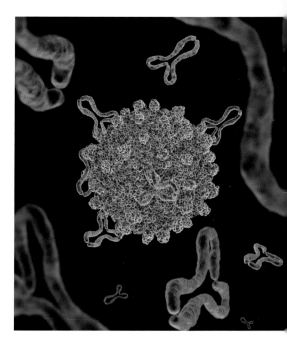

ANTIBODIES

Antibodies are also known as immunoglobulins. They are produced by your B-lymphocytes. Each immunoglobulin forms a Y-shaped molecule made up of four protein chains: two identical heavy chains, and two identical light chains linked together.

Each B-lymphocyte makes one particular type of immunoglobulin that recognizes only one particular foreign protein (antigen). The open end of each immunoglobulin interacts with a specific antigen (for example, a particular bacterial protein). The tail end of the immunoglobulin remains constant within each class of antibody. This portion either binds with complement (opposite) or interacts/binds with immune cells (for example, macrophages, neutrophils and lymphocytes).

TYPES OF ANTIBODY

Immunoglobulins (Ig) are divided into five classes depending on the type of heavy chain they contain.

IgA makes up 15–20 per cent of the total antibody pool. It is mainly found in secretions that protect internal surfaces, such as the respiratory and intestinal tract.

IgD forms less than one per cent of the antibody pool. It is mainly found on B-lymphocyte surfaces, where it acts as a receptor for antigens.

IgE is normally present only in trace amounts. It is involved in the defence against helminthic (worm) infestations and in allergic reactions.

IgG is the most prevalent type of antibody (70–75 per cent of the total). It is the major antibody involved in immune responses against previously encountered infections.

IgM accounts for around 10 per cent of total antibodies. It consists of five antibodies bound together, and is the first type of antibody formed when the body encounters a new infection.

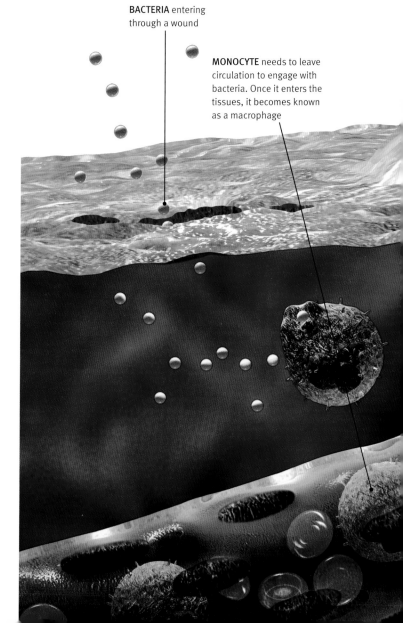

BACTERIA entering through a wound

MONOCYTE needs to leave circulation to engage with bacteria. Once it enters the tissues, it becomes known as a macrophage

Immunization against diseases

The immune system can be stimulated to produce antibiodies by immunization. When you are immunized, the immune system is injected with harmless proteins that have been extracted from inactivated viruses or bacteria. This stimulates the body's B-lymphocytes to make antibodies to the disease and form a pool of B-memory cells that respond to those particular proteins. If that particular virus or bacterium is encountered again, the immune system is able to destroy it quickly before it causes a serious illness. This is known as active immunization and it takes several weeks for antibody levels to increase to a protective level.

Passive immunization involves injecting pre-formed antibodies, harvested from immune donors, to provide rapid protection for non-immune people exposed to a potentially dangerous infection. The level of protection slowly reduces as the donated antibodies are naturally cleared from the system.

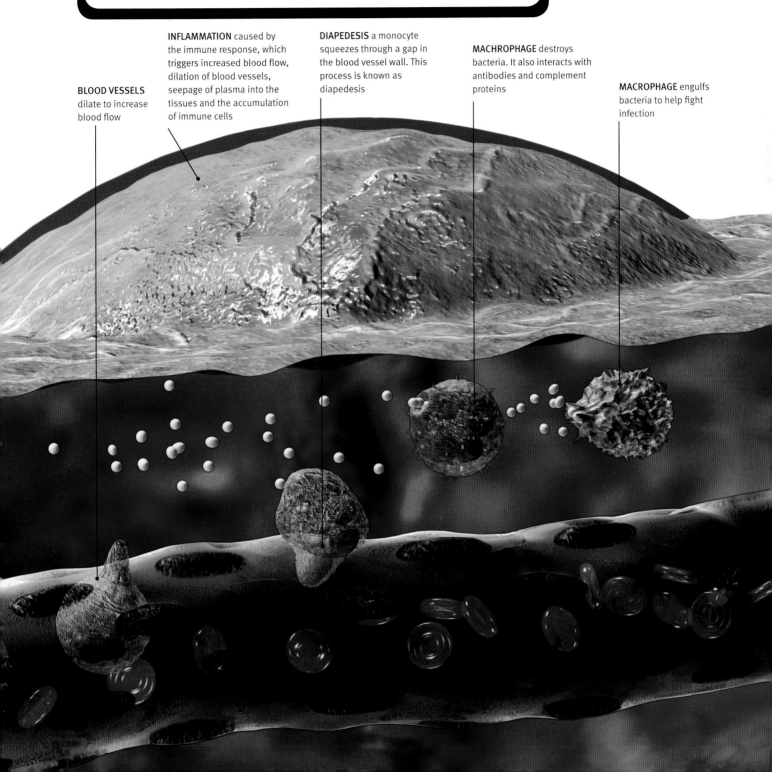

INFLAMMATION caused by the immune response, which triggers increased blood flow, dilation of blood vessels, seepage of plasma into the tissues and the accumulation of immune cells

DIAPEDESIS a monocyte squeezes through a gap in the blood vessel wall. This process is known as diapedesis

MACHROPHAGE destroys bacteria. It also interacts with antibodies and complement proteins

BLOOD VESSELS dilate to increase blood flow

MACROPHAGE engulfs bacteria to help fight infection

Complement proteins

The complement system involves a series of over 20 plasma, or complement, proteins, that circulate in the blood, see below. These proteins bind to antigens and antibodies in a specific sequence. Each step in the sequence triggers a specific set of reactions so that an 'enzyme cascade' occurs.

Complement proteins contribute to your immunity in a number of ways. The first complement proteins (C1 complex) bind directly to the surface of a bacterium, or infected cell, or onto the tail ends of IgM or IgG antibodies that have locked onto foreign antigens. The complement protein coats the unwanted material and alerts any nearby phagocytic immune cell (such as a macrophage or neutrophil) to its presence, which ingests and destroys the coated material.

If there is no phagocyte, the next complement protein in the sequence binds to the C1 complex to trigger the complement cascade. Successive complement proteins bind to each other and the action of the cascade 'punches' a hole in the wall of the invading organism (or the infected host cell) so that fluids rush in and the cell bursts.

Complement proteins act rather like a protein bomb, blowing a hole in the wall of bacteria and/or infected cells to destroy them.

COMPLETE COMPLEMENT PROTEIN

SECONDARY STRUCTURE: ALPHA HELIX

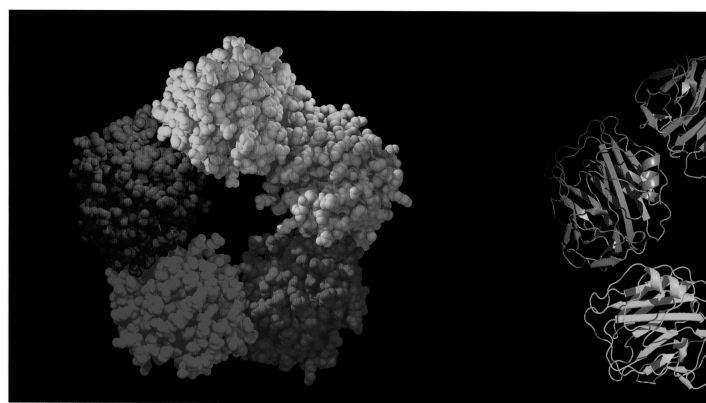

Interferons

These are special proteins that protect you from viral infections. Interferons suppress viral replication as well as super-stimulating the immune cells to a powerful antiviral response.

Interferon production is triggered when a cell is infected with a virus, or when an immune cell detects cytokines (chemical signals) secreted by other immune cells that have encountered a virus. Secreted interferons bind to neighbouring cells and stimulate the rapid production of unusual, short-lived molecules made up of nucleotides – the base units of DNA. These nucleotides activate a latent (inactive) nuclear enzyme (called ribonuclease L, or RNase L), which destroys all of the viral ribonucleic acid RNA within the cell. This stops the viral proteins synthesizing. Interferons made by an infected cell attach to neighbouring uninfected cells. By triggering RNase L production in these cells, it renders them incapable of supporting a viral infection, so the spread of infection is limited. At the same time, interferon activates an enzyme (protein kinase) that breaks down any viral proteins made before the interferon bound to the cell.

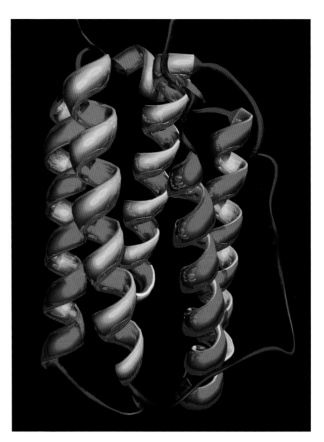

Molecular model showing the structure of a molecule of interferon

SECONDARY STRUCTURE: BETA SHEET

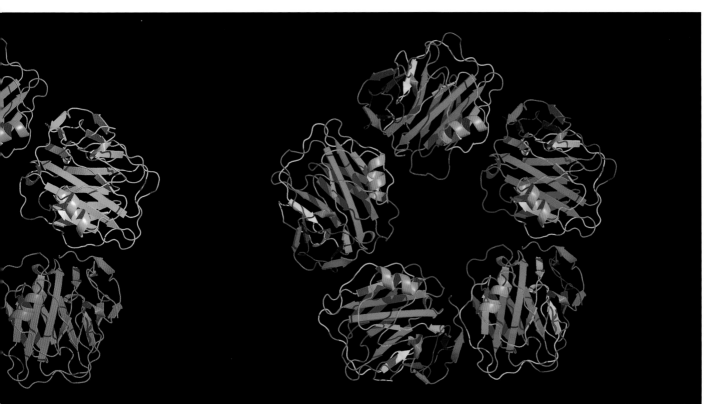

Inflammation and wound healing

Inflammation – which literally means to 'set on fire', as it causes tissues to become red, hot, swollen and painful, with loss of function – is triggered by tissue damage or infection and is an important biological response. Without inflammation, your wounds would never heal. It is a tightly regulated process, however, as unchecked long-term (chronic) inflammation could in itself lead to permanent tissue damage.

INFLAMMATION IS ESSENTIAL

A wound is a disruption in the skin or other body tissue. Wounds heal through three phases: inflammation, followed by the proliferation of new tissue, then its remodelling to repair the damage.

Inflammation triggers the release of chemicals such as histamine and bradykinin, which increase local blood flow and blood vessel permeability. Dilated capillaries leak a protein-rich fluid called exudate into the affected tissues, so the area becomes hot, swollen, red and painful. Pain is an important response as it alerts the brain that something is wrong, and allows reflex movement that takes the area away from any harmful stimulus.

The exudate contains a number of protein systems that act together:
- The kinin system, whose proteins trigger the inflammatory process with the dilation of blood vessels, redness, heat, swelling and pain.
- The coagulation system, whose proteins undergo a series of reactions to form a fibrin scaffold and blood-clotting.
- The fibrinolysis system, whose proteins break down excessive blood clots.
- The complement system, whose proteins activate immune reactions against infection (see page 137).
- Antibodies that work together with complement proteins and immune cells to clear infection.

MOIST WOUND HEALING

In the absence of a wound dressing, red blood cells and platelets form a clot (see right) on the fibrin scaffold, which dries to produce a scab (eschar). This plugs the tissue gap, protects regenerating cells and guards against bacterial infection. It is not waterproof, however, and dries out by evaporation to stick to the living fibrous tissue underneath, and causes the wound to contract. The proliferating epithelial cells have to break down the scab to repair the wound. This old-fashioned 'leave it open to the air' approach to wound healing often leads to scarring. The principle of moist wound healing did not arise until the 1970s when it was recognized that wounds protected by a dressing that allows the exudate to stay unclotted and moist, in fact heal more rapidly. This is because proliferating epithelial cells are able to pass across the moist wound surface in a leapfrog manner instead of having to burrow under a dried scab to dissolve it away. When a wound is allowed to stay moist, the formation of a new epithelial surface occurs twice as fast as in a dry wound, there is less pain, less risk of infection and less scarring.

The image right shows the protein called fibrin forming a mesh across a wound to minimize blood loss.

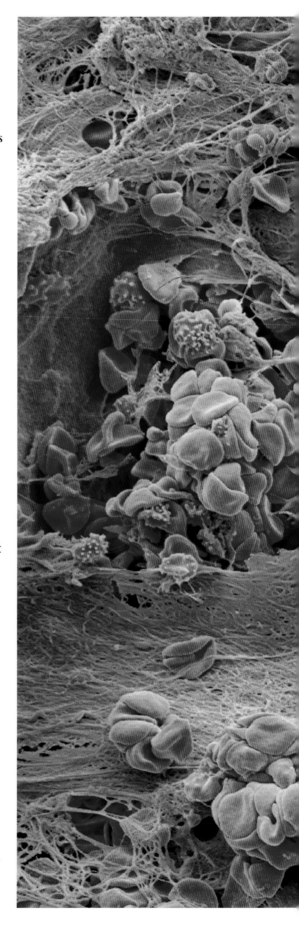

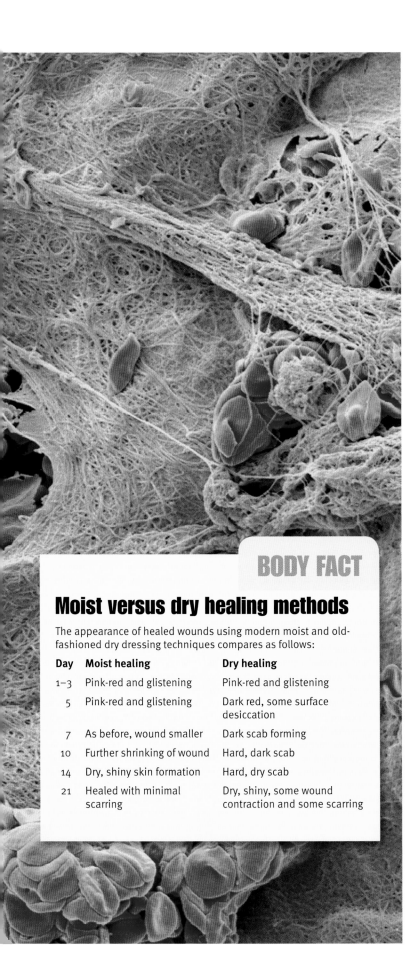

BODY FACT

Moist versus dry healing methods

The appearance of healed wounds using modern moist and old-fashioned dry dressing techniques compares as follows:

Day	Moist healing	Dry healing
1–3	Pink-red and glistening	Pink-red and glistening
5	Pink-red and glistening	Dark red, some surface desiccation
7	As before, wound smaller	Dark scab forming
10	Further shrinking of wound	Hard, dark scab
14	Dry, shiny skin formation	Hard, dry scab
21	Healed with minimal scarring	Dry, shiny, some wound contraction and some scarring

Healing process

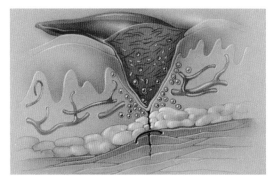

Immediately after an injury bleeding occurs, specialized cells release chemicals and tissue growth factors, which attract fibroblasts (fibre-producing cells). This triggers the inflammatory process. Blood flow to the area increases.

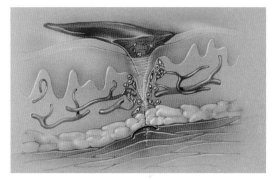

After several hours the wound is plugged with fibrin: red blood cells and platelets that form a scab. The fibroblasts proliferate and migrate into a wound on the fibrin scaffold. Epithelial cells start to migrate down beneath the scab. Phagocytic cells remove debris, and more cells arrive via the enhanced blood circulation. Clotting around the edges partially isolates the region.

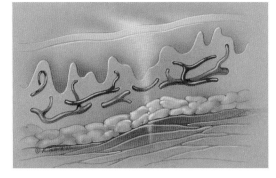

New blood vessels grow into the underlying area. Fibroblasts produce new connective tissue fibres such as collagen. The migration and proliferation of epithelial cells in the base of the wound forms a new covering to seal the surface. The scab is shrinking in size.

Within around three weeks, the wound is fully healed, but shrinking of the scab and collagen fibres leaves behind a slight depression and temporary scar.

ENDOCRINE SYSTEM

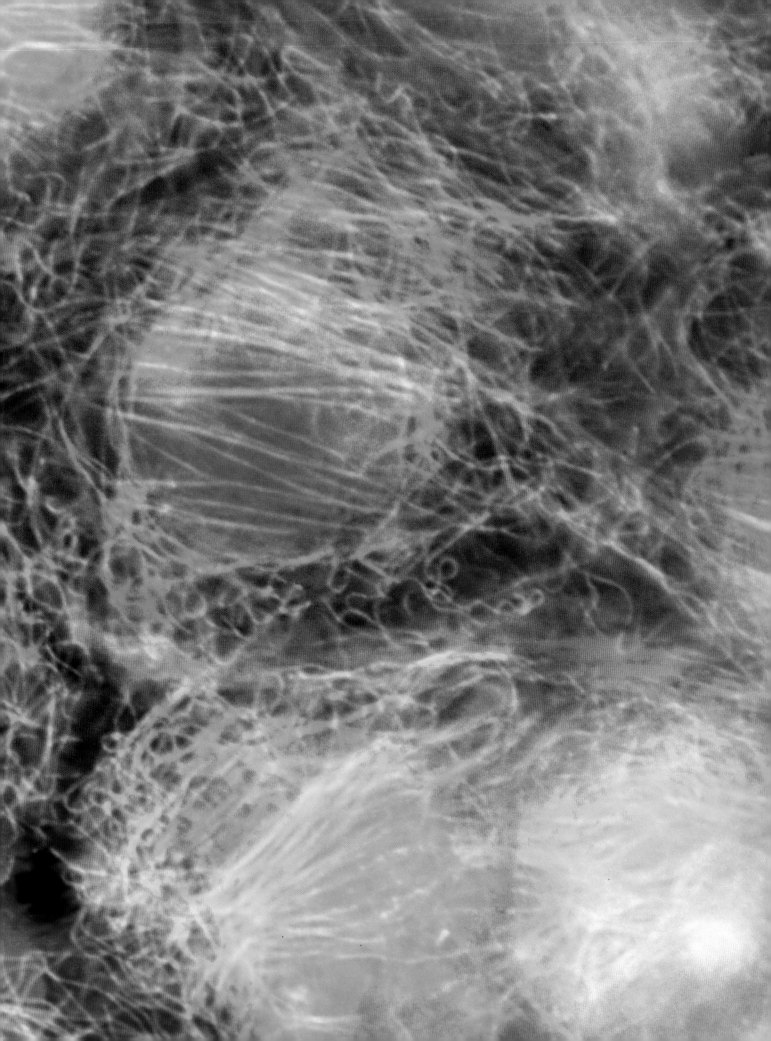

Endocrine glands

Your endocrine system is made up of ductless glands that secrete chemical messengers called hormones directly into your bloodstream. Hormones coordinate functions in different parts of your body. They regulate everything from your appetite, metabolism, growth and development, sexual reproduction and stress responses to your sleep/wake cycles, fluid balance and even your moods. Your body needs to produce just the right amount of hormones to meet conditions within your body from minute to minute. This mechanism is partly regulated by the pituitary gland – often referred to as the master gland – as its hormones control the levels of hormone production in other glands as well as its own.

HORMONES

There are two main types of hormone. Peptide hormones, made from amino acids, bind to receptors on the surface of a cell to produce a response. Steroid hormones, whose chemical structure includes four fused carbon rings and is related to cholesterol, enter the cell and bind to receptors within the cell cytoplasm. The hormone-receptor complex then enters the cell nucleus where it binds to chromatin (unravelled DNA) to activate particular genes. This, in turn, increases the cell's synthesis of certain proteins.

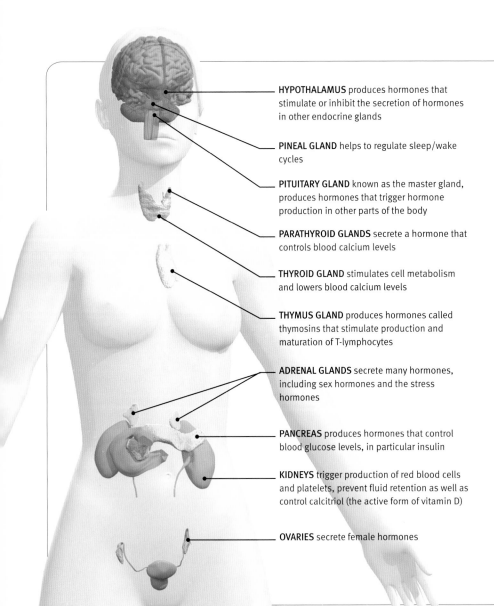

HYPOTHALAMUS produces hormones that stimulate or inhibit the secretion of hormones in other endocrine glands

PINEAL GLAND helps to regulate sleep/wake cycles

PITUITARY GLAND known as the master gland, produces hormones that trigger hormone production in other parts of the body

PARATHYROID GLANDS secrete a hormone that controls blood calcium levels

THYROID GLAND stimulates cell metabolism and lowers blood calcium levels

THYMUS GLAND produces hormones called thymosins that stimulate production and maturation of T-lymphocytes

ADRENAL GLANDS secrete many hormones, including sex hormones and the stress hormones

PANCREAS produces hormones that control blood glucose levels, in particular insulin

KIDNEYS trigger production of red blood cells and platelets, prevent fluid retention as well as control calcitriol (the active form of vitamin D)

OVARIES secrete female hormones

Hormone production

Hormones have many different functions and are produced in specific glands and also in certain organs that possess glandular tissue. For example the kidneys produce hormones, but are also part of the urinary system; the intestines process food but also produce hormones that enhance this process.

The key hormone-producing gland is the pituitary, but the hypothalamus and pineal glands in the brain play an important part, too. Other important glands are the thyroid, thymus, adrenal glands and the pancreas. The stomach, duodenum and small intestines produce hormones such as cholecystokinin, which triggers the release of digestive enzymes from the pancreas, and bile from the gallbladder. It also sends satiety signals to the brain to reduce hunger. In addition, the male and female sex organs produce hormones that coordinate the reproductive process.

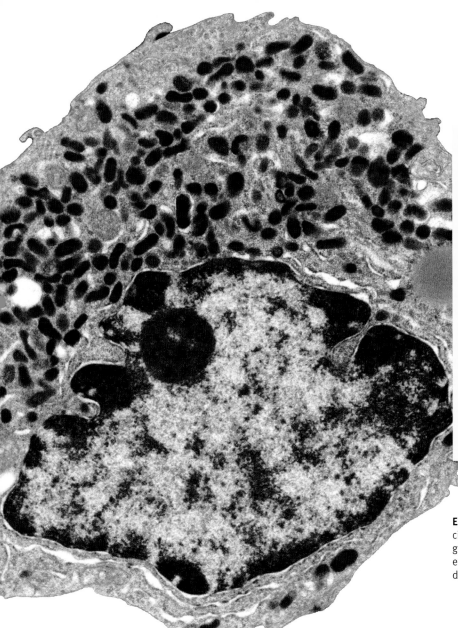

ENDOCRINE CELL Hormones are released into the circulatory system via endocrine cells in the glandular tissue. Shown here is an intestinal endocrine cell. The hormones within this cell form dark-staining secretory vesicles.

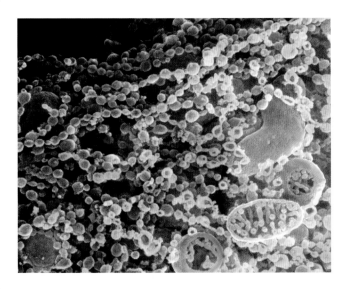

Male and female hormones

The main sex glands are the testes in males and the ovaries in females. These glands are responsible for egg production in women and sperm in men.

The ovaries secrete oestrogens (oestradiol, oestriol and oestrone), progesterone, small amounts of androgen (male hormones) and inhibin – a hormone that feeds back to the pituitary gland to reduce follicle stimulating hormone (FSH) production. The image, left, shows hormone vesicles (yellow) within an ovarian cell.

The testes secrete androgens such as testosterone, plus small amounts of oestrogen (oestradiol), as well as inhibin.

Hypothalamus and pituitary axis

Within your body, the endocrine glands that send hormone signals to each other in sequence are referred to as an axis. Your hypothalamus and pituitary form an axis with a number of other endocrine glands, creating, for example, the hypothalamic-pituitary-adrenal axis, and the hypothalamic-pituitary-thyroid axis.

HYPOTHALAMUS

This is the part of the brain that links the endocrine and central nervous systems. It is located directly below the thalamus and contains a number of neuronal clusters such as the supraoptic nucleus, arcuate nucleus and mammillary bodies. It is linked to the pituitary gland via the tube-like infundibulum. Some of the endocrine hormones produced by the hypothalamus pass to the anterior pituitary in the hypophyseal portal system, in which the capillaries of the hypothalamus are directly connected to the pituitary capillaries by a system of small veins (venules). Some hypothalamic hormones are released directly into the posterior pituitary via neuron axons.

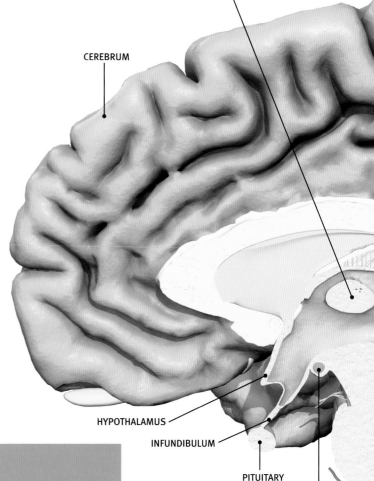

THALAMUS

CEREBRUM

HYPOTHALAMUS

INFUNDIBULUM

PITUITARY GLAND

MAMMILLARY BODY

HORMONES OF THE HYPOTHALAMUS
This gland produces nine hormones

HORMONE	FUNCTION
Thyrotropin-releasing hormone (TRH)	Stimulates release of TSH from the anterior pituitary
Gonadotropin-releasing hormone (GRH)	Stimulates release of FSH and LH from the anterior pituitary
Growth hormone-releasing hormone (GHRH)	Stimulates release of GH from the anterior pituitary
Corticotropin-releasing hormone	Stimulates release of ACTH from the anterior pituitary
Somatostatin (growth hormone-inhibiting hormone)	Inhibits release of TSH and GH from the anterior pituitary
Prolactin-releasing hormone	Stimulates release of prolactin from the anterior pituitary
Prolactin-inhibiting hormone	Inhibits release of prolactin from the anterior pituitary
Oxytocin is made in the hypothalamus, but sent to the posterior pituitary for storage	It acts as a neurotransmitter in the brain and stimulates contraction of the uterus during childbirth and ejection of milk during breast feeding
Vasopressin is made in the hypothalamus, but is sent to the posterior pituitary for storage and release	Stimulates retention of water in the kindeys, and contraction of blood vessels to raise blood pressure

PITUITARY GLAND

This gland is also known as the hypophysis. It is a small, pea-like protrusion from the hypothalamus at the base of the brain. It sits within the pituitary fossa of the sphenoid bone and has two main lobes: the anterior pituitary and the posterior pituitary, which are separated by a slim layer of cells known as the intermediate lobe.

Hormone levels

- Between the ages of 20 and 60 years, the production of growth hormone decreases by as much as 75 per cent.
- Oxytocin has been described as the hormone of mother love and faithful relationships – it is the hormonal equivalent of super-glue, helping to bind people together emotionally.

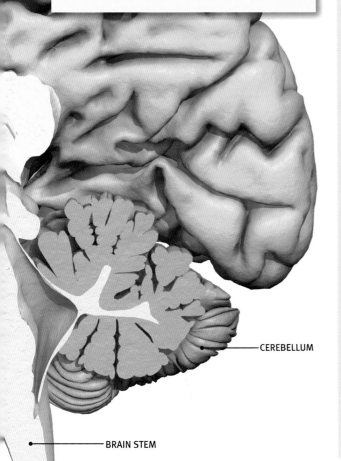

CEREBELLUM

BRAIN STEM

PITUITARY GLAND HORMONES
This gland produces a number of hormones from its different parts

HORMONE	FUNCTION
ANTERIOR PITUITARY	
Adrenocorticotropic hormone (ACTH)	Stimulates synthesis of corticosteroid hormones in the adrenal glands
Thyroid-stimulating hormone (TSH)	Stimulates synthesis of thyroxine and triodothyronine in the thyroid gland
Prolactin	Stimulates milk production (lactation) in the mammary glands; also released during orgasm
Growth hormone (somatotropin)	Stimulates cell growth and division
Follicle-stimulating hormone (FSH)	Stimulates maturation of eggs (ova) in the ovaries, and sperm in the testes
Luteinizing hormone (LH)	Stimulates ovulation in females, and production of testosterone in the testes
Endorphins	Opiate (heroin-like) chemicals that reduce pain perception and provide a natural 'high' after strenuous exercise
Lipotrophins	Stimulate mobilization of fat from adipose tissue stores
INTERMEDIATE LOBE	
Melanocyte-stimulating hormone (MSH)	Stimulates production of melanin pigment in the skin
POSTERIOR PITUITARY	
Oxytocin	Stimulates contraction of the uterus during childbirth and ejection of milk during breast-feeding; released at orgasm
Antidiuretic hormone (vasopressin)	Stimulates retention of water in the kidneys, and contraction of blood vessels to raise blood pressure

Regulation of hormone secretion

The hypothalamic-pituitary axis regulates the secretion of certain ('target') endocrine glands through a process of negative feedback (see homeostasis, pages 129 and 170). For example, if blood levels of thyroid hormones are lower than normal, the hypothalamus releases TRH. This triggers the release of TSH from the pituitary gland, which, in turn, increases the output of thyroxine (T_4) and triiodothyronine (T_3) from the thyroid gland. The production of TSH is also under negative feedback control by T_4 and T_3, so TSH production falls as blood levels of T_4/T_3 rise.

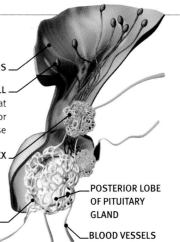

HYPOTHALAMUS

NEUROSECRETORY CELL
produces hormones that are sent to the posterior piuitary for release

CAPILLARY COMPLEX

POSTERIOR LOBE OF PITUITARY GLAND

ANTERIOR LOBE

BLOOD VESSELS

Thyroid gland

The thyroid and adrenal glands are important glands in the endocrine system. The thyroid is a butterfly-shaped gland at the front of the neck. The thyroid forms at the back of the throat prior to birth, and it slowly moves into its final position as other tissues grow around it. If present, a thin strip of tissue, the pyramidal process, represents the remains of the connection between the thyroid's initial and final positions.

THYROID, FRONT VIEW

THYROID, REAR VIEW

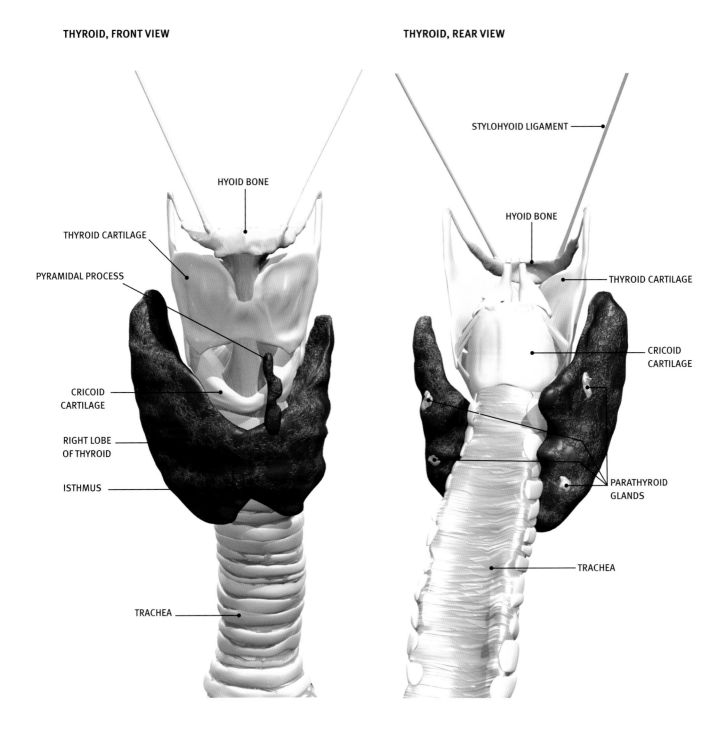

HYOID BONE

THYROID CARTILAGE

PYRAMIDAL PROCESS

CRICOID CARTILAGE

RIGHT LOBE OF THYROID

ISTHMUS

TRACHEA

STYLOHYOID LIGAMENT

HYOID BONE

THYROID CARTILAGE

CRICOID CARTILAGE

PARATHYROID GLANDS

TRACHEA

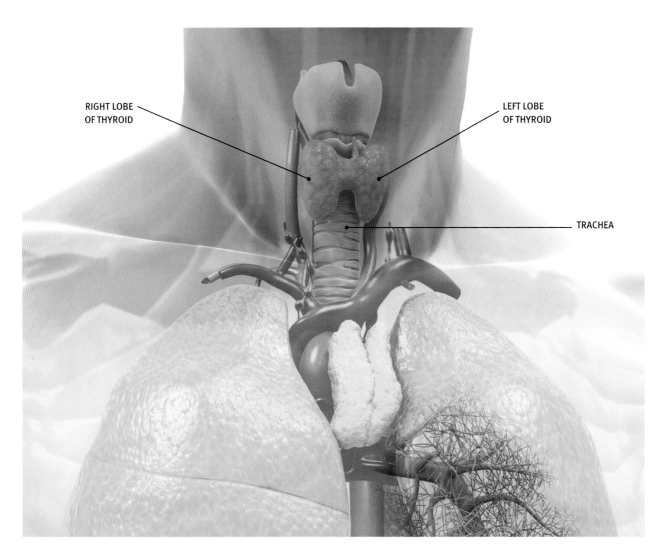

RIGHT LOBE OF THYROID

LEFT LOBE OF THYROID

TRACHEA

FUNCTION OF THE THYROID

The thyroid gland secretes three hormones. Thyroxine (T_4) and triiodothyronine (T_3) are iodine-containing hormones that control the speed of cell metabolism. This affects the growth and function of every system in the body. The thyroid also produces calcitonin, a hormone that lowers blood calcium levels when they become raised. It does this by reducing calcium absorption in the intestines, reducing calcium reabsorption from filtered fluids in the kidneys and restricting calcium release from bone stores.

There are usually four parathyroid glands, behind the thyroid, at the top and bottom of each lobe, which share its blood supply. Their positions are variable. Parathyroid glands secrete parathyroid hormone (or parathormone), which raises blood calcium levels when they fall below the normal range. It does this by by increasing the release of calcium from bone stores, increasing calcium reabsorption from filtered fluids in the kidney and by increasing calcium absorption from the gut.

Thyroid follicles

Thyroid tissue consists of rings of cells, called follicles, that are just one cell deep. Thyroid hormones are stored in the centre of these follicles, ready for release into the circulation when needed. Parafollicular cells between the follicles secrete calcitonin.

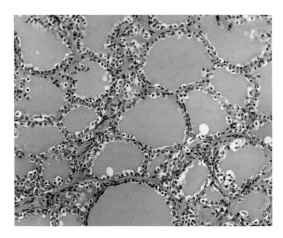

Adrenal gland

The adrenal glands sit just above the kidneys. They secrete several hormones (see opposite). The inner part, known as the medulla, is linked to the sympathetic nervous system (see page 68).

'FIGHT OR FLIGHT' RESPONSE

In times of danger, the sympathetic nervous system initiates the 'fight-or-flight' response by triggering the release of catecholamine hormones from the adrenal medulla. Adrenaline, noradrenaline and dopamine produce the following rapid changes designed to improve your chances of survival:

- Blood glucose level rises
- Pupils dilate so your field of vision increases
- Bowels and bladder (and sometimes stomach) empty so you are lighter for running
- Circulation to the gut shuts down, and more blood is diverted to your muscles
- Pulse and blood pressure go up, and you breathe more deeply to increase blood and oxygen supply to your muscles and brain
- Memory and ability to think straight improve
- Sensitivity to pain is reduced
- Sweat glands are switched on, and the muscles tense, ready for action
- Blood-clotting and blood-vessel constriction occur more easily to reduce bleeding from wounds

If stress continues, the adrenal glands increase their output of the steroid hormone cortisol – a rise that appears to be essential for survival.

BODY FACT

Glands and their hormones

- A quarter of your body's iodine stores are found in the thyroid gland.
- The pyramidal process is the thin strip of tissue that indicates the thyroid's original position.
- Some people have only three parathyroid glands, while others have six.
- Thyroxine (T4) is a weak prohormone that is converted into the more active triodothyronine (T3).
- Adrenaline, noradrenaline and dopamine act both as hormones and as neurotransmitters (nerve cell communication chemicals).
- Blood levels of adrenaline/epinephrine increase as much as a thousand-fold within one minute during acute stress.

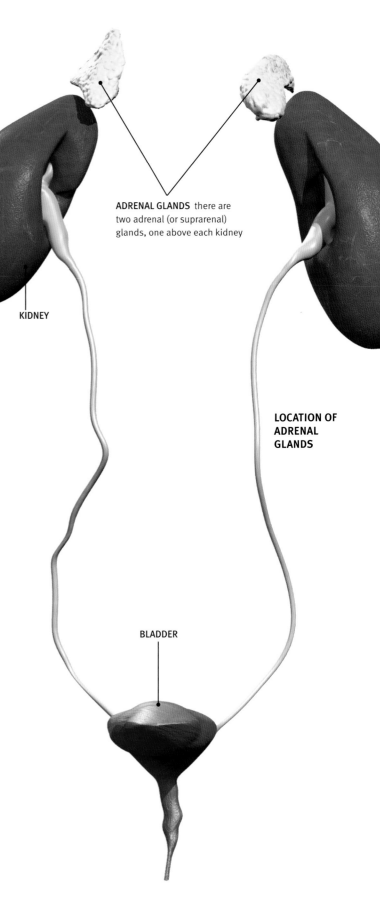

ADRENAL GLANDS there are two adrenal (or suprarenal) glands, one above each kidney

KIDNEY

LOCATION OF ADRENAL GLANDS

BLADDER

ADRENAL HORMONE	FUNCTION
Aldosterone	Increases excretion of potassium in urine, and increases retention of water and sodium. Secretion of aldosterone is regulatedby the renin-angiotensin system.
Cortisol	Stimulates the metabolism to increase circulating levels of free amino acids, fatty acids and glucose. Strengthens heart contractions, increases water retention and inhibits inflammatory and allergic reactions. Its secretion is regulated by adrenocorticotropic hormone (ACTH) from the anterior pituitary gland
Sex hormones, mainly androgens: testosterone; dihydrotestosterone; androstenedione and dehydroepiandrosterone (DHEA)	In the male, these regulate sexual maturation, male secondary sexual characteristics and sex drive. In women, small amounts of androgens affect sex drive. Most are converted into oestrogens (oestradiol, oestriol and oestrone) by an enzyme called aromatase
Adrenaline/epinephrine	Underpins the 'fight-or-flight' response
Noradrenaline/norepinephrine	Underpins the 'fight-or-flight' response
Dopamine	Increases heart rate and blood pressure

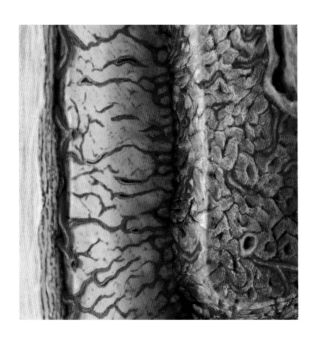

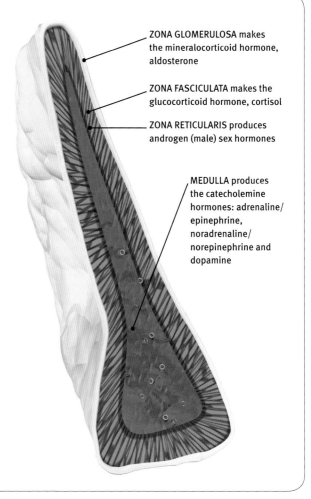

ZONA GLOMERULOSA makes the mineralocorticoid hormone, aldosterone

ZONA FASCICULATA makes the glucocorticoid hormone, cortisol

ZONA RETICULARIS produces androgen (male) sex hormones

MEDULLA produces the catecholemine hormones: adrenaline/epinephrine, noradrenaline/norepinephrine and dopamine

CROSS-SECTION OF THE ADRENAL GLAND
The outer portion of the adrenal gland, the adrenal cortex is responsible for the synthesis of three different hormones: aldosterone, cortisol and sex hormones. The inner portion of the adrenal gland is the adrenal medulla which is responsible for the synthesis of epinephrine, norepinephrine and a small amount of dopamine.

Pancreas

Your pancreas is an organ that lies beneath the liver, nestled in the curve of the duodenum (see pages 170–171). It functions as both an exocrine gland, secreting digestive enzymes into the pancreatic duct, and as an endocrine gland, secreting hormones directly into the bloodstream.

EXTERNAL APPEARANCE

The surface texture is lumpy and nodular, and is divided anatomically into three sections: the head, body and tail.

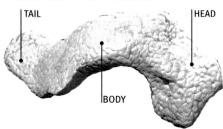

REAR VIEW OF THE PANCREAS

TAIL — HEAD

BODY

PANCREATIC SECRETIONS

Each day about 1 litre (2 pints) of pancreatic juice is poured out by the exorine cells, collected in the pancreatic duct and delivered to the duodenum. The juice is slightly alkaline and helps neutralize the acidity of the stomach contents that have just entered the duodenum.

Pancreatic juice is highly corrosive to other tissues, and can cause severe inflammation if it leaks outside the pancreas and bowel.

The secretory function of the pancreas is regulated by a hormone, secretin, produced in the duodenum in response to chyme (partially digested food from the stomach). It is also set in motion by the vagus nerve, activated when food reaches the stomach. This means that the correct enzymes are in place when food reaches the duodenum.

ACINAR CELLS

These cells, seen right, make up most of the pancreas and secrete enzymes into tiny ducts. They form clusters (acini) that produce bicarbonate and digestive enzymes, trypsin, chymotrypsin and exopeptidases, which break down protein. They also produce pancreatic lipase, which breaks down fat molecules, and pancreatic amylase, which breaks down starch into smaller units containing two glucose molecules (disaccharides) or three glucose molecules (trisaccharides). These secretions pass down the pancreatic duct to enter the duodenum via the ampulla of Vater (see page 170).

BODY FACT

Your productive pancreas

- Your pancreas contains around one million islets of Langerhans (see opposite).
- The islets of Langerhans make up only 2 per cent of the weight of your pancreas.
- Beta cells make up around 75 per cent of cells within the islets of Langerhans.
- Beta cells communicate electrically with one another (but not with other types of islet cells) through gap junctions connecting their membranes.
- Acinar cells are responsible for the remaining 98 per cent of the weight of the pancreas and are involved in the production of digestive enzymes.

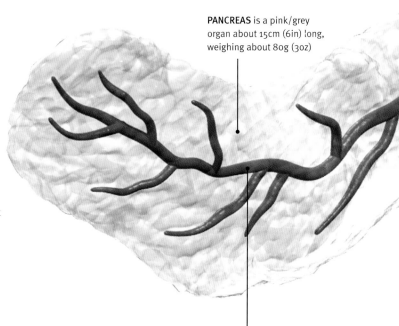

PANCREAS is a pink/grey organ about 15cm (6in) long, weighing about 80g (3oz)

PANCREATIC DUCT begins in the tail and then runs down the centre. Lobular ducts feed into it at regular intervals

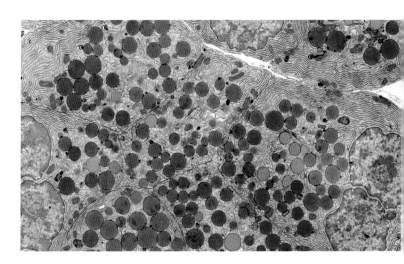

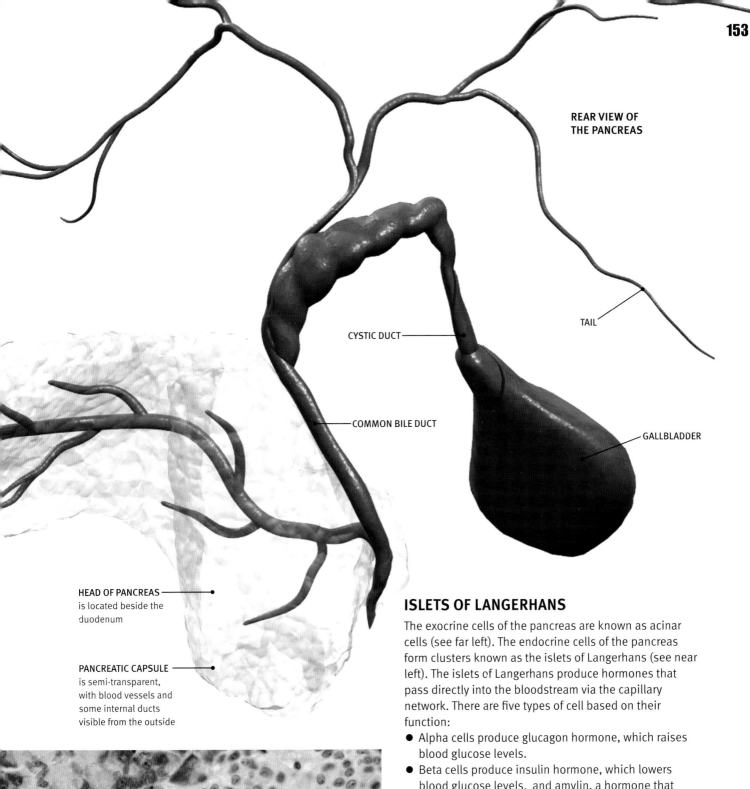

TAIL

CYSTIC DUCT

COMMON BILE DUCT

GALLBLADDER

HEAD OF PANCREAS
is located beside the duodenum

PANCREATIC CAPSULE
is semi-transparent, with blood vessels and some internal ducts visible from the outside

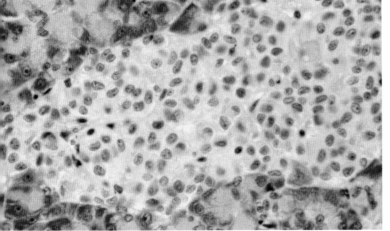

ISLETS OF LANGERHANS

The exocrine cells of the pancreas are known as acinar cells (see far left). The endocrine cells of the pancreas form clusters known as the islets of Langerhans (see near left). The islets of Langerhans produce hormones that pass directly into the bloodstream via the capillary network. There are five types of cell based on their function:

- Alpha cells produce glucagon hormone, which raises blood glucose levels.
- Beta cells produce insulin hormone, which lowers blood glucose levels, and amylin, a hormone that slows gastric emptying and digestion to reduce the amount of glucose absorbed into the circulation; it also inhibits secretion of glucagon.
- Delta cells produce somatostatin, which suppresses the release of insulin and glucagon.
- Epsilon cells produce ghrelin, which stimulates the appetite.
- F cells (mainly found in the head of the pancreas) produce pancreatic polypeptide, which regulates the exocrine and endocrine activities of the pancreas. These cells and their hormones interact with each other to help regulate their activity.

DIGESTIVE SYSTEM

VOLUMINOUS VILLI
Coloured scanning electron micrograph of the lining of the small intestine showing its highly folded surface (purple). The folds (known as villi), project into the interior cavity to increase the surface area. The small intestine runs from the stomach to the large intestine and is where digestion is completed and water and nutrients are absorbed into the blood.

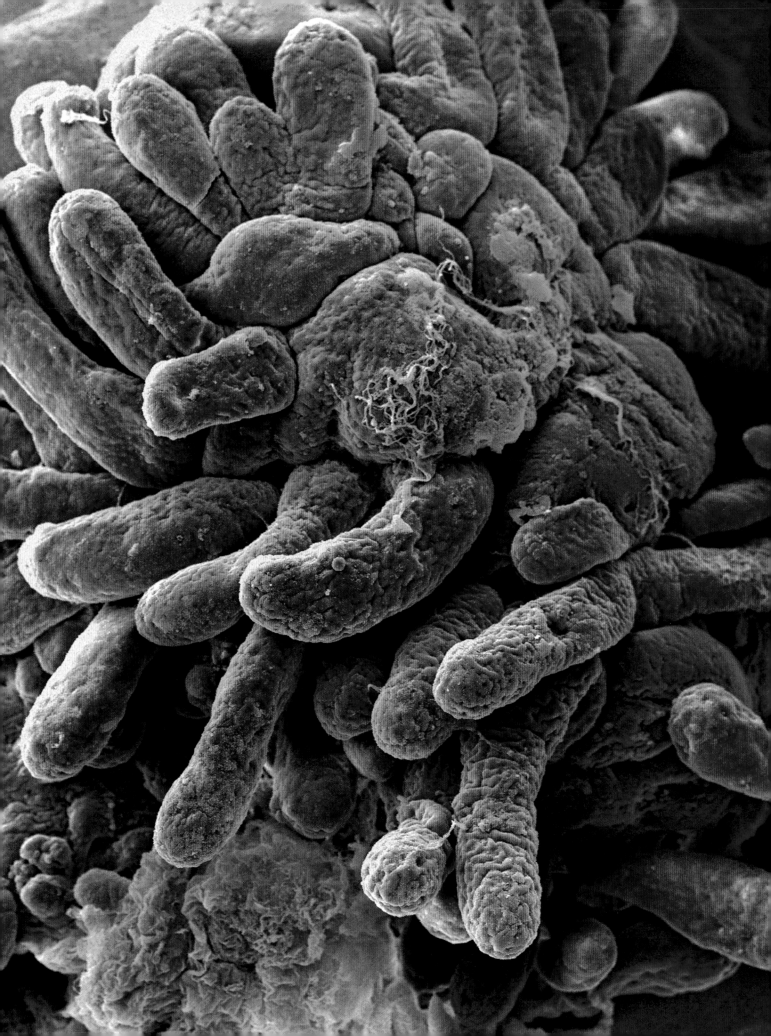

Digestive organs

Your gastrointestinal tract forms a long tube that starts at your mouth and ends at your anal sphincter. It acts as a food-processing system, accepting complex food molecules at one end, and breaking them down (using a combination of mechanical and chemical methods) into simpler, more soluble components for absorption. Waste products are disposed of – usually in neat packages – at the other end.

The mechanical breakdown of food occurs via the chewing action of the teeth, and the churning motion of muscles in the stomach wall.

Chemical disruption is carried out by enzymes and hydrochloric acid secreted by the stomach wall, and by enzymes and alkalis in the juices secreted by the duodenal wall, liver and pancreas. These acids, alkalis and enzymes dissolve chemical bonds and break down complex food molecules (proteins, carbohydrates, fats) into simpler units (amino acids, sugars, fatty acids) that can be absorbed.

Most nutrients are absorbed across the walls of the jejunum and ileum. Excess fluids are absorbed within the colon, leaving behind a solid waste for excretion.

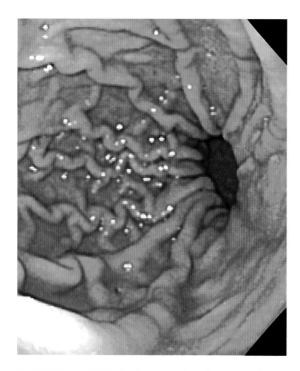

STOMACH WALL Folds in the stomach wall secrete acid, enzymes and gastric intrinsic factor, which is a glycoprotein necessary for the absorption of vitamin B.

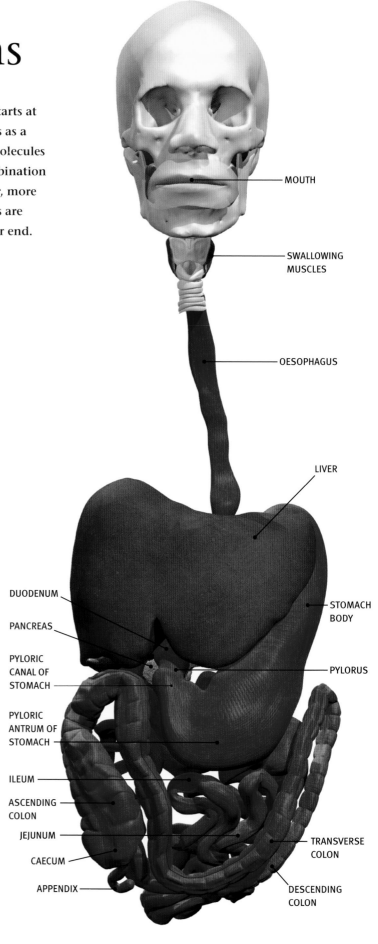

MOUTH

SWALLOWING MUSCLES

OESOPHAGUS

LIVER

DUODENUM

PANCREAS

PYLORIC CANAL OF STOMACH

PYLORIC ANTRUM OF STOMACH

ILEUM

ASCENDING COLON

JEJUNUM

CAECUM

APPENDIX

STOMACH BODY

PYLORUS

TRANSVERSE COLON

DESCENDING COLON

Gut facts

- Your digestive system is around 9m (30ft) long.
- The oesophagus is the narrowest part of your gut.
- The stomach is the widest part of your gut.
- The omenta (singular: omentum) contribute to the 'beer belly' of people who store excess fat around their middle.
- The lesser omentum encases the hepatic artery, common bile duct and portal vein.

Swallowing

The tongue rolls chewed food into a ball (bolus) ready for swallowing, pushing it to the back of the mouth where it triggers the swallowing reflex.

The palatopharyngeal folds on each side of the pharynx come closer together to ensure only a small bolus can pass through, while the back of the tongue lifts up to seal the nasopharynx and prevent a simultaneous in-breath, which could lead to choking.

The larynx and hyoid bone are pulled upwards and forwards, closing the epiglottis to prevent food entering the trachea.

The pharyngeal constrictor muscles contract to initiate an automatic wave of peristalsis that propels food down the oesophagus into the stomach.

Rings of muscle (the upper and lower oesophageal sphincters), which normally hold both ends of the oesophagus closed, open to let food through, then close again. The swallowing reflex is coordinated by centres in the brainstem (the medulla oblongata and the pons).

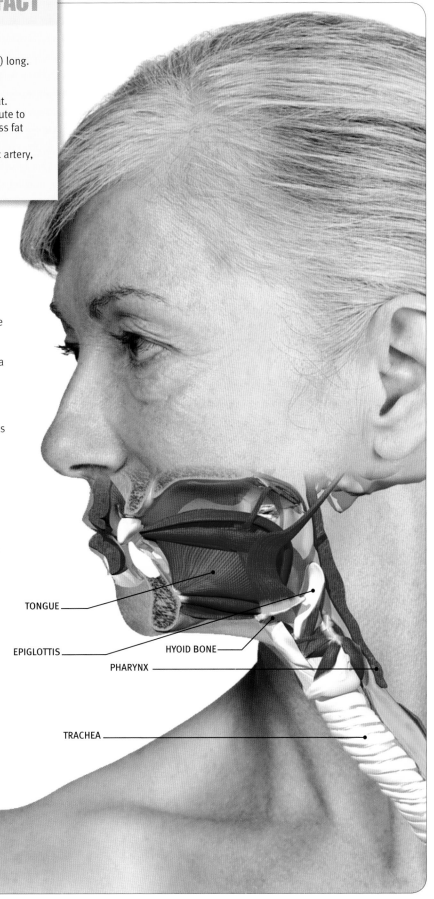

TONGUE

EPIGLOTTIS

HYOID BONE

PHARYNX

TRACHEA

Peritoneum

The intestines and the abdominal and pelvic cavities are lined by a single transparent membrane called the peritoneum. This forms a large sac with two layers. One layer lines the walls of the cavities (the parietal peritoneum) and the other layer pushes in to cover the abdominal and pelvic organs (the visceral peritoneum). A small amount of lubricating fluid separates the two layers to prevent rubbing. The parietal and visceral peritoneum are fused to form double sheets each called a mesentery. These provide access for the vessels, nerves and lympatics to supply the digestive tract and stabilize the relative positions of each part. This prevents entanglement during digestive movements (peristalsis) or sudden changes in body movement.

Each mesentery contains a rich supply of blood and lymphatic vessels, helping to prevent infection entering the body via the intestines, and storing intra-abdominal fat.

A sheet of visceral peritoneum hangs down from the greater curvature of the stomach to form an apron-like sheet of tissue called the greater omentum. A smaller sheet of peritoneum hangs down from the lesser curvature of the stomach.

The peritoneum holds the abdominal contents in place and allows them to slide over each other without friction.

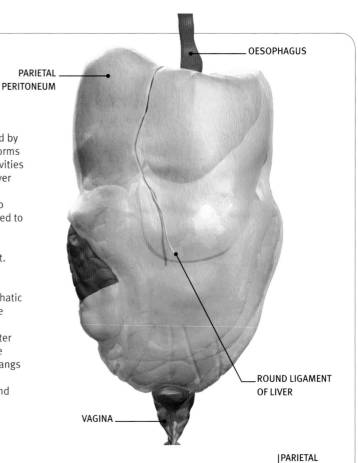

OESOPHAGUS

PARIETAL PERITONEUM

ROUND LIGAMENT OF LIVER

VAGINA

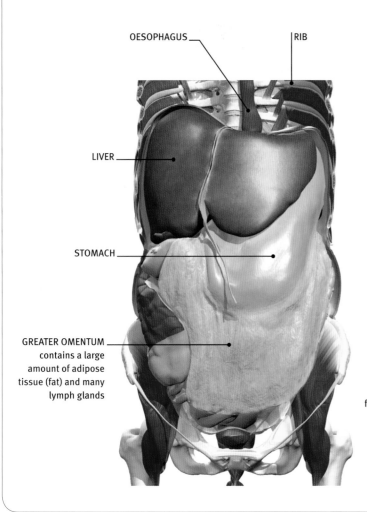

OESOPHAGUS

RIB

LIVER

STOMACH

GREATER OMENTUM contains a large amount of adipose tissue (fat) and many lymph glands

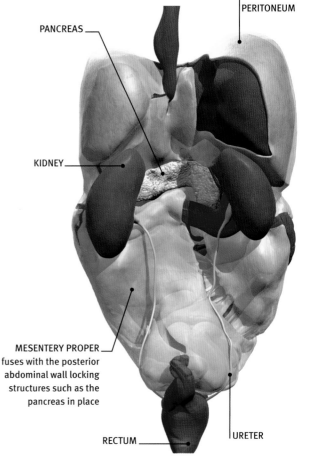

PARIETAL PERITONEUM

PANCREAS

KIDNEY

MESENTERY PROPER fuses with the posterior abdominal wall locking structures such as the pancreas in place

RECTUM

URETER

Peristalsis

The rhythmic contraction of smooth muscle propels food through the digestive tract. In the three diagrams below, chewed food is forced down the oesophagus eventually ending up in the small intestine. In the illustration, right, the thick outer layer (orange ring) contains the circular and longitudinal muscles involved in moving food from one end of the intestines to the other. Smooth muscle and villi (red and yellow areas) mix food as it passes through the lumen (white area).

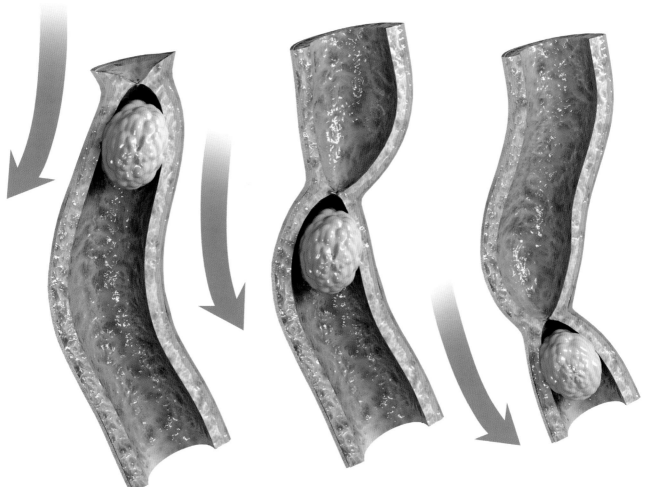

STAGE 1
Circular muscles contract behind the food bolus and relax ahead of it

STAGE 2
Longitudinal muscles contract ahead of the bolus, shortening the bowel segment

STAGE 3
A wave of contraction in the circular muscle layer forces the food bolus forwards

Mouth

Digestion starts in your mouth, where biting and chewing breaks food down into suitable portions for swallowing.

TEETH

Adults normally have thirty-two permanent teeth. Each tooth consists of a crown above the gum, which is covered in enamel, and a root, which is covered in cementum. Canines, incisors and most premolars (except the maxillary first premolars) usually have one root. Maxillary first premolars and mandibular molars usually have two roots, while maxillary molars usually have three.

The central part of the tooth consists of a pulp chamber with pulp canals extending down each root, which contains blood vessels and nerves.

The main bulk of the tooth is dentin – a porous, yellow connective tissue that has microscopic channels (dentinal tubules), which radiate out to the tooth surface.

Teeth are attached to bone by periodontal ligaments embedded in the cementum. A periodontal membrane separates each tooth from the underlying bone.

CHEWING

When food enters the mouth it undergoes analysis by receptors for taste, temperature and pressure. It is processed mechanically by action of the teeth, tongue and palate, then lubricated and softened by mixing with mucus and salivary secretions. Limited digestion of carbohydrates by salivary amylase (ptyalin), an enzyme, also occurs.

Once food has been shredded or torn to the necessary consistency by the teeth and moistened with salivary sections, it is ready to be swallowed. The muscles of the tongue roll the food into a ball called a bolus, which is then pushed to the back of the throat. From there, muscle action and nerve reflexes pass it down the gullet (oesophagus) towards the stomach for further processing (see page 157).

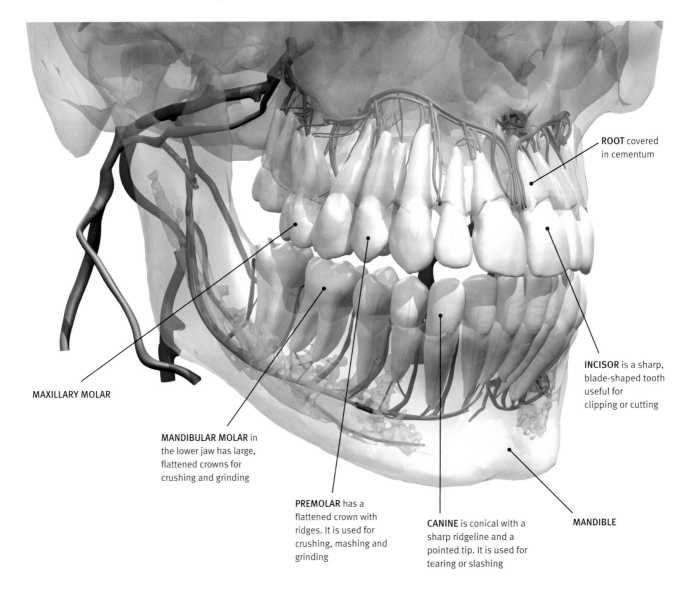

ROOT covered in cementum

INCISOR is a sharp, blade-shaped tooth useful for clipping or cutting

MAXILLARY MOLAR

MANDIBULAR MOLAR in the lower jaw has large, flattened crowns for crushing and grinding

PREMOLAR has a flattened crown with ridges. It is used for crushing, mashing and grinding

CANINE is conical with a sharp ridgeline and a pointed tip. It is used for tearing or slashing

MANDIBLE

Tooth enamel

Enamel covers all exposed surfaces of the teeth. It is the hardest tissue in the body, but it is nonliving and cannot repair itself once damaged. It is shiny and hard and protects the underlying tooth layers from food acids, heat and cold.

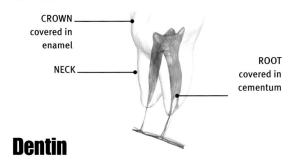

CROWN covered in enamel

NECK

ROOT covered in cementum

Dentin

The second hardest tissue in the body, dentin is the yellow substance under tooth enamel. It has a slight flexibility that protects teeth from breaking during chewing.

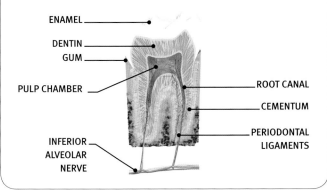

ENAMEL

DENTIN

GUM

PULP CHAMBER

ROOT CANAL

CEMENTUM

PERIODONTAL LIGAMENTS

INFERIOR ALVEOLAR NERVE

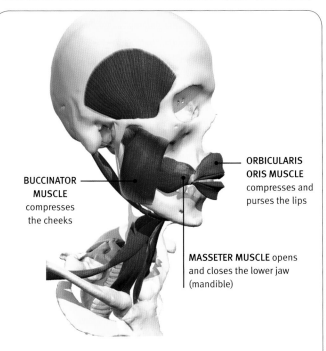

BUCCINATOR MUSCLE compresses the cheeks

ORBICULARIS ORIS MUSCLE compresses and purses the lips

MASSETER MUSCLE opens and closes the lower jaw (mandible)

Muscles of mastication

These close the jaws and slide or rock the lower jaw from side to side to force food back and forth between the vestibule and the rest of the oral cavity. This process is helped by the muscles of the mouth.

Salivary glands

The salivary glands secrete saliva into the mouth through the salivary ducts. Saliva moistens your food while salivary enzymes initiate the digestive process. Salivary amylase starts breaking down starch to form simpler carbohydrates, such as maltose, and salivary lipase starts breaking down dietary fats.

The two parotid glands, which overlie the temporomandibular joint on each side, are the largest, although they produce only around a quarter of a person's total saliva. Most (70 per cent) is secreted by the submandibular glands beneath the floor of the mouth. A small amount (five per cent) of saliva is made by the sublingual glands beneath the tongue. Hundreds of tiny 'minor' salivary glands are also found within the oral cavity, and these secrete lubricating mucus into the mouth.

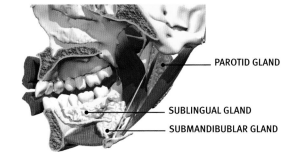

PAROTID GLAND

PAROTID DUCT

SUBMANDIBUBLAR GLAND

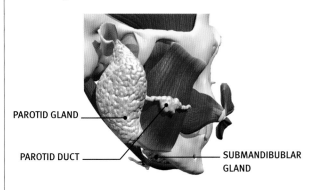

PAROTID GLAND

SUBLINGUAL GLAND

SUBMANDIBUBLAR GLAND

BODY FACT

Digest this!

- You produce between 750 and 1500ml (1.25–2.5 pints) saliva every day.
- Very little saliva is produced during sleep.
- You secrete the salivary enzyme lipase continuously. This is swallowed to build up in your stomach between meals – 20 per cent of dietary fat is digested in the stomach by this enzyme.
- Tooth enamel is the hardest substance in your body.
- Children have a set of 20 deciduous 'milk' teeth, which are replaced by the 32 adult teeth.
- Chewing is known as mastication, while swallowing is known as deglutition.
- Your breathing stops for a brief time during swallowing – this is known as deglutition apnoea.

Stomach

Your stomach is a hollow, J-shaped muscular sac located in the upper left-hand side of your abdomen, just beneath your diaphragm. The upper part is known as the fundus, the main part is called the body, and the lower part is the pyloric antrum – a funnel-shaped region that leads into the pyloric canal and the pyloric sphincter. The last of these separates the stomach from the first part of the small intestines, the duodenum. The area where the oesophagus joins the stomach is known as the cardiac region, and is at the level of the seventh costal cartilage of the ribs.

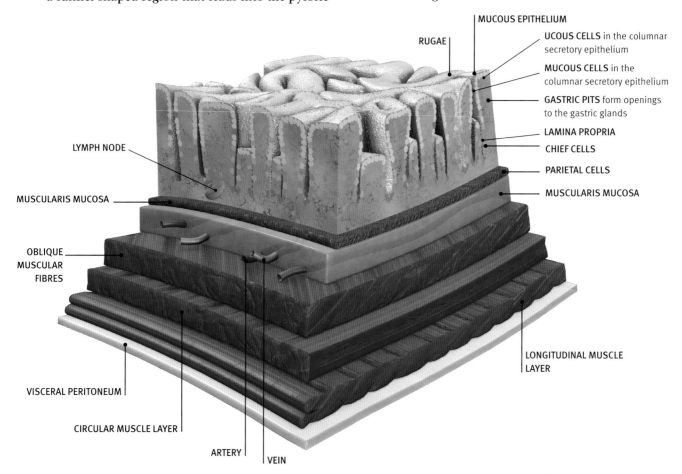

MUCOUS EPITHELIUM

RUGAE

UCOUS CELLS in the columnar secretory epithelium

MUCOUS CELLS in the columnar secretory epithelium

GASTRIC PITS form openings to the gastric glands

LAMINA PROPRIA

CHIEF CELLS

PARIETAL CELLS

MUSCULARIS MUCOSA

LYMPH NODE

MUSCULARIS MUCOSA

OBLIQUE MUSCULAR FIBRES

LONGITUDINAL MUSCLE LAYER

VISCERAL PERITONEUM

CIRCULAR MUSCLE LAYER

ARTERY

VEIN

LAYERS OF THE STOMACH

Beneath the visceral peritoneum is the muscularis externa, consisting of three layers of muscle (longitudinal, circular and oblique).

The submucosa, or middle layer, contains a capillary network that supplies the stomach wall.

The gastric mucosa has three layers: a thin layer of smooth muscle (muscularis mucosae), the lamina propria (loose connective tissue containing capillaries, lymphatic vessels and nerves) and the inner simple, columnar secretory epithelium. The mucosa is folded to form millions of gastric pits.

STOMACH MUSCLES

In addition to the usual circular and longitudinal layers, the stomach contains additional smooth muscle, which helps to strengthen the stomach wall. It is these smooth muscles in the stomach wall that produce the churning motions necessary to break up food and mix it with gastric juices in order to form chyme.

STOMACH SECRETIONS

The gastric pits contain glands that secrete a variety of substances. Mucous cells produce mucin, which mixes with water to produce mucus. Parietal (oxyntic) cells secrete hydrochloric acid and intrinsic factor, which is vital for the absorption of vitamin B12 in the small intestines (terminal ileum). Chief (peptic or zymogenic) cells secrete pepsinogen (a proenzyme converted into pepsin by the action of hydrochloric acid, which breaks down proteins into chains of amino acids called peptides), gastric lipase (an enzyme that breaks down dietary fats) and rennin (an enzyme that curdles milk by converting caseinogen into insoluble casein). Renin production declines after infancy as its function is taken over by pepsin.

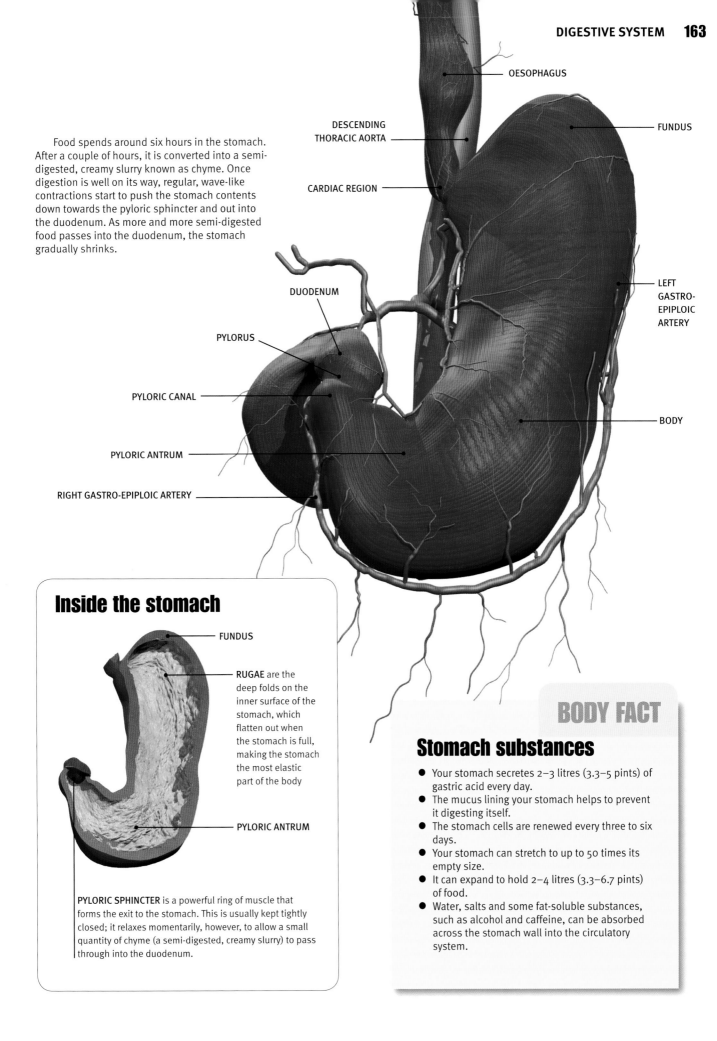

OESOPHAGUS

FUNDUS

DESCENDING THORACIC AORTA

CARDIAC REGION

Food spends around six hours in the stomach. After a couple of hours, it is converted into a semi-digested, creamy slurry known as chyme. Once digestion is well on its way, regular, wave-like contractions start to push the stomach contents down towards the pyloric sphincter and out into the duodenum. As more and more semi-digested food passes into the duodenum, the stomach gradually shrinks.

DUODENUM

LEFT GASTRO-EPIPLOIC ARTERY

PYLORUS

PYLORIC CANAL

BODY

PYLORIC ANTRUM

RIGHT GASTRO-EPIPLOIC ARTERY

Inside the stomach

FUNDUS

RUGAE are the deep folds on the inner surface of the stomach, which flatten out when the stomach is full, making the stomach the most elastic part of the body

PYLORIC ANTRUM

PYLORIC SPHINCTER is a powerful ring of muscle that forms the exit to the stomach. This is usually kept tightly closed; it relaxes momentarily, however, to allow a small quantity of chyme (a semi-digested, creamy slurry) to pass through into the duodenum.

BODY FACT

Stomach substances

- Your stomach secretes 2–3 litres (3.3–5 pints) of gastric acid every day.
- The mucus lining your stomach helps to prevent it digesting itself.
- The stomach cells are renewed every three to six days.
- Your stomach can stretch to up to 50 times its empty size.
- It can expand to hold 2–4 litres (3.3–6.7 pints) of food.
- Water, salts and some fat-soluble substances, such as alcohol and caffeine, can be absorbed across the stomach wall into the circulatory system.

Small intestines

Your small intestines form a long tube that is highly coiled to fit into your abdominal cavity. During your life, it is semicontracted and measures around 3m (10ft) long, but if it was fully relaxed it would extend to 6m (20ft) or more in length.

PERISTALSIS

The walls of your small intestines have an outer longitudinal layer, and an inner circular layer of smooth muscle. When the longitudinal muscle contracts, the bowel length shortens; when the circular muscle contracts, the bore of the gut narrows. Coordinated contraction of these muscle layers pushes food through the intestinal tract in wave-like movements known as peristalsis (see page 159).

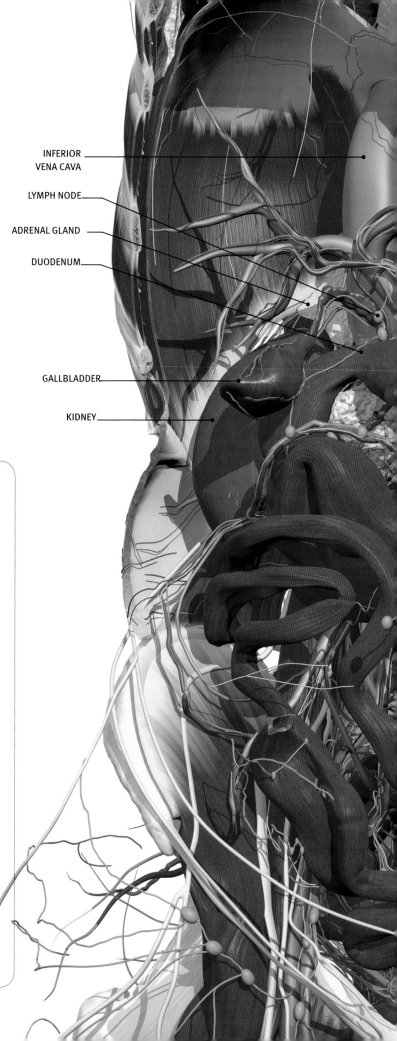

INFERIOR VENA CAVA

LYMPH NODE

ADRENAL GLAND

DUODENUM

GALLBLADDER

KIDNEY

Duodenum

The first part of the small intestines is the duodenum. This curved, C-shaped tube encircles the head of the pancreas, and is around 25cm (10in) long. It is fixed to the back wall of the abdominal cavity by the peritoneal membrane, and to a sinewy structure called the left crus of the diaphragm by the suspensory ligament of Treitz.

The descending part of the duodenum receives pancreatic juices from the pancreatic duct, and bile from the liver via the common bile duct (see page 173). The pancreas secretes digestive enzymes (trypsin, elastase, lipase and amylase) into the duodenum via the pancreatic duct.

The submucosa of the duodenum is packed with Brunner's glands. These secrete copious amounts of alkaline mucus, containing bicarbonate, and this neutralizes the acidity of the digested food slurry (chyme) arriving from the stomach.

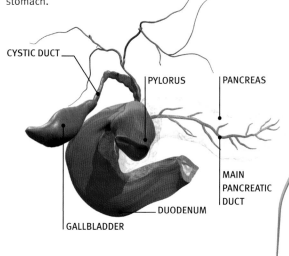

CYSTIC DUCT

PYLORUS

PANCREAS

MAIN PANCREATIC DUCT

DUODENUM

GALLBLADDER

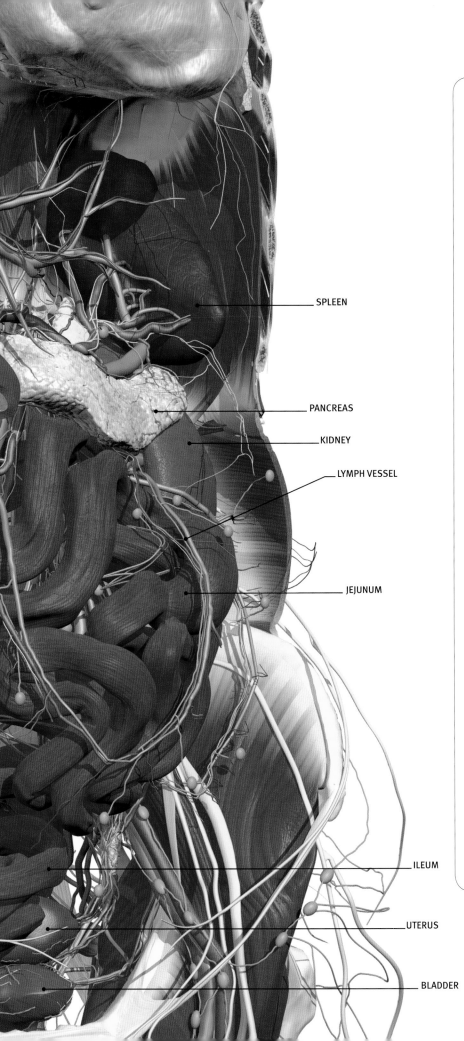

SPLEEN

PANCREAS

KIDNEY

LYMPH VESSEL

JEJUNUM

ILEUM

UTERUS

BLADDER

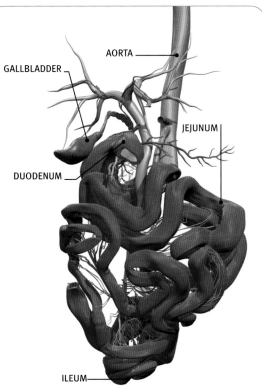

AORTA

GALLBLADDER

JEJUNUM

DUODENUM

ILEUM

Jejunum and ileum

The jejunum is the name given to the first 40 per cent of the small intestine below the duodenum. It is usually defined as starting at the level of the ligament of Treitz. Although called a ligament, it is actually a suspensory muscle, which contracts to open the duodenal-jejunal flexure and allow chyme to pass through.

The small intestines secrete juices (succus entericus) containing several enzymes. Sucrase breaks down sucrose into glucose and fructose; lactase breaks down lactose (milk sugar) into glucose and galactose; peptidases break down peptides into amino acids; lipase breaks down triglycerides into free fatty acids and glycerol. The contents of the jejunum and ileum are usually neutral or slightly alkaline (pH 7–8).

The ileum is the name given to the last 60 per cent of the small intestines. There is no distinct border with the jejunum and this division is somewhat arbitrary. In general, the ileum is paler in colour than the jejunum, and its walls contain immune areas called Peyer's patches (see page 132). The ileum joins the caecum of the colon at the ileocaecal valve.

The ileum and jejunum are suspended from the back wall of the abdomen by a double layer of peritoneum called the mesentery.

Large intestines

Your large intestines form a wide tube around 1m (3ft) long. Like your small intestines, the muscles in its wall are usually contracted, but if it was fully relaxed it would measure 1.5m (5ft) long. The major functions of the large intestines are the reabsorption of water and electrolytes and the compaction of the intestinal contents into faeces, the absorption of important vitamins and the storing of faecal material before defaecation.

BODY FACT

Heavy bacteria

- Your bowels contain around 11 trillion bacteria, weighing a total of 1.5kg (3.3lbs).
- Over half the weight of your stools consists of bacteria.
- Bowel bacteria ferment and break down undigested fibre. They produce useful amounts of vitamin K, biotin and folate, which can be absorbed and used in the body.
- Substances formed by bacterial metabolism – mainly indole and skatole – are largely responsible for the characteristic odour of faeces.
- The brown colour of faeces is due to pigments formed when the bowel bacteria interact with bile (see page 141).

BOWEL MOVEMENTS

Peristalsis within the colon is coordinated by the slow wave of the colon, which gets faster as it passes along the colon. The large intestines absorb excess fluid, salts and minerals from the bowel contents. Of around 2 litres (3.3 pints) of bowel contents received into the colon each day, only 200–250ml (7–9fl oz) of semi-solid waste remains for voiding.

Waste enters the rectum for expulsion through the anal canal. When the rectum is distended with faeces, reflex contractions stimulate a powerful urge to open the bowels. The internal anal sphincter is able to relax automatically, while the external sphincter, which is under voluntary control, stays tightly shut until you allow the sphincter to open.

While some people normally open their bowels once every two or three days, others defaecate once daily and some regularly pass motions as often as three times a day. Although fewer than one in two people open their bowels once a day, this is the most common bowel habit.

MUSCULAR WALLS

The walls of the large intestine have two main muscle layers, which are arranged differently from those in the small intestines. The outer layer of muscle fibres form three, longitudinal bands known as the taenia coli. These bands draw the colonic wall into a series of out-pouchings known as haustra.

Abdominal quadrants

The abdomen can be divided anatomically into four quadrants. Each quadrant contains a number of digestive and other organs. Abdominal pain is often referred to by doctors by the quadrant within which it is localized, for example, left upper quadrant pain.

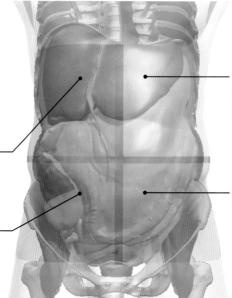

RIGHT UPPER QUADRANT houses the liver, gallbladder, right kidney, duodenum, ascending colon, transverse colon and small intestine

RIGHT LOWER QUADRANT houses the appendix, caecum, ascending colon, part of the transverse colon, and small intestine

LEFT UPPER QUADRANT houses the stomach, spleen, left kidney, pancreas, descending colon, transverse colon and small intestine

LEFT LOWER QUADRANT houses the descending colon, transverse colon and small intestine

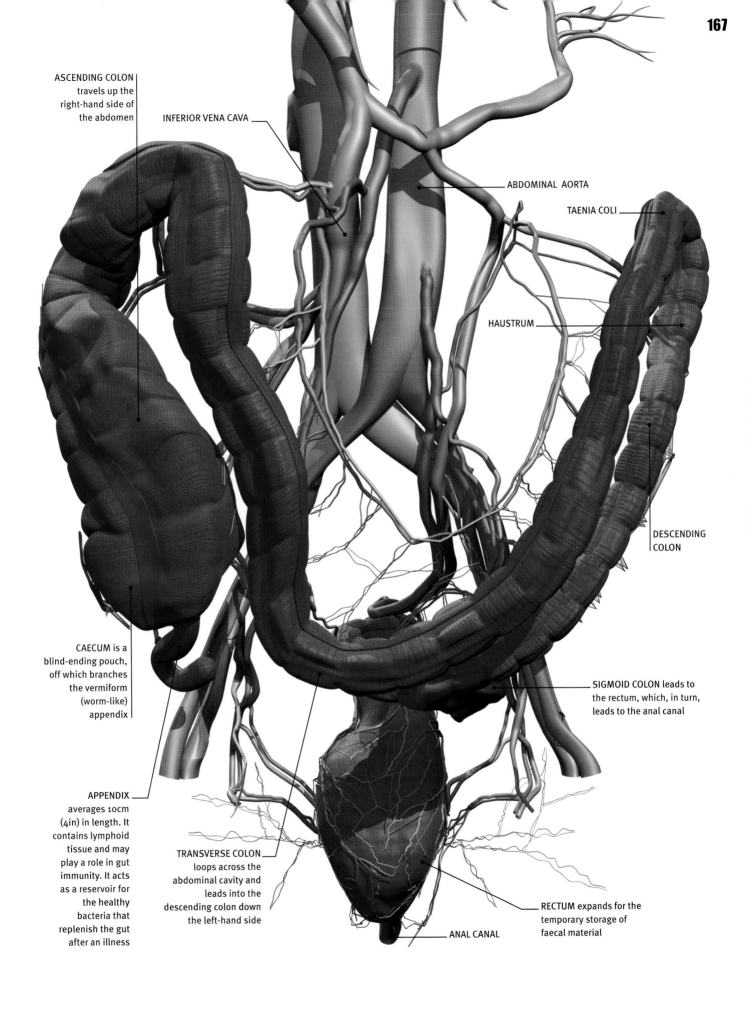

ASCENDING COLON
travels up the
right-hand side of
the abdomen

INFERIOR VENA CAVA

ABDOMINAL AORTA

TAENIA COLI

HAUSTRUM

DESCENDING
COLON

CAECUM is a
blind-ending pouch,
off which branches
the vermiform
(worm-like)
appendix

SIGMOID COLON leads to
the rectum, which, in turn,
leads to the anal canal

APPENDIX
averages 10cm
(4in) in length. It
contains lymphoid
tissue and may
play a role in gut
immunity. It acts
as a reservoir for
the healthy
bacteria that
replenish the gut
after an illness

TRANSVERSE COLON
loops across the
abdominal cavity and
leads into the
descending colon down
the left-hand side

RECTUM expands for the
temporary storage of
faecal material

ANAL CANAL

HEPATIC SYSTEM

BILE-FILLED GALLBLADDER
Coloured X-ray of a gallbladder (purple) and bile ducts (green).
Bile is made in the liver and stored in the gallbladder, passing
through the bile ducts and onto the small intestine to aid in the
digestion of fats.

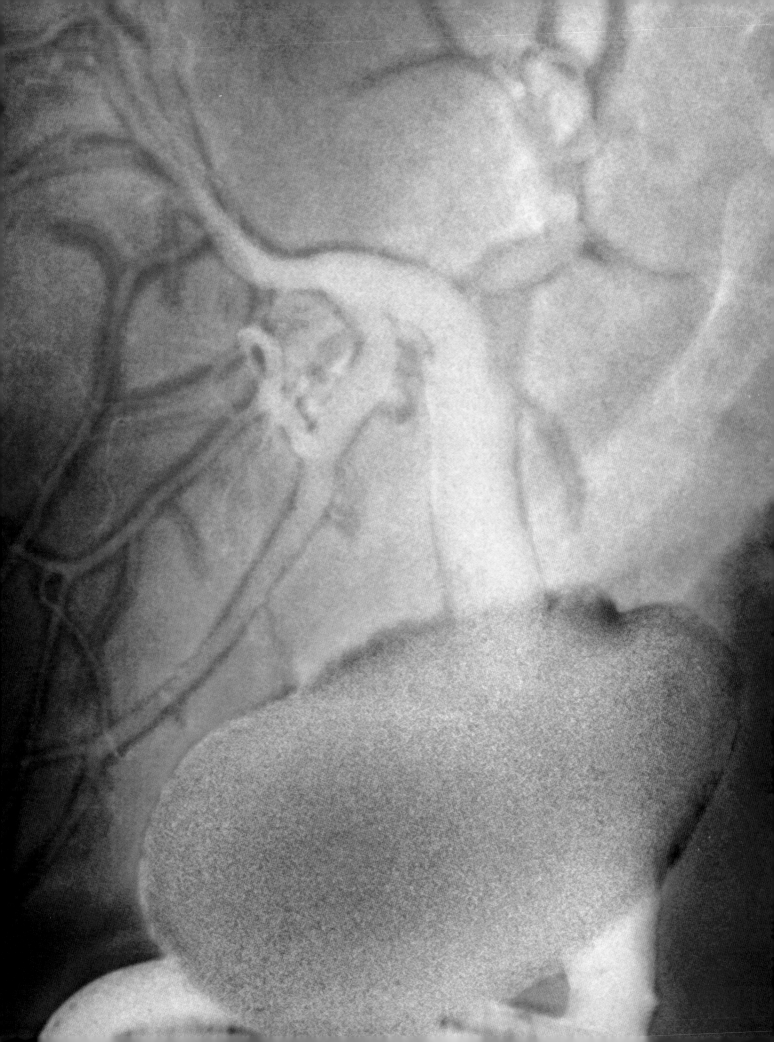

Hepatic system

Your hepatic system consists of your liver, gallbladder and pancreas. The liver secretes bile, which helps to break down dietary fats. It also receives and processes the absorbed products of digestion, and deactivates poisons such as alcohol. The gallbladder stores bile and the pancreas secretes digestive enzymes.

HOMEOSTASIS

Latin for 'staying the same,' homeostasis is the maintenance of standard conditions – temperature, water content and concentration of thousands of different substances – within the body and is probably the most important function of the hepatic system. Most of the work is done by the liver, which filters and regulates 1 litre (1⅔ pints) of blood every minute (see pages 174–175).

BODY FACT

Your body needs bile

- You make 750–1,500ml (1.25–2.5 pints) of bile per day.
- Your gallbladder removes water from bile to make it up to five times more concentrated.
- One in 200 people has additional, accessory bile ducts running between the liver and the cystic duct or gallbladder.
- The gallbladder is not essential to life. When removed surgically (cholecystectomy), bile trickles into the duodenum continuously, rather than being squirted in intermittently and most people continue to digest fats normally.
- Around 95 per cent of bile salts secreted into the intestinal tract are reabsorbed in the terminal ileum and reused.
- Bilirubin is yellow and biliverdin is green. Chemical action by bacteria in the colon converts these to the brown colour in faeces. If bile outflow from the liver is blocked, the faeces develop a pale, putty colour.
- Bruises turn yellow-green in colour due to the conversion of haemoglobin to bilirubin and biliverdin by macrophages during the healing of damaged tissues.

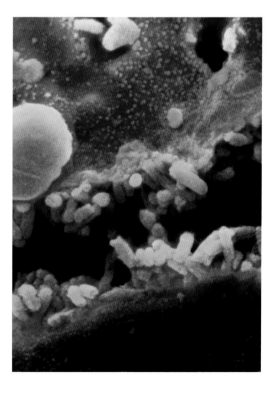

Bile

The liver produces bile, which trickles down the common hepatic duct. Some continues on into the common bile duct, and some is diverted through the cystic duct, where it is stored and concentrated between meals.

Bile is a bitter-tasting, yellow-green, alkaline fluid. It contains water, bicarbonate, bile pigments, bile salts, cholesterol and phospholipids such as lecithin. These have a detergent-like action, emulsifying large globules of fat to produce microscopic drops known as micelles. Micelles are more readily digested by the pancreatic lipase enzyme.

The bile pigments, bilirubin and biliverdin, are produced in hepatocytes (liver cells) from the breakdown of haemoglobin during the recycling of old red blood cells (erythrocytes).

The bile salts, sodium glycolate and sodium taurocholate, are produced in hepatocytes from cholesterol. They coat the micelles to make them more soluble for absorption into the lacteals of the intestinal villi (see page 154).

When semi-digested food (chyme) enters the duodenum, it triggers the secretion of a hormone, cholecystokinin, by cells in the duodenal mucosa. Cholecystokinin causes the gallbladder to contract and the pancreas to release digestive enzymes. It also inhibits further gastric emptying and opens the sphincter of Oddi – the valve that allows bile and pancreatic juices to flow from the ampulla of Vater into the duodenum. Cholecystokinin also has an effect on the brain to induce feelings of being full (satiety).

REAR VIEW OF HEPATIC SYSTEM

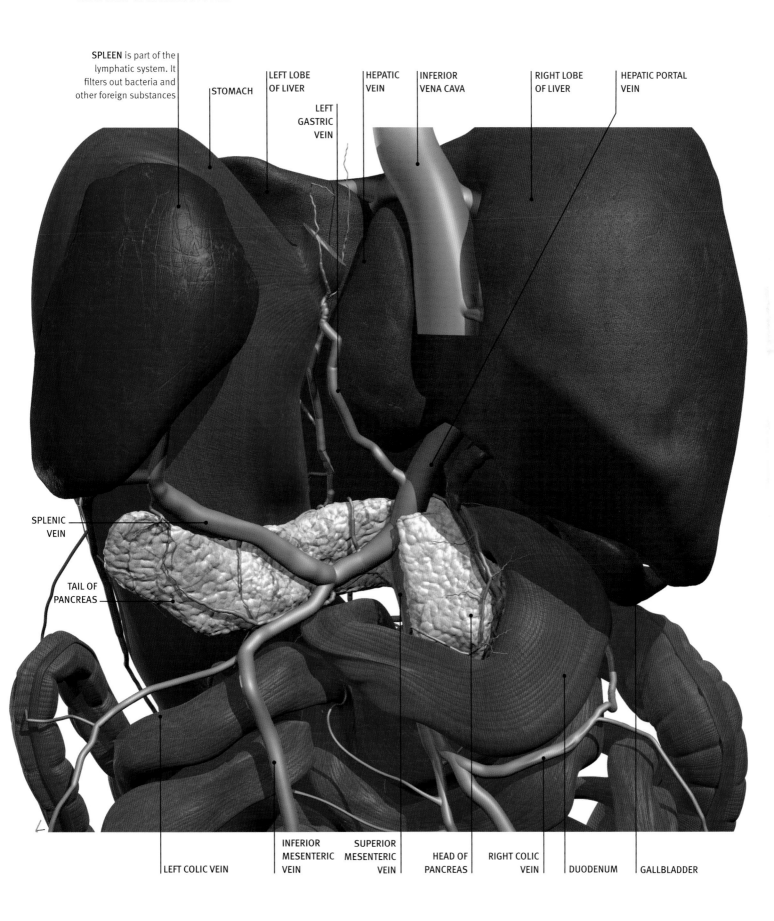

SPLEEN is part of the lymphatic system. It filters out bacteria and other foreign substances

STOMACH

LEFT LOBE OF LIVER

LEFT GASTRIC VEIN

HEPATIC VEIN

INFERIOR VENA CAVA

RIGHT LOBE OF LIVER

HEPATIC PORTAL VEIN

SPLENIC VEIN

TAIL OF PANCREAS

LEFT COLIC VEIN

INFERIOR MESENTERIC VEIN

SUPERIOR MESENTERIC VEIN

HEAD OF PANCREAS

RIGHT COLIC VEIN

DUODENUM

GALLBLADDER

Gallbladder

Your gallbladder (also called the cholecyst) is a pouch-like organ whose purpose is to store bile – a green-yellow, detergent-like substance made in the liver. Bile breaks down dietary fat into small globules – a process called emulsification – so it is easier to absorb. The organ is about 7–10cm (2¾in–4in) long and has a capacity of 30–50ml (1–2fl oz).

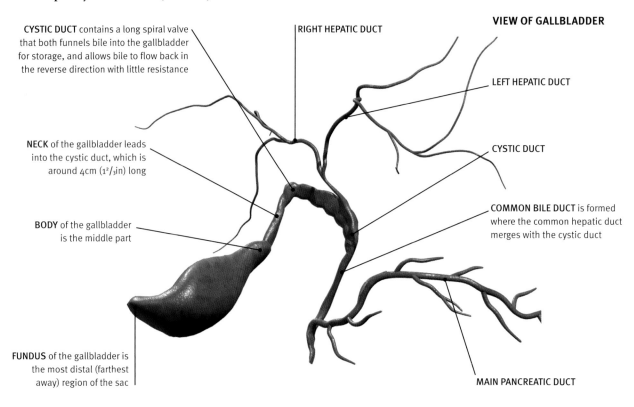

VIEW OF GALLBLADDER

CYSTIC DUCT contains a long spiral valve that both funnels bile into the gallbladder for storage, and allows bile to flow back in the reverse direction with little resistance

RIGHT HEPATIC DUCT

LEFT HEPATIC DUCT

CYSTIC DUCT

NECK of the gallbladder leads into the cystic duct, which is around 4cm (1²/₃in) long

COMMON BILE DUCT is formed where the common hepatic duct merges with the cystic duct

BODY of the gallbladder is the middle part

FUNDUS of the gallbladder is the most distal (farthest away) region of the sac

MAIN PANCREATIC DUCT

Blood supply to the gallbladder

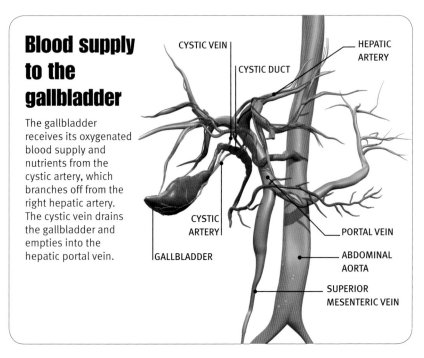

CYSTIC VEIN

CYSTIC DUCT

HEPATIC ARTERY

The gallbladder receives its oxygenated blood supply and nutrients from the cystic artery, which branches off from the right hepatic artery. The cystic vein drains the gallbladder and empties into the hepatic portal vein.

CYSTIC ARTERY

GALLBLADDER

PORTAL VEIN

ABDOMINAL AORTA

SUPERIOR MESENTERIC VEIN

Gallstones

These are mineral and salt deposits that crystallize in the gallbladder and form stones. Most are composed of cholesterol, often mixed with calcium and some bile pigment. They are rare in the young, but by the age of 70 one man in 10 and one woman in four will have a gallstone. Some people have many stones of varying sizes. Women are more prone due to the effects of female hormones on the composition of bile and on the gallbladder. Taking the oral contraceptive pill also increases the risk of stones developing. Stones may remain in the gallbladder and be asymptomatic for years. However, if a stone blocks the cystic duct, the neck of the gallbladder or the bile duct, the gallbladder can become painful, swollen and inflamed and need removing.

Liver

Your liver is situated in your upper abdomen, immediately below the diaphragm, but above your stomach and pancreas. It is covered in a layer of visceral peritoneum, which attaches it to both the front wall (via the falciform ligament) and the back wall (via the hepatic coronary ligaments) of your abdomen. The round ligament of the liver passes down to the umbilicus (the so-called belly-button).

HEPATOCYTES

The liver contains billions of cells called hepatocytes. These are arranged into six-sided columns called lobules, which are separated from each other by a layer of connective tissue.

The hepatocytes:

- Break down haemoglobin to produce bile pigments (bilirubin and biliverdin).
- Make bile, a green-yellow liquid that emulsifies fats in the duodenum to aid digestion.
- Process dietary fats to make triglycerides and cholesterol.
- Process dietary amino acids to make proteins (for example, albumen and globulin the blood-clotting proteins) and glucose.
- Make new amino acids from other building blocks (for example, lactic acid).
- Convert ammonia, a waste product of amino acid metabolism, into urea.
- Make new glucose from glycerol, lactic acid and certain amino acids (for example, alanine).
- Store excess glucose as glycogen – a starchy emergency fuel from which it releases glucose to maintain blood sugar levels when needed (for example, during the overnight fast).
- Store fat-soluble vitamins (A, D, E and K plus vitamin. B12) and some minerals (for example, iron and copper),
- Generate heat to warm passing blood.
- Remove poisons (for example, alcohol) from the blood and detoxify them.
- Act as an immune 'sieve', filtering out antigens carried from the intestines in the hepatic portal vein.

Hepatocytes detoxify and remove poisons in three main ways: by chemically altering them, so they become water-soluble for easier elimination through the kidneys; by secreting them into the bile so that they pass out of the body through the intestines; and by phagocytosis – a process in which macrophages derived from bone marrow engulf and digest toxins, bacteria and viruses. The macrophages within the liver are known as Kupffer cells.

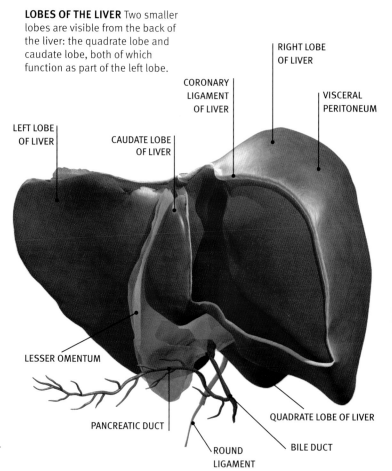

LOBES OF THE LIVER Two smaller lobes are visible from the back of the liver: the quadrate lobe and caudate lobe, both of which function as part of the left lobe.

RIGHT LOBE OF LIVER

CORONARY LIGAMENT OF LIVER

VISCERAL PERITONEUM

LEFT LOBE OF LIVER

CAUDATE LOBE OF LIVER

LESSER OMENTUM

PANCREATIC DUCT

ROUND LIGAMENT

BILE DUCT

QUADRATE LOBE OF LIVER

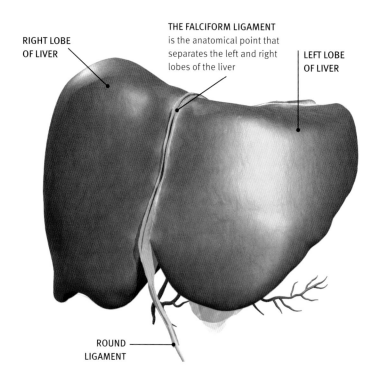

RIGHT LOBE OF LIVER

THE FALCIFORM LIGAMENT is the anatomical point that separates the left and right lobes of the liver

LEFT LOBE OF LIVER

ROUND LIGAMENT

Liver continued

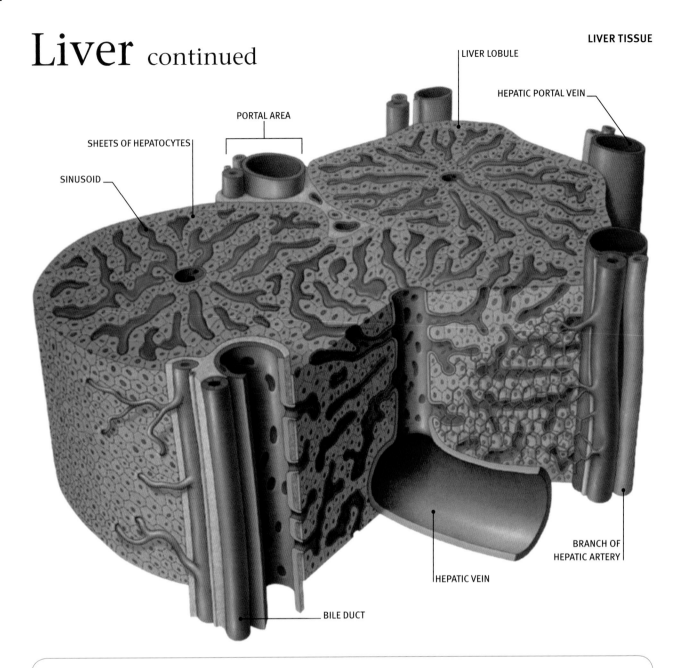

LIVER LOBULE

HEPATIC PORTAL VEIN

PORTAL AREA

SHEETS OF HEPATOCYTES

SINUSOID

HEPATIC VEIN

BRANCH OF
HEPATIC ARTERY

BILE DUCT

Liver tissue

Liver cells are organized into about 1 million liver lobules, each about 1mm in diameter. The hepatocytes form a set of 'plates' arranged like the spokes of a wheel; spaces between the plates (siusoids) contain blood that is delivered by the hepatic portal vein and hepatic artery. Liver cells absorb chemicals from blood and release proteins into the blood. The electron micrograph of liver tissue, right, shows the tiny liver cells.

Bile is a fluid that is produced by the liver and collected into bile canaliculi between the liver's hepatocytes. It flows out to the portal area and is collected into the bile duct.

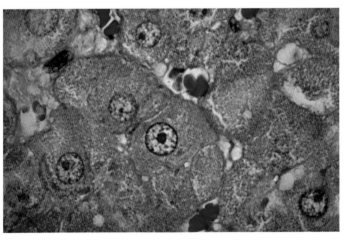

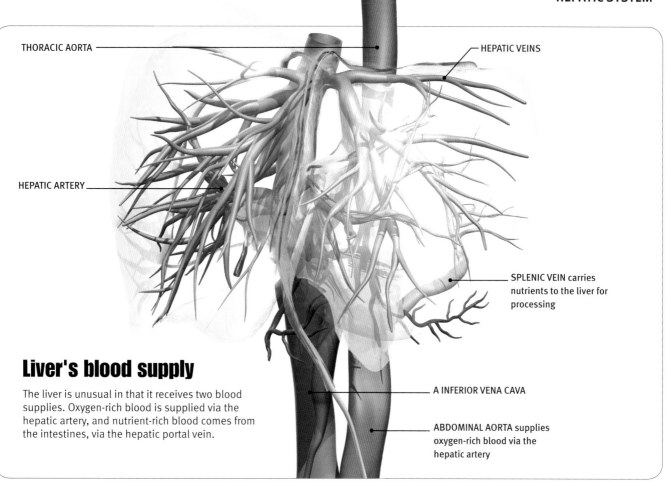

THORACIC AORTA

HEPATIC VEINS

HEPATIC ARTERY

SPLENIC VEIN carries nutrients to the liver for processing

Liver's blood supply

The liver is unusual in that it receives two blood supplies. Oxygen-rich blood is supplied via the hepatic artery, and nutrient-rich blood comes from the intestines, via the hepatic portal vein.

A INFERIOR VENA CAVA

ABDOMINAL AORTA supplies oxygen-rich blood via the hepatic artery

Liver lives on

- The liver is your largest internal organ and the largest gland in your body. The adult liver weighs around 1.5kg (3lbs).
- Your liver is capable of regeneration – even if surgeons remove 75 per cent of a liver lobe, it can usually grow back.
- In an embryo, the liver is the main site of red blood cell formation until the bone marrow takes over this function.
- The round ligament of your liver is the remains of the left umbilical vein, which transports blood from the placenta to the liver in the embryo.
- About 75 percent of blood arriving at your liver is venous blood from the hepatic portal vein.
- Your liver is unique in that it receives both oxygenated blood (from the hepatic artery) and deoxygenated blood (from the hepatic portal vein). Blood from both sources mixes within spaces (sinusoids) between the liver cells and drains into the hepatic vein, which, in turn, drains into the inferior vena cava.

Hepatic portal system

Blood drains from the liver directly into the inferior vena cava via the hepatic veins.

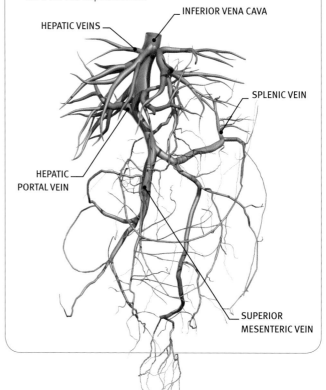

HEPATIC VEINS

INFERIOR VENA CAVA

SPLENIC VEIN

HEPATIC PORTAL VEIN

SUPERIOR MESENTERIC VEIN

URINARY SYSTEM

COLOURFUL KIDNEYS
A digital rendering of the major organ of the urinary system. The thin dark blue outer layer or cortex surrounds the orange, yellow and light blue areas of the medulla, which contains the urine making and collecting structures. Urine leaves the kidney through the long blue tubes or ureters. Each kidney receives blood from the short, dark blue tubes or renal arteries, seen in the centre.

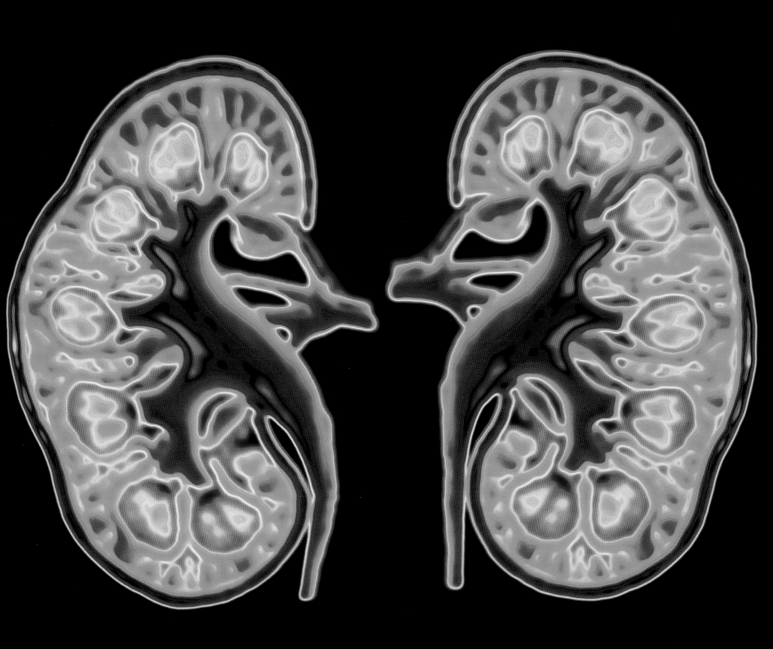

Urinary structures

Your urinary system filters your blood to remove excess fluid, salts and soluble wastes. It consists of your kidneys, where fluid and wastes are filtered from your blood and concentrated to form urine; thin tubes (ureters), down which urine trickles from the kidneys; the distensible sac (bladder), where urine is stored; and the urethra, the tube through which urine drains from the bladder to the outside world. Your kidneys receive blood via the renal arteries and, after filtration, the blood passes back through the renal veins to the inferior vena cava.

URINE

Urine contains around 95 per cent water, plus water-soluble wastes such as urea (a by-product of protein metabolism in the liver), creatinine (produced during muscle metabolism), uric acid (a waste produced by the recycling of old DNA and RNA) and excess salts such as sodium, potassium, chloride, phosphate and sulphate.

Urine is normally sterile and varies in colour from pale straw to a dark orange-yellow depending on your level of hydration. Urine has a faint smell that becomes stronger the more concentrated it is. Women may notice that the odour of their urine varies with the time of the month due to the presence of hormone breakdown products.

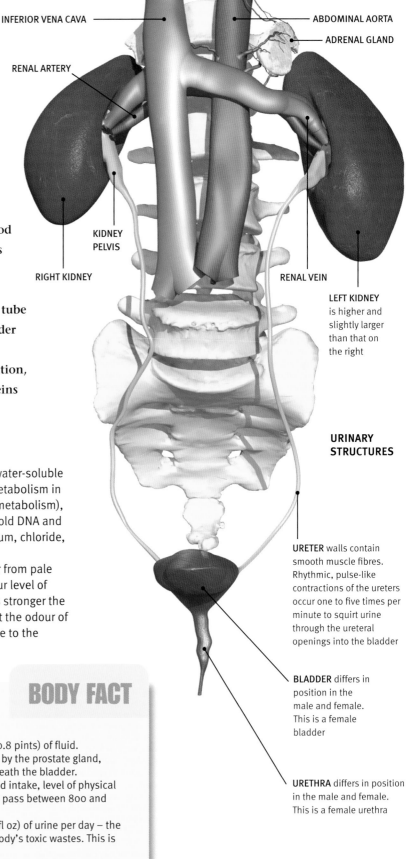

INFERIOR VENA CAVA

ABDOMINAL AORTA

ADRENAL GLAND

RENAL ARTERY

KIDNEY PELVIS

RIGHT KIDNEY

RENAL VEIN

LEFT KIDNEY is higher and slightly larger than that on the right

URINARY STRUCTURES

URETER walls contain smooth muscle fibres. Rhythmic, pulse-like contractions of the ureters occur one to five times per minute to squirt urine through the ureteral openings into the bladder

BLADDER differs in position in the male and female. This is a female bladder

URETHRA differs in position in the male and female. This is a female urethra

BODY FACT

Full to bursting

- Your bladder can stretch to hold over half a litre (0.8 pints) of fluid.
- In men, the neck of the bladder is also supported by the prostate gland, which wraps around the urethra immediately beneath the bladder.
- The volume of urine varies depending on your fluid intake, level of physical exercise and ambient temperature – most people pass between 800 and 2,500ml (1.3–4.2 pints) of urine over 24 hours.
- It is essential that you produce at least 440ml (15fl oz) of urine per day – the estimated amount needed to excrete all of your body's toxic wastes. This is known as the obligatory water loss.
- After filtration, 60 per cent to 80 per cent of filtered water and salts nutrients are reabsorbed back into the blood stream.
- Urine is yellow due to the pigments, urochrome and urobilin, produced from the breakdown of red haemoglobin.
- Low blood volume triggers release of antidiuretic hormone (also called vasopressin) from the pituitary gland. Antidiuretic hormone increases the reabsorption of water from filtered fluids in the kidney.

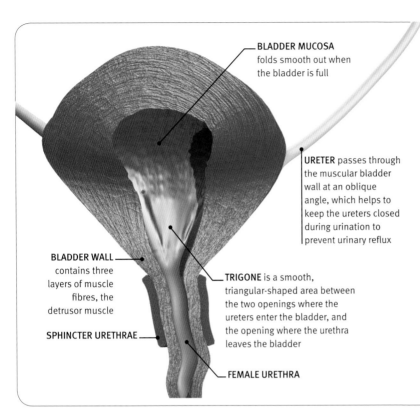

BLADDER MUCOSA
folds smooth out when
the bladder is full

URETER passes through
the muscular bladder
wall at an oblique
angle, which helps to
keep the ureters closed
during urination to
prevent urinary reflux

BLADDER WALL
contains three
layers of muscle
fibres, the
detrusor muscle

TRIGONE is a smooth,
triangular-shaped area between
the two openings where the
ureters enter the bladder, and
the opening where the urethra
leaves the bladder

SPHINCTER URETHRAE

FEMALE URETHRA

Bladder

Urine produced in your kidneys trickles down the ureters into your bladder. Your bladder is a hollow, muscular sac that stores urine without affecting its concentration or the balance of its constituents. It is situated behind your pubic bone at the front of your pelvic cavity. When empty, it is shaped like a pyramid, with its apex pointing upwards and forwards towards your pubic bone. When full, it is ovoid in shape and bulges up behind your front abdominal wall.

The wall of the bladder consists of thick detrusor muscle. Whorls of interlacing smooth muscle fibres form spiral, longitudinal and circular bundles, which allow the bladder wall to expand or contract. Muscle bundles at the base of the bladder pass on either side of the urethra and are referred to as the internal urethral sphincter.

The inner wall of the bladder (mucosa) is lined by multiple layers of cells and can contract or expand (they are called transitional epithelium). It forms folds (rugae) that are pronounced when the bladder is empty, but which flatten out as the bladder fills and stretches.

Urethra

Urine passes from the bladder to the outside world through a single tube known as the urethra.

The male urethra is about five times longer than that of the female. Because the female urethra is relatively short, women are more prone to urinary infections. Because the prostate gland encircles the male urethra (see page 184) at the base of the bladdder, as men age their prostates enlarge causing problems with urination.

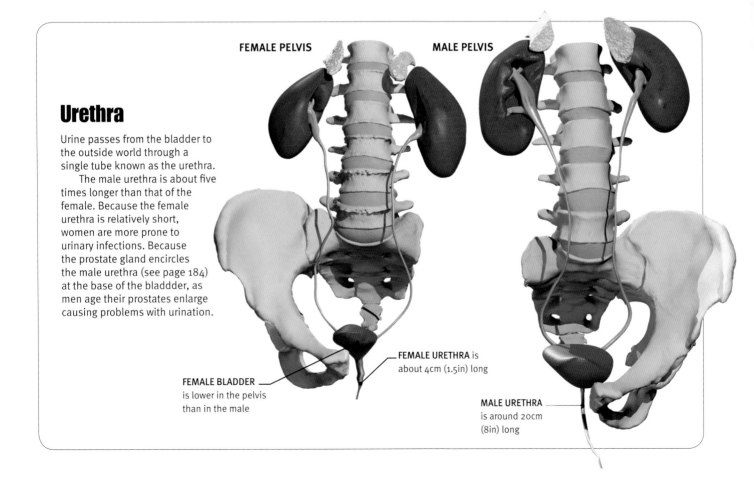

FEMALE PELVIS

MALE PELVIS

FEMALE BLADDER
is lower in the pelvis
than in the male

FEMALE URETHRA is
about 4cm (1.5in) long

MALE URETHRA
is around 20cm
(8in) long

Kidneys

Your kidneys are two bean-shaped organs located at the back of your abdomen, behind the peritoneum.

They measure 9–12cm (3.5–4.5in) in length. They have four main functions: the filtration of blood; the excretion of water-soluble wastes; the regulation of blood volume; and the composition and production of some hormones (erythropoietin and renin). They also play a vital role in the regulation of your blood salt levels, blood pressure and blood acidity.

The term 'renal' is from *renes*, the Latin word for kidneys.

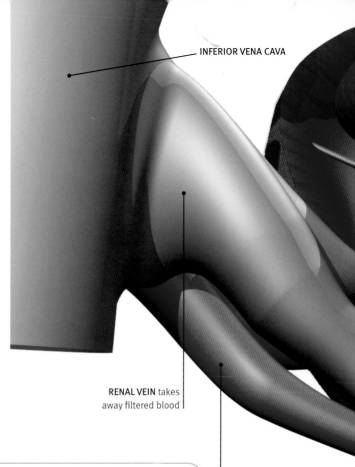

INFERIOR VENA CAVA

RENAL VEIN takes away filtered blood

RENAL ARTERY branches off from the abdominal aorta and brings in blood for filtering

RENAL PELVIS collects urine from the kidneys via the calyces and drains it into the ureters

URETER drains away filtered fluids, salts and other water-soluble wastes

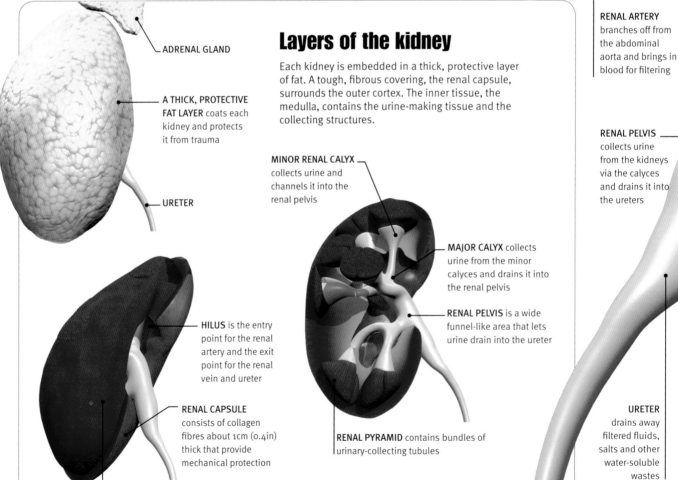

ADRENAL GLAND

A THICK, PROTECTIVE FAT LAYER coats each kidney and protects it from trauma

URETER

Layers of the kidney

Each kidney is embedded in a thick, protective layer of fat. A tough, fibrous covering, the renal capsule, surrounds the outer cortex. The inner tissue, the medulla, contains the urine-making tissue and the collecting structures.

MINOR RENAL CALYX collects urine and channels it into the renal pelvis

MAJOR CALYX collects urine from the minor calyces and drains it into the renal pelvis

RENAL PELVIS is a wide funnel-like area that lets urine drain into the ureter

HILUS is the entry point for the renal artery and the exit point for the renal vein and ureter

RENAL CAPSULE consists of collagen fibres about 1cm (0.4in) thick that provide mechanical protection

RENAL PYRAMID contains bundles of urinary-collecting tubules

MEDULLA

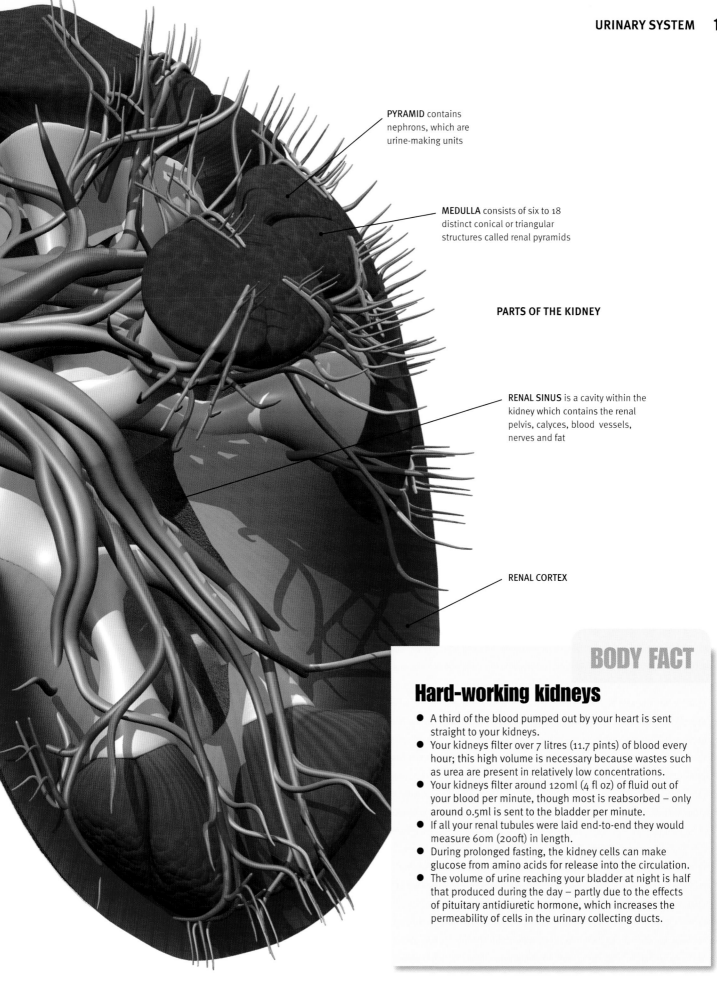

PYRAMID contains
nephrons, which are
urine-making units

MEDULLA consists of six to 18
distinct conical or triangular
structures called renal pyramids

PARTS OF THE KIDNEY

RENAL SINUS is a cavity within the
kidney which contains the renal
pelvis, calyces, blood vessels,
nerves and fat

RENAL CORTEX

BODY FACT

Hard-working kidneys

- A third of the blood pumped out by your heart is sent straight to your kidneys.
- Your kidneys filter over 7 litres (11.7 pints) of blood every hour; this high volume is necessary because wastes such as urea are present in relatively low concentrations.
- Your kidneys filter around 120ml (4 fl oz) of fluid out of your blood per minute, though most is reabsorbed – only around 0.5ml is sent to the bladder per minute.
- If all your renal tubules were laid end-to-end they would measure 60m (200ft) in length.
- During prolonged fasting, the kidney cells can make glucose from amino acids for release into the circulation.
- The volume of urine reaching your bladder at night is half that produced during the day – partly due to the effects of pituitary antidiuretic hormone, which increases the permeability of cells in the urinary collecting ducts.

REPRODUCTIVE
SYSTEM

SMALL BUT POWERFUL SPERM CELLS
These tiny male sex cells are responsible for fertilizing the female ovum. The rounded head contains the male DNA and the long tail propels it along to the ovum. Some 300 million of these are released at a time from the testes, but only one sperm will eventually fertilize the egg.

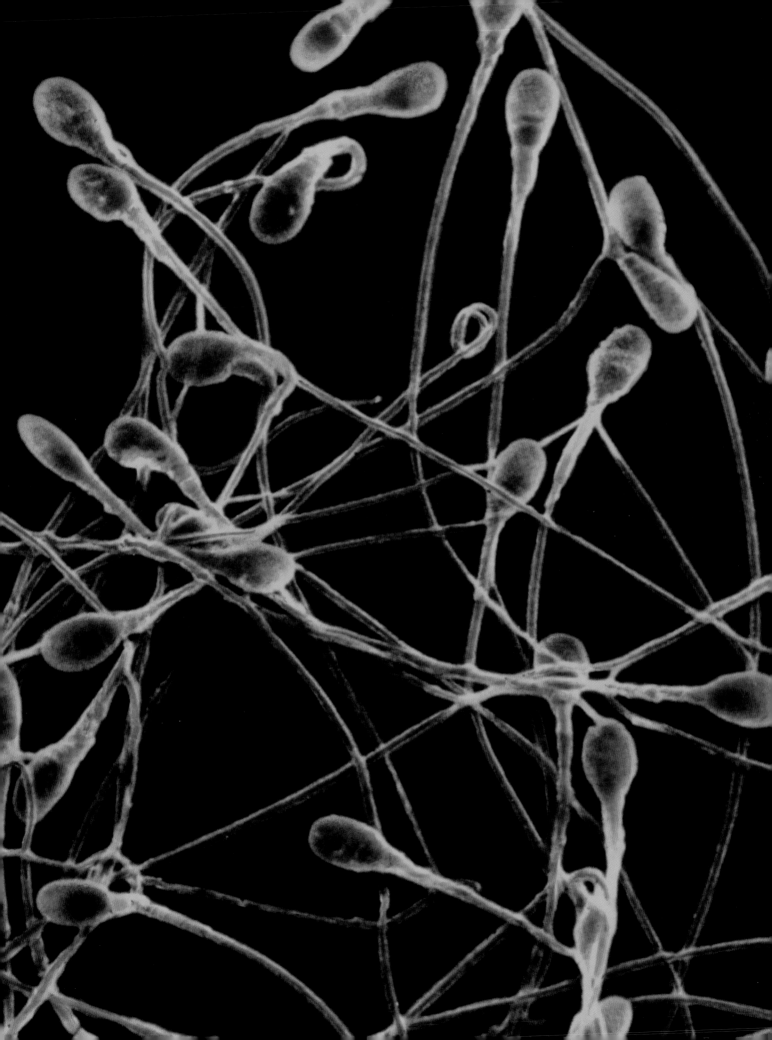

Male reproductive system

The male reproductive system consists of the penis, testes and several accessory glands, plus the tubes that connect them. The testes and glands together produce a fluid called semen.

EXTERNAL GENITALS

The external sex organs – the penis and the scrotum – are known as the genitals or genitalia. The scrotum is a loose pouch of skin that is rich in muscle fibres. It is separated from the anus by a fibrous area of tissue known as the perineum.

The skin is more wrinkled and dark than other body skin and often has a reddish hue. A thin internal membrane divides the scrotum into two separate compartments, each of which contains a testis. The testes are situated outside the pelvis to keep them 4–7°C cooler than normal body temperature, which is vital for the normal production of spermatozoa (sperm cells).

PENIS

The penis contains three cylinders of erectile tissue: two upper corpora cavernosa (singular: corpus cavernosum) and a corpus spongiosum, which runs centrally up the underside. These cylinders are surrounded by a tough, fibrous coat (the tunica albuginea).

It is covered in a loose sleeve of thin, hairless skin containing muscle fibres that folds over on itself to form the prepuce (foreskin). The prepuce is tethered to the glans penis on the underside to form a ridge of skin, the frenulum, which contains a small artery. The foreskin helps to keep the glans penis moist and sensitive. In circumcised males, the foreskin is surgically removed (usually soon after birth for religious reasons). After circumcision, the skin of the glans penis loses its soft, moist texture, more fibrous protein (keratin) is laid down and the glans becomes more like normal skin. Some sexual sensitivity may be lost.

EJACULATORY DUCTS AND SEMINAL VESICLES

The ejaculatory ducts form where the ductus, or vas, deferens (plural: ducta deferentia) and seminal vesicles meet behind the bladder. The ejaculatory ducts pass through the prostate gland at the base of the bladder to direct semen into the penis.

The seminal vesicles are two coiled sacs about 5cm (2in) long. They secrete a pale yellow fluid rich in fructose (sugar), that nourishes the spermatozoa, and proteins

that allow the semen to clot (so that it stays in the vagina for longer). The fluids pass into a duct that joins the ductus deferens on each side to form the left and right ejaculatory ducts.

URETHRA

This passes through the prostate gland and penis, acting as a conduit for both urine and semen, though not at the same time.

BULBO-URETHERAL (COWPER'S) GLANDS

Situated beneath the prostate gland, these glands produce a slippery fluid just before ejaculation. The fluid helps to flush away any residual urine within the urethra, as well as providing lubrication.

BODY FACT

The penis unravelled

- If unravelled, each epididymis would be about 6m (20ft) long.
- During a vasectomy, the two narrow, muscular tubes (the ductus or vas deferens) are cut and tied.
- The central opening of each ductus deferens is only around the width of a coarse hair.
- The cremaster (literally, suspender) muscle in the spermatic cord is responsible for the cremasteric reflex – the involuntary drawing up of the testicles towards the inguinal canal when it is cold, and during times of stress. (see page 188).
- The prostate contains millions of tiny glands separated from one another by muscle and fibre cells.
- When flaccid, the average adult penis is 8.3cm (3.25in) long and 8.1cm (3.20in) in circumference; when erect, it is 13.6cm (5.25in) long and 10.9cm (4.33in) in circumference.
- Most men experience one to five erections during an average night's asleep, each of which lasts approximately 30 minutes. These nocturnal erections occur during the REM (rapid eye movement) phase of sleep.

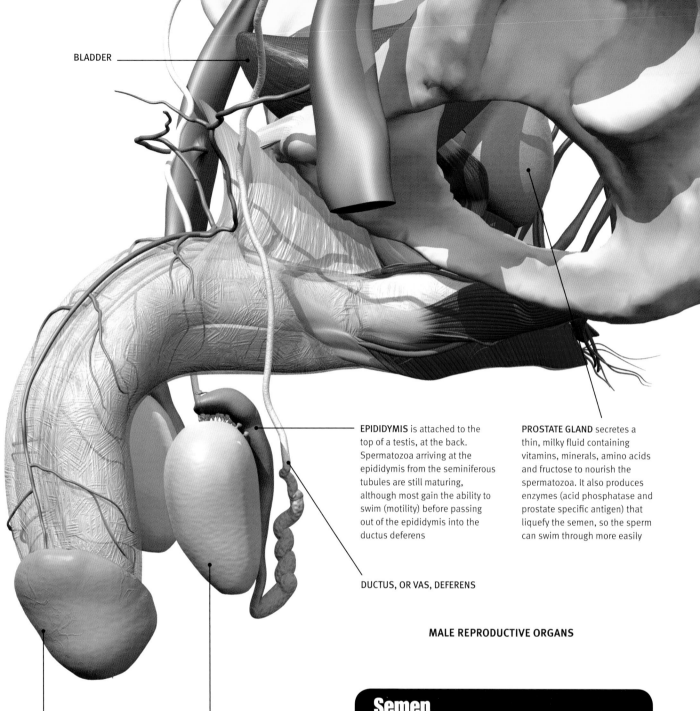

BLADDER

EPIDIDYMIS is attached to the top of a testis, at the back. Spermatozoa arriving at the epididymis from the seminiferous tubules are still maturing, although most gain the ability to swim (motility) before passing out of the epididymis into the ductus deferens

PROSTATE GLAND secretes a thin, milky fluid containing vitamins, minerals, amino acids and fructose to nourish the spermatozoa. It also produces enzymes (acid phosphatase and prostate specific antigen) that liquefy the semen, so the sperm can swim through more easily

DUCTUS, OR VAS, DEFERENS

MALE REPRODUCTIVE ORGANS

PENIS forms a shaft topped by the glans penis – the most sensitive part. The opening of the male urethra (the meatus) is usually at the tip of the glans penis, or just beneath it. During sexual arousal, the penis swells and lengthens

TESTIS contain the vas deferens, plus several arteries, veins and nerves. The testes remain inactive until puberty, when they start producing male hormones (androgens such as testosterone) and spermatozoa (sperm cells)

Semen

A white-yellow, pearly secretion that contains fluids from the testes, epididymis, seminal vesicles, prostate and bulbo-urethral glands. It also contains spermatozoa plus nutrients such as fructose, vitamins and minerals. Hormone-like prostaglandins in the semen encourage 'pouting' of the female cervix, so that the sperm can swim through more easily. They may also intensify contraction of the female upper reproductive tract to propel sperm forwards. Semen contains around 100 million spermatozoa per millilitre – an average of 330 million sperm per ejaculation.

Female reproductive system

The female reproductive system consists of the clitoris, vagina, cervix, uterus, uterine tubes and ovaries. It not only produces ova or eggs but also provides a 'home' for the developing fetus.

FEMALE SEX ORGANS

There are internal and external organs. The external organs, the vulva (see below), are separated from the anus by a fibrous area of tissue known as the perineum. The internal organs are the vagina, uterus, ovaries and fallopian tubes. The vagina connects the vulva to the upper reproductive tract. Its elastic, corrugated walls usually touch together, so the vaginal canal is H-shaped if shown in cross-section. It produces a discharge that is usually a pale cream colour. It contains antibodies and lactic acid-secreting lactobacilli, which help to protect against infection.

In young girls, the hymen, a thin, perforated mucous membrane, partly covers the entrance to the vagina. This often breaks down naturally after puberty, when playing sports or inserting a tampon. It allows discharge and menstrual flow to pass through. If it is still present the first time someone has sexual intercourse, it may tear and bleed slightly, although lack of pain and bleeding during first intercourse is equally common and the state of the hymen is not a reliable indicator of virginity.

Vaginal Secretions

The vagina is kept clean and moist by the secretions of the cervix and the vaginal lining. These secretions contain antibodies and lactic acid-secreting lactobacilli, which help to protect against infection. The secretions change in character as a result of the different hormones secreted during the menstrual cycle (see page 190) and these changes can be used as a natural way to determine fertility. During the first half of the cycle, as oestrogen levels rise, cervical mucus increases in quantity and becomes clearer and more stretchy. This type of mucus provides a nurturing alkaline medium for sperm and is known as fertile mucus. In fact, a woman is most fertile during the two or three days during which this mucus appears. In the latter part of the menstrual cycle, as ovulation occurs and oestrogen levels fall, cervical mucus diminishes and becomes more opaque.

External organs

Also known as the vulva, these consist of the labia minora and majora, the clitoris and the mons pubis (an area of fatty tissue that protects the pubic bone). In adult females this is covered by pubic hair, which helps to regulate airflow and warmth around the genitals, and traps pheromones – chemicals involved in sexual attraction (see page 85).

CLITORIS is the female equivalent of the penis and has a similar structure

BULBOSPOGIOSUS MUSCLE over which lies the labia majora which surround the labia minora on each side

LABIA MINORA are a pair of thin, red skin folds that surround the entrance to the vagina. They vary in size and shape and one is often longer than the other

VAGINAL ORIFICE is the external opening of the vagina into the vestibule bulbospogiosus muscle over which lies the labia majora which surround the labia minora on each side

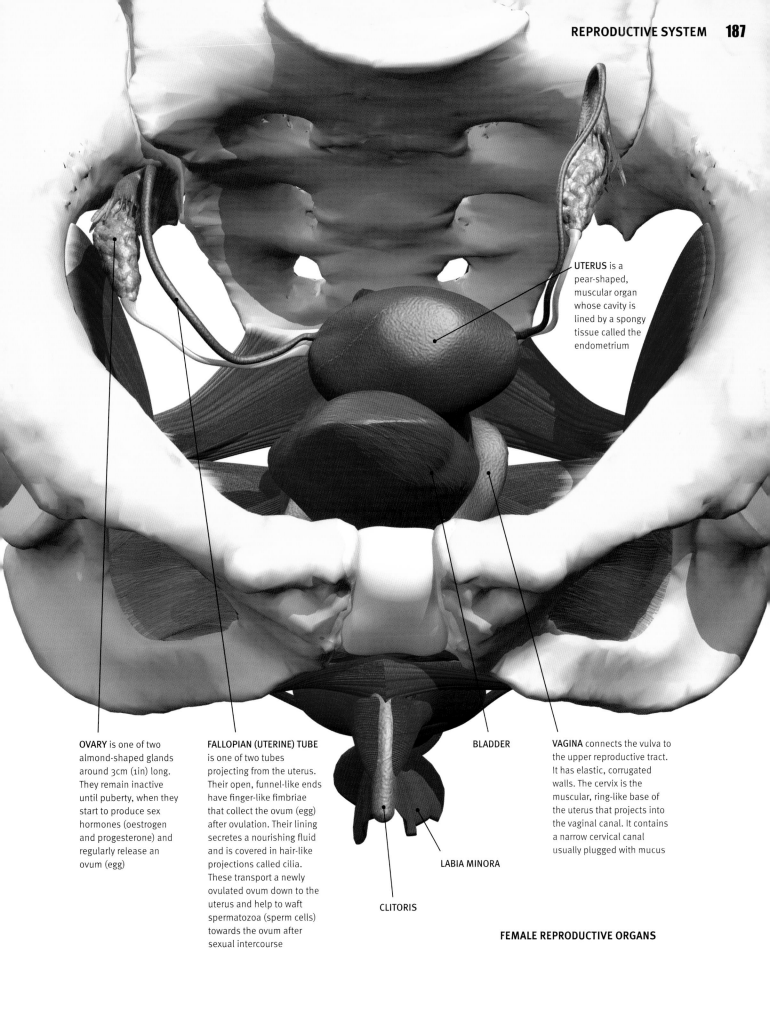

UTERUS is a pear-shaped, muscular organ whose cavity is lined by a spongy tissue called the endometrium

OVARY is one of two almond-shaped glands around 3cm (1in) long. They remain inactive until puberty, when they start to produce sex hormones (oestrogen and progesterone) and regularly release an ovum (egg)

FALLOPIAN (UTERINE) TUBE is one of two tubes projecting from the uterus. Their open, funnel-like ends have finger-like fimbriae that collect the ovum (egg) after ovulation. Their lining secretes a nourishing fluid and is covered in hair-like projections called cilia. These transport a newly ovulated ovum down to the uterus and help to waft spermatozoa (sperm cells) towards the ovum after sexual intercourse

BLADDER

VAGINA connects the vulva to the upper reproductive tract. It has elastic, corrugated walls. The cervix is the muscular, ring-like base of the uterus that projects into the vaginal canal. It contains a narrow cervical canal usually plugged with mucus

LABIA MINORA

CLITORIS

FEMALE REPRODUCTIVE ORGANS

Sex cells

The testis in the male and ovary in the female produce the sex cells or gametes. Sex cells are unique: the nucleus of each spermatozoon (sperm cell) and ovum (egg) contains only 23 chromosomes, unlike your other body cells, which contain 46, arranged as 23 pairs. Sex cells are created by a special process known as meiosis. During fertilization, when the head of a spermatozoon enters an ovum, their genetic information combines to create a 46-chromosome blueprint for a new human life.

TESTICLE

A testicle is made up of a testis and an epididymis. Each testis contains thousands of long, convoluted loops called seminiferous tubules. These are lined with primitive germ cells, called spermatogonia, which become active only during puberty. Production of spermatozoa then starts, and continues throughout a man's life. Sperm is produced in the seminiferous tubules and is propelled along by eddy currents to the efferent ductules and then into the epididymis. (Spermatozoa arriving at the epididymis are still maturing and are unale to swim until they are ready to pass out of the epididymis into the ductus deferens).

Meiosis

Spermatozoa and ova contain a random half-selection of the genes present in all other body cells. This is the result of a specialized division called meiosis.

During the first stage of meiosis, the chromosomes exchange random blocks of genes within each pair to introduce variation in the offspring. During the second stage of meiosis, the rearranged chromosomes separate, so that each new divided cell contains only 23 chromosomes rather than 23 pairs.

When spermatogonia (male germ cells) divide during meiosis, four spermatozoa result, but when oogonia (female germ cells) progress through meiosis, the final two divisions are unequal. One daughter cell gets half the genetic material but most of the cell cytoplasm. The smaller offspring cells (called polar bodies) fragment and disappear. As a result, each oogonium gives rise to only one ovum. This conserves nutrients and, as these final divisions are completed just before and after ovulation, helps to prevent a multiple pregnancy.

As a result of the swapping of genes that occurs during meiosis, each spermatozoon or ovum contains a unique set of genes – a random half-selection of the 20,000–25,000 genes present in the parent cell. Some may have a similar selection of genes to others – accounting for family similarities between future brothers and sisters – but no two are ever identical.

Spermatozoa

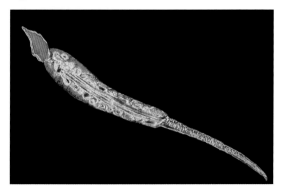

Each of the spermatozoa (singular: spermatozoon) measures 0.05mm (0.002in) in length. The head contains a sac of enzymes, the acrosome, which dissolves the 'shell' of an ovum during fertilization, and the nucleus contains a random half-set of a man's genetic material (DNA). The sperm's middle section (midpiece) contains mitochondria, wrapped around the tail in a spiral sheath, which produce energy for sperm motility. Its tail contains 20 long filaments – a central pair surrounded by two rings each containing nine fibrils, within a protective sheath. The gradual thinning and tapering of the tail helps the spermatozoon produce its whip-like swimming motion.

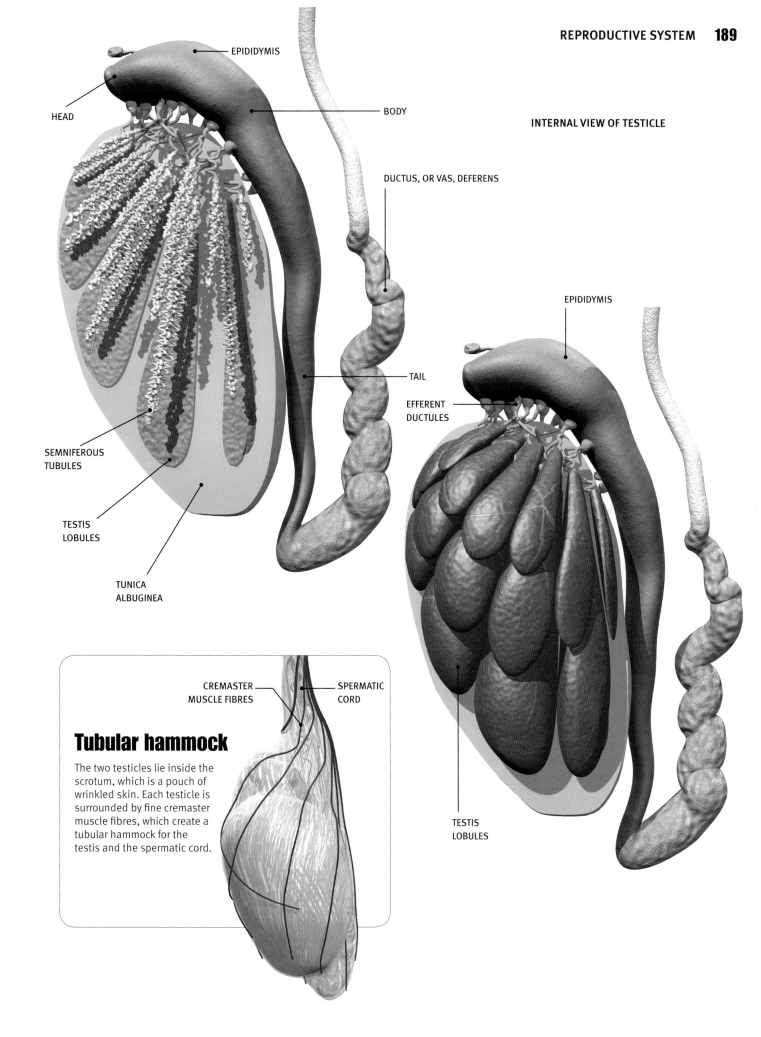

EPIDIDYMIS

HEAD

BODY

INTERNAL VIEW OF TESTICLE

DUCTUS, OR VAS, DEFERENS

EPIDIDYMIS

TAIL

EFFERENT DUCTULES

SEMNIFEROUS TUBULES

TESTIS LOBULES

TUNICA ALBUGINEA

TESTIS LOBULES

CREMASTER MUSCLE FIBRES

SPERMATIC CORD

Tubular hammock

The two testicles lie inside the scrotum, which is a pouch of wrinkled skin. Each testicle is surrounded by fine cremaster muscle fibres, which create a tubular hammock for the testis and the spermatic cord.

Sex cells continued

OVULATION

Every month about 100–150 eggs begin to ripen inside their fluid-filled follicles, although usually only one egg reaches maturity. This occurs midway through the menstrual cycle due to the release of gonadotrophin-releasing hormone (GnRH) by the hypothalamus. GnRH stimulates the pituitary gland to secrete follicle-stimulating hormone (FSH) and luteinizing hormone (LH), thus stimulating the development of several dormant follicles in the ovaries, which start to secrete oestrogen. Eventually, one follicle (the dominant follicle) puts on a growth spurt and matures to bring forth its ovum. Rising oestrogen (and inhibin) levels have a negative-feedback effect on the pituitary gland to reduce FSH secretion and the non-dominant follicles stop growing.

OVULATION Ovulation is triggered by a spike in the amount of FSH and LH released from the pituitary gland. The mature ovum, shown here in red, is released when ovulation takes place.

BODY FACT

Menstrual cycle

- Some women experience mid-cycle pain around the time of ovulation due to pressure within the swollen ovarian follicle.
- Usually, only one ovum is released each month.
- Contrary to popular belief, an ovum is not released alternately from each ovary. Ova are released from either ovary in an irregular and unpredictable pattern.
- Only 12 per cent of women experience a regular, 28-day menstrual cycle.
- A period usually lasts from one to eight days, with three to five days being most common.
- The average blood loss during menstruation is 30–35ml (around 1fl oz).

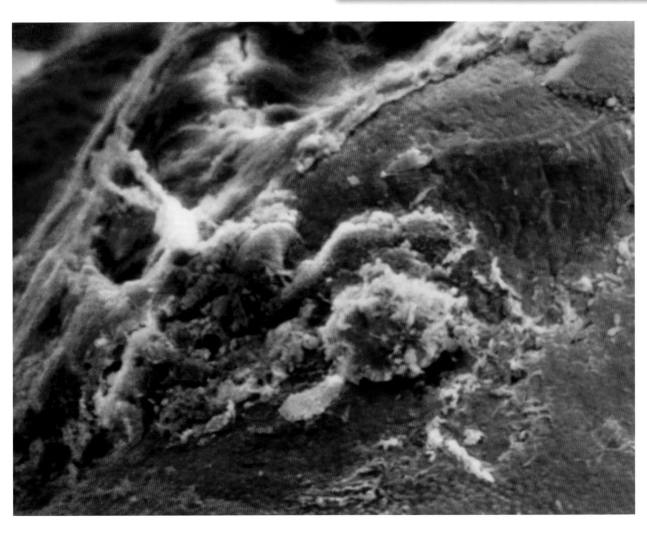

Ovary

One ovary lies on each side of the uterus. Each contains around half of the approximately one to two million immature eggs (ova), with which the average female is born. Each immature egg (ovum) is found within a structure known as an ovarian follicle. At the onset of puberty, ova are matured in the ovary. Generally, a single ovum is released each month until the menopause, which usually occurs between the ages of 45 and 55 (the average age when ovulation and menstruation stop is 51 years). The ovary also produces sex hormones in response to hormones released by the pituitary gland at the base of the brain (see pages 146–147).

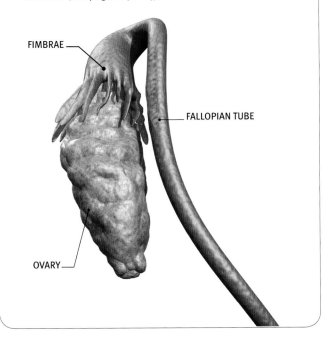

FIMBRAE

FALLOPIAN TUBE

OVARY

OVA (SINGULAR: OVUM) The ovum is the largest cell in the body, and is just visible to the naked eye. Its large nucleus (known as the germinal vesicle) contains a random half-set of a woman's genetic material (DNA). The ovum (above) is enclosed within a thick, transparent 'shell' called the zona pellucida.

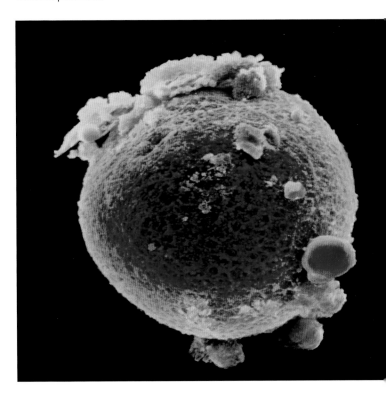

After 10–14 days of growth, the pituitary gland secretes a surge of FSH and LH, which triggers the release of the ovum (ovulation) around nine hours later (see the false-colour scanning electron micrograph, left). The ovum is collected by the fimbriae of a uterine tube and transported down to the uterus.

After ovulation, the empty ovarian follicle collapses and fills with blood. Cells surrounding the follicle proliferate into it to form a yellow cyst, the corpus luteum. The cyst swells to around 2cm (0.8in) across. During this time, it continues making oestrogen and increasing amounts of progesterone.

If the ovum is fertilized and a pregnancy occurs, the developing placenta secretes a hormone, human chorionic gonadotrophin (hCG). This tells the corpus luteum to continue making progesterone, which maintains the endometrium.

If pregnancy does not occur, the corpus luteum does not receive the hCG signal, and stops making progesterone. The endometrial lining then starts to shed, as a menstrual period. The corpus luteum is eventually replaced by scar tissue. By the end of a period, blood levels of the two ovarian hormones, oestrogen and progesterone, are at their lowest. This triggers increasing production of GnRH to start the next menstrual cycle all over again.

Although most women are completely unaware of ovulation, around 25 per cent experience lower abdominal pain, usually on the side near the ovary that's ovulating. The pain is called *mittelschmerz*, which is a German phrase meaning 'middle pain'. It is due to pressure within the swollen ovarian follicle.

Conception

Once an egg is released, it makes its way down the Fallopian tube, ready for fertilization. The ovum plays an active role in the process by releasing chemicals that attract spermatozoa. Only one of the approximately 300 million ejaculated sperm needs to reach the ovum and breach its shell (zona pellucida). As the sperm penetrates the egg, it sheds its tail. The head of the sperm fuses with the nucleus of the ovum to form a zygote.

FERTILIZATION

This occurs in the upper third of the Fallopian tube. Spermatozoa bind to the zona pellucida membrane that surrounds the ovum, releasing enzymes (the acrosome reaction) to dissolve their way through. Though several sperm may attach to the zona pellucida, only one breaks through to enter the ovum. This triggers an electrochemical reaction that hardens the zona pellucida and prevents other sperm entering the egg. As the successful sperm enters the egg, it loses its tail and its head enlarges. The head of the sperm then fuses with the nucleus of the ovum to form a single cell – the zygote – containing 46 chromosomes (23 from each parent) of genetic information. The fertilized ovum goes through several stages of development, involving constant subdivision during the approximately seven days that it takes it to reach the uterus and implant in the walls (endometrium). Its progress is helped along by the cilia (hair-like feelers) that line the Fallopian tube.

> ## BODY FACT
>
> ### The great race
>
> - Sperm swim at a rate of 3mm (0.1in) per hour.
> - A sperm lashes its tail 800 times to swim 1cm (0.4in).
> - Sperm reach the uterine tubes within 30 to 60 minutes of ejaculation into the female tract, helped along by steady currents.
> - The average survival time for a spermatozoon in the upper female reproductive tract is three to four days.
> - If the ovum is not fertilized within 12–24 hours after ovulation, it starts to disintegrate.

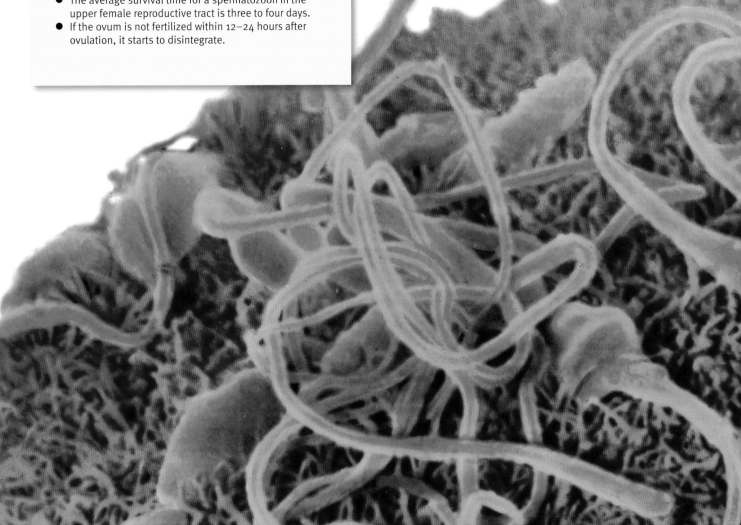

Zygote

This picture shows a fertilized egg in the process of becoming a zygote – the pronuclei from the sperm and egg are fusing to produce its full complement of 46 chromosomes. The zygote will soon begin its first cell division. It then continues subdividing until it forms a solid ball the size of a pinhead, by which time it consists of 16–32 cells. It is now known as a morula. It then transforms into a fluid-filled ball, which is called a blastocyst (see page 194).

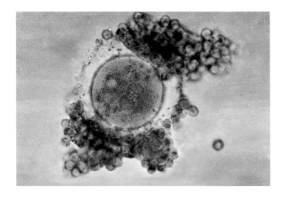

Gender

Within each normal body cell, the 46 chromosomes are arranged as 23 pairs. One pair, the sex chromosomes, determines an individual's gender. There are two types: a larger X chromosome, which carries genes for female characteristics; and a smaller Y chromosome, which carries genes for male characteristics. Females have two X chromosomes (XX) and males have one X and one Y (XY). When the sex chromosomes split during meiosis, each spermatozoon receives either an X chromosome or a Y chromosome (hence sperm may be referred to as X or Y sperm). The ova only ever contain an X chromosome. When a spermatozoon containing a Y chromosome fertilizes the X ovum, a boy (XY) results. When a spermatozoon containing an X chromosome fertilizes the X ovum, a girl (XX) results.

FERTILIZATION Sperm try to penetrate the zona pellucida that surrounds the ovum. Only one of the millions of sperm released will penetrate the egg and fuse with the nucleus to form a single cell.

Creation of the embryo

The amazing business of conception starts when a sperm cell (spermatozoon) fuses with an egg cell (ovum), but the process is not complete until implantation occurs and the placenta starts to develop.

CHANGES TO THE ZYGOTE

The zygote divides repeatedly as it passes down the uterine tube. Its next recognizable stage is when it forms a ball of eight to 16 cells, which is called the morula. The morula continues dividing at 15-hour intervals; by the time it reaches the uterus – some 90 or so hours later – it has approximately 64 cells. Of these, only a few cells develop into the embryo; the rest will form the placenta and the membranes that surround the fetus.

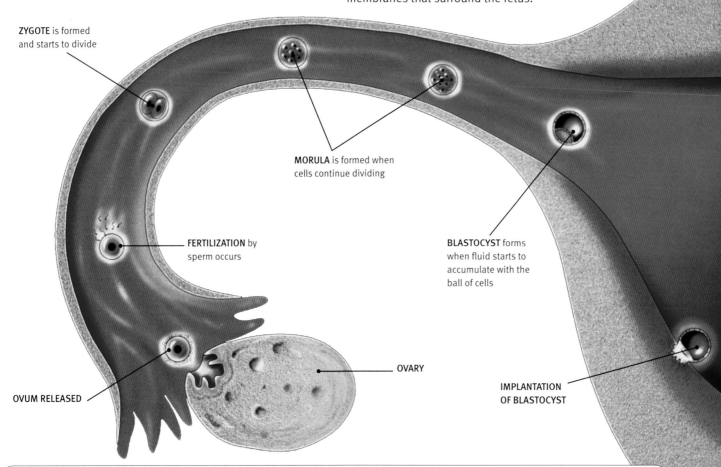

ZYGOTE is formed and starts to divide

MORULA is formed when cells continue dividing

BLASTOCYST forms when fluid starts to accumulate with the ball of cells

FERTILIZATION by sperm occurs

OVUM RELEASED

OVARY

IMPLANTATION OF BLASTOCYST

Morula and blastocyst

Shown near right is a coloured scanning electron micrograph of a morula – a human embryo at the eight cell stage, three days after fertilization. The cluster of eight large rounded cells are known as blastomeres. The smaller spherical structures will degenerate. The surface of each cell is covered in little hair-like microvilli.

About a day later, the ball of cells starts to accumulate fluid and becomes known as a blastocyst (far right).

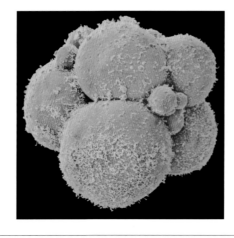
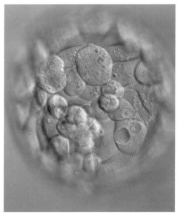

Fluid gradually accumulates inside the morula producing a fluid-filled ball of cells, known as a blastocyst. The surface of the blastocyst consists of a single layer of large, flat cells known as trophoblasts.

The blastocyst 'hatches' out of the *zona pellucida* around five days after fertilization has occurred. The *zona pellucida* helps to prevent premature implantation within the uterine tube.

IMPLANTATION

The hatched blastocyst arrives in the uterus ready for implantation in the uterine lining (endometrium) six to seven days after fertilization. At that time it is less than 0.2mm (.01in). Progesterone has stimulated the rich blood vessels that supply the endometrium to grow in preparation to receive the blastocyst, which floats freely in the uterus for a few days, continuing to develop. Approximately nine days after fertilization, the blastocyst starts to attach itself to the uterine wall by means of sponge-like projections of the trophoblast cells, which burrow into the endometrium. By now the blastocyst is made up of a few hundred cells.

Once the blastocyst hatches and embeds itself in the endometrium, the outer layer of cells (the trophoblasts) develop into the chorionic villi, which will eventually produce the placenta and the membranes of the amniotic sac. The inner cells of the blastocyst (the embryoblast) develop into the embryo. It takes about 13 days for the blastocyst to implant firmly. The trophoblast cells release enzymes that penetrate the lining of the uterus and cause tissue to break down. This provides the nourishing mix of blood cells on which the blastocyst feeds.

At the site of implantation, the endometrium thickens with blood to form the decidua, into which the placenta grows. The developing placenta produces human chorionic gonadotrophin (hCG), which causes the corpus luteum to persist (see page 191) and continue secreting oestrogen and progesterone hormones. However, the placenta slowly takes over this role and the corpus luteum fades away after the first few months of pregnancy.

BODY FACT

Heredity

- The SRY gene on the Y chromosome codes for a protein that causes the sex organs in an embryo to develop into testes rather than ovaries.
- Blocks of genes that are close together on a chromosome tend to be inherited together as they are less likely to get separated during meiosis reshuffling than genes that are farther apart.
- Inherited traits are not always passed on in a straightforward way – they may 'skip' a generation if they are inherited with other genes that mask their effects.
- Some genes are inherited on the male Y chromosome and show their effects only in men.

Heredity

Genes are passed on from generation to generation. A baby gets half of its genes from its mother, and half from the father. A quarter of a baby's genes therefore came from each of its four grandparents, an eighth from each great-grandparent, and so on, right back through the generations.

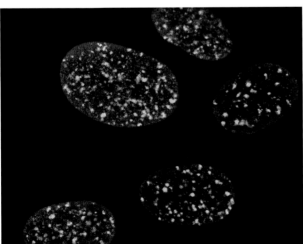

Some genes have strong effects and are described as dominant. Other genes have weak effects that are readily masked by the dominant genes, and are described as recessive.

Traits such as eye colour usually result from a number of different genes acting together. In general, however, people with blue eyes have inherited recessive genes that result in very little production of pigment within their irises. Someone with brown eyes, though, will have inherited at least one dominant gene that causes the production of melanin pigment within their irises.

Not all genes are dominant or recessive – sometimes each of the genes inherited for a trait have equal weight. For example, if you inherit the gene for blood group A from one parent, and the gene for blood group B from another parent, your blood group is AB – not A or B as would be the case if one were dominant and one recessive.

An individual's final height depends on the interaction of many genes, such as those controlling growth hormone production and bone development. Height also depends on environmental factors such as nutrition and the effects of illness at different stages in development – both in the womb and during childhood.

This light micrograph (left) of the human nuclei shows the cell's genetic material.

Pregnancy

Although the length of pregnancy is calculated from the first day of the last menstrual period, conception occurs around two weeks later, after ovulation. A baby's gestational (development) age is therefore two weeks less than the calculated length of pregnancy. For example, when a woman is six weeks' pregnant, the gestational age of her baby is four weeks. The average gestation for human beings is 266 days (38 weeks) from conception to childbirth (equivalent to 280 days, or 40 weeks, of pregnancy).

TRIMESTERS

The 40 weeks of pregnancy are divided into three stages called trimesters. The first trimester lasts from weeks 1–12, the second trimester from weeks 13–27 and the third trimester from weeks 28–40.

SIGNS OF PREGNANCY

The symptoms and signs of early pregnancy can include:
- A missed or unusually light period.
- Nausea and sometimes vomiting.
- Breast tingling and tenderness.
- Enlargement and darkening of the areolae around the nipples.
- Needing to go to the toilet more frequently.
- Feeling increasingly tired.
- A metallic taste in your mouth.
- Increased vaginal discharge.

BODY FACT

Truth about pregnancy

- Pregnancy is a time of homonal activity: existing hormone production rises dramatically and new hormones are created. Pregnancy tests assess urinary (or blood) levels of hCG (human chorionic gonadotrophin).
- A good intake of folic acid is vital during the first few weeks of pregnancy, when rapid cell division starts to form the embryo's spinal cord and brain.

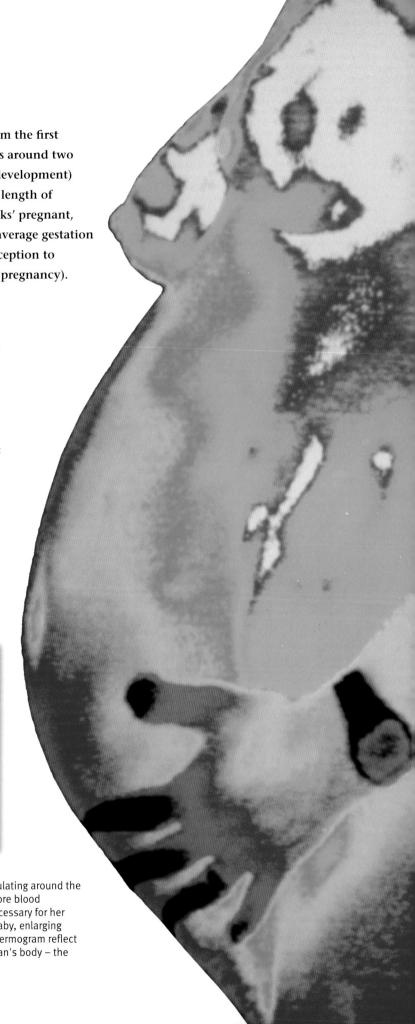

HEAT GENERATOR During pregnancy, the volume of blood circulating around the body increases so that by week 30 a woman has 50 per cent more blood circulating within her bloodstream. This massive increase is necessary for her body to provide an adequate blood supply to the developing baby, enlarging uterus and growing placenta. The colours in this false-colour thermogram reflect the volume of blood supply in various parts of a pregnant woman's body – the lighter the tone, the warmer the part (greater volume of blood).

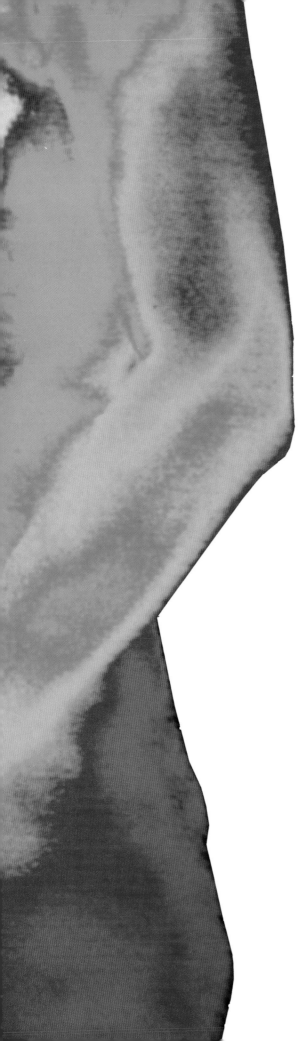

The pregnant uterus

Home to the fetus throughout pregnancy, the uterus is a hollow muscular organ that enlarges to keep pace with a developing baby or babies. The uterine mucosa, or lining, is composed of simple columnar cells characterized by a vast number of microvilli on their surface. During pregnancy these cells thicken in response to hormones produced by the ovaries increasing their size and secretory activity. The blood circulation in the underlying connective tissue also increases in order to provide more nutrient substances to the fetus. After birth, the uterus shrinks to little more than its original size.

Multiple pregnancy

If a fertilized egg splits into two (or more), two (or more) separate identical embryos are formed resulting in a twin, triplet or quadruplet pregnancy. Alternatively two (or more) eggs may be fertilized by different sperm producing two or more non-identical siblings. Some multiple pregancies are a combination – identical twins from a single egg and a singleton sibling from another egg. Depending on when the fertilized egg divides, identical twins may or may not share the same placenta and amniotic sac. Non-identical twins always have their own placentas. The uterus is able to accommodate multiple babies (octuplets have been the largest multiple produced) but generally for a shorter period than singletons, which is why most multiple pregnancies end in a premature delivery. The scan here shows triplets – mono-dichorionic twins (ones sharing a placenta) and a singleton baby in his own chorionic sac.

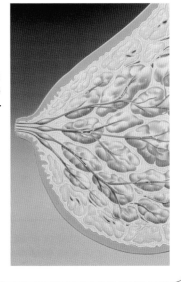

Breast glands during pregnancy

The female breast consists mainly of 15–20 lobes of milk-secreting glands (here, coloured pink) embedded in fatty tissue (yellow). Ducts of these glands have their outlet at the nipple. The breast contains no muscle, but bands of fine ligaments weave between the fat and gland-lobules; they are attached to the skin and determine the breast's shape. During pregnancy, oestrogen and progesterone are secreted by the ovary and placenta. These hormones stimulate the milk-producing glands of the breast to develop, enlarge and become active in preparation for breast-feeding. After the birth, these glands first produce the antibody-rich 'milk' called colostrum, then breastmilk.

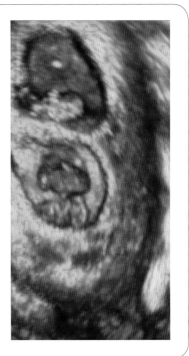

First trimester

The first trimester of pregnancy lasts from weeks one to 12. During the first eight weeks of development, the basic outline of all the organs and structures that make a baby recognizably human are laid down. Once these structures are in place, the embryo becomes known as a fetus, and its tiny body systems continue to grow. By the end of the 12th week, all of a baby's major organs and body systems are formed.

FOUR WEEKS OF PREGNANCY (two weeks' gestation)

The mass of cells, the embryoblast, divides into three germ layers: the ectoderm, which develops into the brain, nervous system, sense organs and integumentary system; the endoderm, which will develop into the intestinal tract, respiratory system, hepatic system, bladder and some endocrine organs such as the thyroid gland; and the mesoderm, which will develop into the skeletal system, muscular system, connective tissues, circulatory system, kidneys, spleen and reproductive system.

SIX WEEKS OF PREGNANCY (four weeks' gestation)

The embryo is only 2–4mm (0.2in) in length with a curved back and a recognizable head. The tiny heart is beating on its own and the tiny blood vessels start circulating blood. Rudimentary arms and legs appear as tiny buds on the body. The neural tube connecting the brain and spinal cord closes and major organs such as the kidneys and liver continue to develop.

EIGHT WEEKS OF PREGNANCY (six weeks' gestation)

About 20mm (0.8 in) from crown to rump, the baby's head is larger than the rest of his body and the facial features continue to develop. Eyes teeth, tongue and nostrils are present while the jaw is fusing to shape the mouth. Arms and legs lengthen and there are rudimentary hands and feet. Most of the internal organs such as the heart, brain, lungs, liver and kidneys are present in basic forms.

Placenta and umbilical cord

The placenta is an organ that develops from the fertilized egg and is attached to the uterus. It links a baby's blood supply to the mother's but keeps it separate. It produces some of the hormones needed to maintain pregnancy and performs functions the baby cannot do for itself, such as supplying nutrients and oxygen, furnishing antibodies to protect against infection and carrying away waste products. The umbilical cord connects the placenta to the baby and is the conduit through which oxygen and nutrients (via one vein) and waste products (via two arteries) are transported.

BODY FACT

Early pregnancy

- During the first eight weeks of development, while the internal organs are forming, the developing baby is referred to as an embryo.
- Once the organs are formed, and the baby starts to grow rapidly, it is referred to as a fetus.
- During the fetal stage of growth, from eight weeks until birth, the fetus increases in size almost 1,000-fold.
- The baby hiccups regularly to exercise its diaphragm muscle and glottis (see page 115).
- The placenta develops from the fertilized egg and becomes fully functional at around 12 weeks of pregnancy.

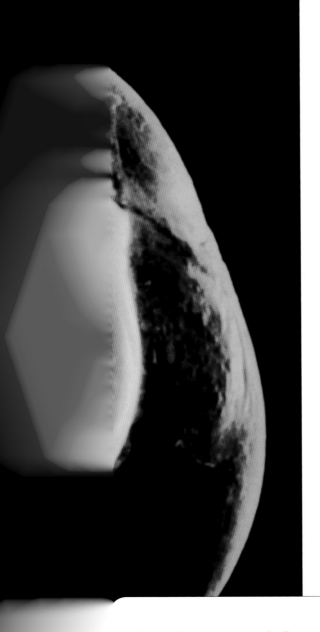

10 WEEKS OF PREGNANCY (eight weeks' gestation)

The embryo is 23–26mm (about 1in) long. All of the essential organs have formed, including the sex organs, and most of them – except the lungs – start to show signs of functioning. The tail that was present in the early embryo is slowly reabsorbed. The eyelids almost cover the tiny eyes, which are beginning to accumulate pigment. The nose has appeared, and the mouth, lips and chin are continuing to form. The nervous system is now advanced enough for the embryo to make tiny wriggling movements. Tastebuds are forming and tooth buds for all the milk teeth are now in place.

The embryonic phase of development has now ended, and the developing baby, at this stage recognizable as a tiny human being, becomes known as a fetus. Growth of the tiny head, brain and organ system is rapid from now on.

12 WEEKS OF PREGNANCY (10 weeks' gestation)

The baby is fully formed from head to toe although organs such as the brain continue to develop. The pituitary gland is beginning to make hormones. Fingers and toes have separated and hair and nails are growing. The bones continue to harden. The genitals are taking on gender characteristics.

There are many things a fetus can do at this stage: move arms, fingers and toes, smile, frown and suck a thumb.

Development of the spinal cord

In the first weeks of gestation, a long thickening forms in the area where the future backbone and spinal cord will develop. This is known as the neural plate and is pear-shaped, with the widest section at the head end.

The centre of the plate develops a long depression known as the neural groove. The walls of the groove grow upwards to form a U-shaped depression. This neural groove continues to deepen and its walls fold over, until they meet above the groove.

The neural groove starts to fuse from the middle outwards. The head end closes first, and the tail end closes around two days later. This forms the hollow neural tube that will develop into the spinal cord.

The head end of the neural tube dilates to form three hollow swellings that will develop into the forebrain, midbrain and hindbrain. Groups of cells grow around the lower neural tube until they meet and fuse at the back. This encloses the developing spinal cord in a series of rings – these will eventually become the protective, bony vertebrae. The picture right is the spine at four weeks' gestation.

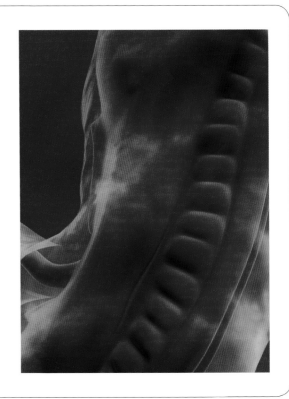

Second trimester

The second trimester of pregnancy lasts from weeks 13–27. It is the time of greatest activity for the fetus, since he has a great deal of room to bend, stretch, twist and kick and make complex movements with his hands. For the mother, it is generally the most enjoyable trimester as the majority of the early symptoms will fade and the baby has not grown so large that he is uncomfortable to carry.

14 WEEKS OF PREGNANCY (12 weeks' gestation)

The fetus measures around 61mm (2.5in) and weighs just 14g (0.5oz). He is fully formed but must grow in size until he is capable of independent life. The eyes are formed, although the eyelids remain fused.

The fetus drinks increasingly large amounts of amniotic fluid. This is absorbed through its immature intestinal tract, into the fetal circulation, and processed through the kidneys to be returned into the amniotic fluid as urine.

The fundus (top) of the mother's enlarging uterus starts to rise above her pelvis and can be felt during an abdominal examination to assess fetal growth. A dark line of skin pigment, running from the middle of the pubis to the navel (belly button), and known as the linea nigra may develop. A few women also develop brown markings on the face called chloasma. These are thought to result from hormone changes and usually disappear or lighten after delivery.

16 WEEKS OF PREGNANCY (14 weeks' gestation)

The fetus is around 108–111mm (just over 4in) from crown to rump and weighs around 80g (3oz). His arms and legs are complete and his joints are working, as are his nervous system and muscles so he can coordinate movements. Bones that have formed are getting harder and retaining calcium. He is very active and can roll over, do somersaults and kick.

Cells are shed and chemicals secreted into the amniotic fluid so that if tests are carried out, such as amniocentesis or choronic villus sampling, information can be gleaned about his health.

18 WEEKS OF PREGNANCY (16 weeks' gestation)

The fetus is 120–140mm (about 5in) from crown to rump and weighs around 150g (5.5oz). The placenta is a similar size to the fetus. He is covered in fine lanugo hair and the nerves are starting to acquire their fatty myelin sheaths. The facial features are well formed, the eyes start to open and the fetus can produce a number of facial expressions. The fetus is often seen to suck his thumb during ultrasound scans. Blood vessels are visible under the paper-thin skin and the cartilage that forms the blueprint for the foetal skeleton starts to harden in places to form bone. The external genitals are visible, and his or her sex is becoming more obvious.

The mother may start to feel some movement as the fetus flexes his spine and limbs and clenches his fists.

BODY FACT

Middle trimester

- The length of fetal gestation is approximately equal to the height of the uterus above the pubic bone measured in centimetres. For example, a fundal height of 24cm (9.5in) is approximately equivalent to a gestational age of 24 weeks (26 weeks of pregnancy).
- Fetal brain cells form at a rate of 100,000 per minute.
- The average maternal increase in weight by the 20th week of pregnancy is 4–6kg (9–13lb), but all women vary.
- If born prematurely, a fetus of 24 weeks' gestation has a small chance of survival in an intensive care baby unit.
- By the end of the second trimester, the fetus still has room to turn somersaults inside the amniotic sac.

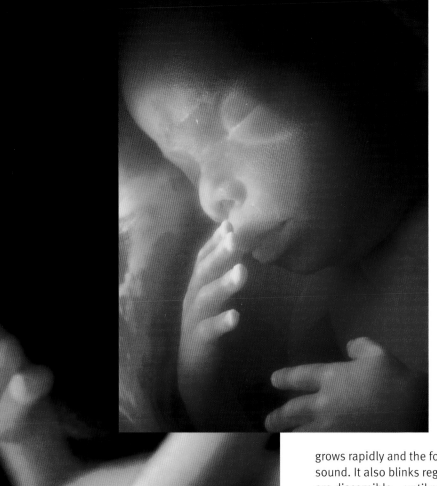

20 WEEKS OF PREGNANCY (18 weeks' gestation)

The fetus measures about 14–16cm (about 6in) and weighs approximately 255g (9oz). He has reached the halfway point of his gestation. This time is crucial for the development of his senses. The nerve cells serving taste, smell, hearing, sight and touch are developing in their particular areas of the brain. The complex connections required for the development of memory and thinking functions are being formed. If the fetus is a girl, she already has roughly two million eggs in her ovaries.

22 WEEKS OF PREGNANCY (20 weeks' gestation)

The fetus measures around 16cm (6in) from crown to rump and weighs around 260g (9oz). The fundus of the uterus now reaches the level of the mother's navel. The eyebrows and scalp hair are becoming visible.The brain grows rapidly and the foetus consistently reacts to light, touch and sound. It also blinks regularly. Distinct phases of sleeping and waking are discernible – until now, the fetus has rarely been still for more than five minutes at a time. The testes in a male foetus descend down from the pelvic cavity into the scrotum. The fetal bone marrow starts taking over the production of red blood cells rather than the liver and spleen. The heart is now beating at around 140–150 beats per minute.

24 WEEKS OF PREGNANCY (22 weeks' gestation)

The fetus measures around 19cm (7.5in) from crown to rump and weighs around 350g (12.2oz). The skin of the fetus is less transparent and he has sweat glands. The fingernails are fully formed and continue to grow. The brain begins to grow very quicly now, especially in the germinal matrix, a structure in the centre of the brain that muanufactures brain cells. If the fetus is a boy, his testes have begun their descent from the pelvis to the scrotum. Primitive sperm have already formed in the testes.

26 WEEKS OF PREGNANCY (24 weeks' gestation)

The fetus measures around 21cm (8in) from crown to rump and weighs about 540g (19oz). The head circumference is around 27.5cm (11in). The cells that control conscious thought are starting to develop and the fetus becomes more sensitive to sound and movement. A loud noise will make him jump and he can cough as well as hiccup. He spends a lot of time asleep, and is developing a pattern of quiet sleep and active sleep that alternate every 20–40 minutes throughout the day and night. The fetus is growing plumper and starting to lose his skin wrinkles. More muscle is forming, but very little body fat is present. A fatty, white grease known as vernix forms on the skin as protection from chemicals such as urea in the amniotic fluid.

Third trimester

The third trimester of pregnancy lasts from weeks 28–40. During this time the fetus grows significantly and more than triples in weight from around 910g to 3.4kg (2–7½lb). The added weight of the baby and pressure on a mother's internal organs and skin can lead to frequent urination, indigestion, heartburn and the appearance of stretch marks.

28 WEEKS OF PREGNANCY (26 weeks' gestation)

The fetus measures 25cm (10in) from crown to rump and weighs around 1.1kg (2.5lb). The fundus (top) of the uterus reaches 6cm (2.25in) above the mother's navel – 26cm (10in) above her pubic bone. The fingernails now reach the end of the fingers and the fetus is putting on increasing amounts of fat in preparation for independent life. There is a dramatic increase in the surface area of the developing brain, which has formed shallow grooves. The fetus's body has grown more than the head during the last few weeks, so the developing baby now looks in better proportion, but space inside the womb is starting to get cramped.

30 WEEKS OF PREGNANCY (28 weeks' gestation)

The fetus measures 27cm (10.75in) from crown to rump and weighs 1.35kg (3lb). The lanugo or early body hair is disappearing; there may be a few fuzzy patches left at birth that will rub off in the ensuing weeks. Head hair is thicker and the eyelids open and close. Instead of the liver, the bone marrow now produces red blood cells. The skeleton is hardening even more and the brain, muscles and lungs continue to mature.

BODY FACT

The final stage

- The type and amount of movement felt by the mother changes during the third trimester as the fetus has less and less space to move freely. Rather than turning somersaults, it starts to wriggle, slither and kick.
- The total maternal weight gain during pregnancy is between 7.5 and 10kg (16–22lb).
- Although 40 weeks is considered full-term for a singleton pregnancy, birth at any time between 38 and 42 weeks is accepted as normal.
- For a twin pregnancy, 37 weeks is considered full-term.
- For a triplet pregnancy, 34 weeks is considered full-term.

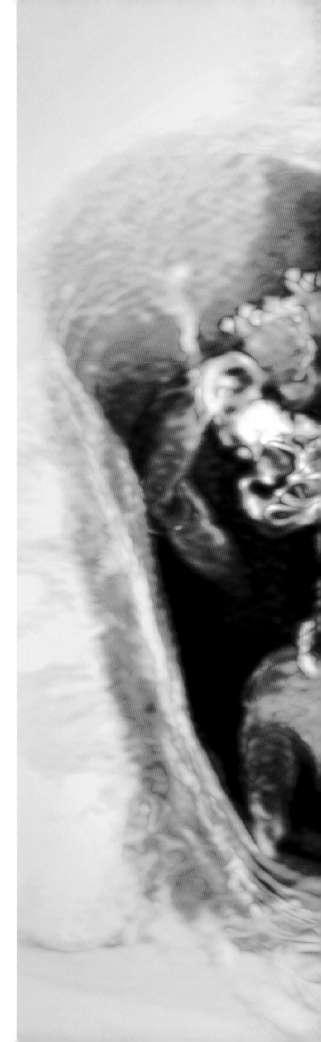

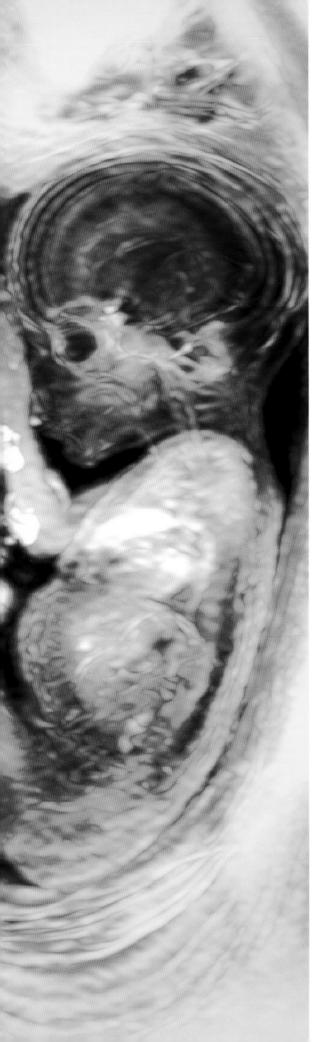

32 WEEKS OF PREGNANCY (30 weeks' gestation)

The fetus measures 29cm (11.5in) from crown to rump and weighs 1.8kg (4lb). The head circumference is around 32cm (12.5in), and the fundus reaches about 30cm (12in) above the pubic bone. Fetal behaviour now shows four activity patterns: quiet (slow wave) sleep, active (REM or rapid eye movement) sleep, quiet awareness and active awareness. During late pregnancy, the placenta starts to produce relaxin, a hormone that softens the cervix and pelvic ligaments in preparation for childbirth.

The fetus now has an excellent chance of survival in a special care baby unit if pre-term delivery occurs.

34 WEEKS OF PREGNANCY (32 weeks' gestation)

The fetus measures 31cm (12.5in) from crown to rump with a total length of about 44cm (16in) and weighs almost 2.275kg (5lb). The immune sysem is developing to fight mild infection. He is too big to float in the amniotic fluid and his movements are slower and bigger.

36–40 WEEKS OF PREGNANCY (34–38 weeks' gestation)

At 36 weeks, the fetus measures over 33cm (13in) from crown to rump and weighs about 2.75kg (6lb) and the fundus reaches about 34cm (13in) above the mother's pubic bone. The fetal head may now be 'engaged' (see below). In another week the fetus will be considered full term and could be born any day. By full-term the fetus measures 37–38cm (just under 15in) and weighs around 3.4kg (7.5lb). The crown–rump length is 37–38cm (15in) and total body length about 48–52cm (19–20in). As much as 15 per cent of fetal weight consists of fat stores. The fundus of the uterus is now 36–40cm (14–16in) above the pubic bone depending on the size of the baby. The hair on the baby's head may vary from a few wisps to hair that is 2–4cm (around 1in) long. Most babies are now in a head-down position ready for birth.

During the last few weeks of pregnancy, 'practice' contractions of the uterus, known as Braxton-Hicks contractions, become more noticeable and are sometimes mistaken for the onset of labour.

Engagement

During late pregnancy as the lower part of the uterus softens and expands, a baby's head descends lower into the mother's pelvis. This is known as engagement. It usually occurs between two and four weeks before labour starts for a first baby and often just before labour begins with subsequent babies. The progress is gradual and may cause bowel and bladder symptoms due to the pressure of the baby on these organs. If, however, a baby is lying bottom down (breech) or across the abdomen (transverse) it may not be possible to have a vaginal delivery.

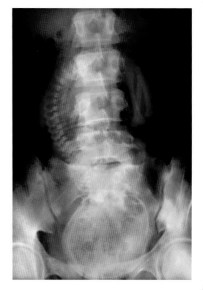

Childbirth

Childbirth (also known as parturition) is triggered by hormones produced in the placenta and the fetal hypothalamus. Some research suggests that the fetus senses a drop in oxygen and glucose concentrations as its needs outpace what the placenta can supply. Levels of a neurotransmitter called neuropeptide Y, which is linked to starvation, also increase towards the end of the pregnancy, along with stress hormones such as fetal ACTH (adrenocorticotropic hormone) and cortisol.

STAGES OF CHILDBIRTH

There are three stages to childbirth. During the first stage or labour, uterine contractions work to fully dilate the cervix to 10cm (4in). The second stage is the passage of the baby out of the uterus, down the birth canal and delivery into the outside world. The third stage is the delivery of the placenta. Sometimes a vaginal delivery involves the use of forceps or a vacuum extractor (ventouse) and/or an episiotomy – an opening made in the perineum under a local anaesthetic to help deliver a baby's head. In a planned caesarean delivery, the baby is delivered through an incision in the abdomen before labour begins, while in an emergency caesarean, labour and the baby progressing down the birth canal may be well underway.

BIRTH PROCESS

Labour is often divided into three phases. These are known as early or latent labour, active or established labour and transition or hard labour. Not all women experience these as distinct and noticeable stages. At either of the early two phases, the amniotic sac will break and amniotic fluid will leak out – usually less than 300ml (10fl oz) is lost. A blood-stained mucus plug, which has blocked the cervical canal during pregnancy, may appear.

The birth canal is curved and varies in diameter – it is widest from side to side at the top, and from front to back at the outlet. The baby's head therefore rotates as it comes down. The bones of the mother's pelvis spring apart (under the influence of the hormone relaxin, which has softened the pubic ligaments) to widen the diameter of the canal. Remaining partially upright or squatting, rather than lying flat, allows gravity to make delivery more efficient.

LABOUR

During early labour contractions are usually short, far apart and irregular – typically every 30 to 45 minutes and lasting 10 to 15 seconds each. As labour progresses to active labour, these contractions become more frequent, with one every one to three minutes, lasting around 60 seconds as birth is imminent. During transition, the time between the end of active labour and the start of pushing, the contractions may become more powerful to push the fetal head down against the cervix, which gradually widens to 10cm (4in). For a first labour, dilating at around 1cm (½in) per hour is common.

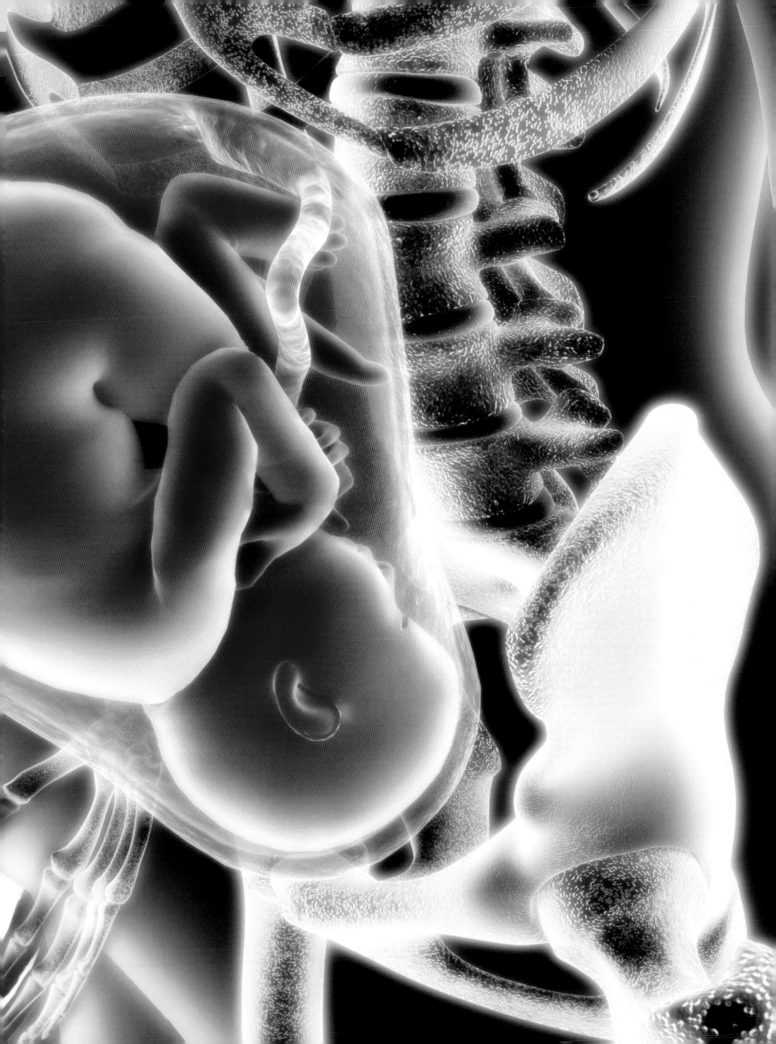

Crowning

This is an endoscopic view of a baby's head just before birth. The hairs on top of the baby's head are clearly visible. The arrival of the head at the vaginal opening is known as 'crowning'. This is normally accompanied by burning pain and pressure on the rectum as the baby's head pushes against the perineum.

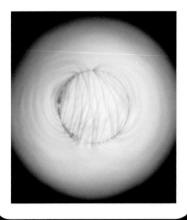

DELIVERY

Once transition is over it is time to push the baby out. This stage usually takes about an hour, but can vary from 10 minutes to three hours. Contractions are long and close together and there is an overwhelming urge to push. Bearing down thins the perineum and the baby's head will appear at the vaginal opening, known as crowning. Once the head is delivered, the body quickly follows. Once the baby is born, the umbilical cord is cut.

About five to 90 minutes after the baby is born, the placenta and amniotic sac are delivered. This process is assisted by injection of a synthetic oxytocin hormone, by breastfeeding soon after delivery and by massaging the fundus of the uterus. The placenta is a disc around 20cm (8in) wide and 2.5cm (1in) thick. It typically weighs around a sixth of the weight of the baby.

Oxytocin

This hormone, which plays a number of roles in labour, delivery and breastfeeding, is secreted by the pituitary gland and also manufactured synthetically in the laboratory for use as a drug. The natural hormone is responsible for the production of uterine contractions during labour: it both stimulates the uterine muscles to contract and the pituitary to release chemicals, known as prostaglandins, which intensify muscle contractions. Oxytocin also stimulates milk flow if breastfeeding and the shrinkage of the uterus after birth. Synthetic oxytocin known as syntocinon is usually injected into a woman's thigh after birth to help the uterus stay contracted and to aid in its delivery.

PAIN RELIEF

A number of pain-relief options are available to women in labour. Natural techniques include the adoption of helpful postures, relaxation and breathing techniques, acupuncture, massage and TENS (transcutaneous electrical nerve stimulation). Methods of medical pain control include breathing a nitrous oxide and oxygen gas mixture ('gas and air'), receiving opioid drugs (such as pethidine or meptazinol) and administering an epidural in which a local anaesthetic is injected into the epidural space surrounding the spinal cord. Some women use a combination of techniques.

BODY FACT

Baby statistics

- Only one in 20 babies is born on the due date calculated at the beginning of pregnancy.
- Childbirth averages seven to nine hours for a first baby, and around four hours for subsequent deliveries.
- More babies are born between three and four in the morning than at any other time.
- Most full-term babies weigh between 2.7kg and 4.3kg (6–9.5lb).
- A baby's irises are almost always blue at birth, with any change in colour occurring within the first three to four months of life.
- A newborn baby needs 14–16 hours of sleep a day – sleep is when growth hormone is secreted and most growth occurs.
- A newborn normally loses weight after birth – often as much as 225g (0.5lb) – but by the age of 10 days, most weigh the same as they did at birth.
- Babies put on an average of 28g (1oz) weight per day.
- A newborn baby grows at a rate of around 2cm (0.75in) per month initially.

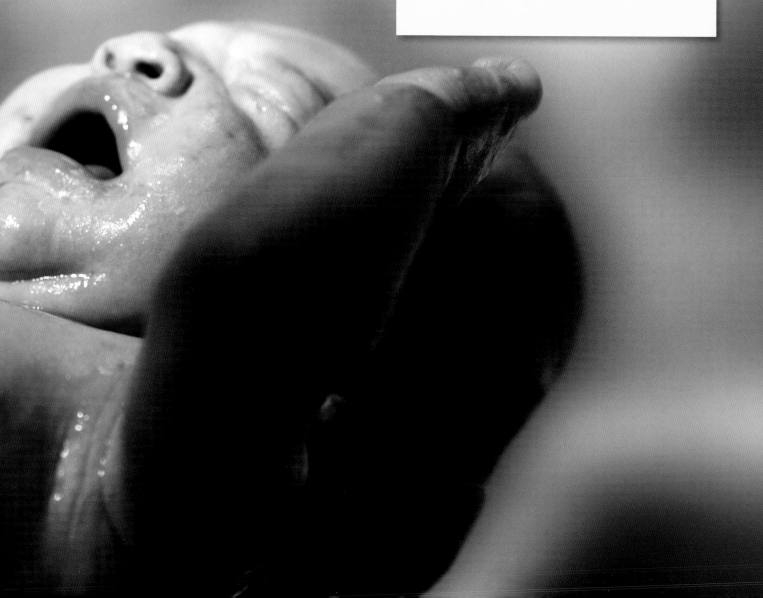

Maturation and the ageing process

A human being develops in the uterus for nine months, grows to maturity in 15–20 years, and may live for the better part of 100 years. During that time, change is constantly occurring within the body systems. Birth, growth, maturation, ageing and death are all part of a continuous process, governed by genetic programming, environmental and physiological processes.

Growth occurs rapidly during the first two years of life. Between birth and the age of four to five months, the weight of a baby doubles, and by the age of 12 to 14 months a baby's weight has tripled. Babies gain around 25cm (10in) in length during the first year and by their second birthday, they have reached half their adult height. Puberty is the stage between childhood and adulthood when secondary sexual characteristics develop under the influence of sex hormones. Even in the absence of disease, the function of body systems alters and decreases as we age, leading ultimately to death. As a result, the elderly are less able to adapt their bodies to changes.

Elements affecting ageing

DEVELOPMENT	Gradual modification of anatomical structures and physiological processes during the period from fertilization to maturity
MATURITY	The state of fully completed growth
INHERITANCE	The transfer of genetically determined characteristics from generation to generation

Effect of ageing on different body systems

DNA AND BODY TISSUES
- Telomeres are a length of DNA at the end of each chromosome. Whenever DNA is copied during cell division, the telomeres shorten. When the telomeres become too short, the cell can no longer copy its DNA and cell division stops. This is an important factor in the ageing process.
- The speed and effectiveness of tissue repair decreases and energy consumption declines. This is caused by hormonal changes, reduced activity and environmental effects.
- Epithelia get thinner, connective tissues more fragile, bruising and bone fractures more common, and cumulative damage can lead to health problems.

MUSCULO-SKELETAL SYSTEM
- Mineral content is reduced, which increases the risk of osteoporosis and fractures.
- Reduction in size and height of vertebrae and intervertebral discs leads to loss of height.
- Cumulative wear and tear at articulating surfaces of joints leads to osteoarthritis.
- Skeletal muscle fibres become smaller in diameter so skeletal muscles reduce in size; strength and endurance are reduced.
- Skeletal muscles are less elastic and develop more fibrous tissue making them less elastic and flexible.
- There are fewer satellite cells so injury repair capability is reduced.

ENDOCRINE SYSTEM
- Reproductive hormone production decreases. In women this is most striking at the time of the menopause when the levels of oestrogen and progesterone decline, leading to a variety of symptoms. The decline in testosterone in men happens more slowly. Sex hormones have widespread effects on the body including brain development, muscle mass, bone mass and density, body shape, and patterns of hair and fat distribution.
- Some hormone levels remain unchanged in old age, but the body tissues become less sensitive to their instructions.

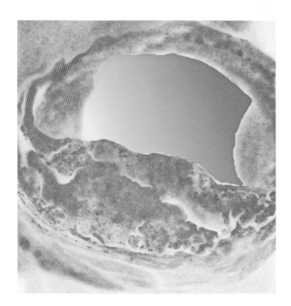

CARDIOVASCULAR SYSTEM

- The arterial walls become less elastic leading to higher systolic blood pressure and a risk of sudden rupture.
- Deposits of calcium and lipids lead to narrowing of arteries (see atheroma, above), which increases risk of heart attack and/or stroke.
- Changes in activity of the electrical conducting system can lead to long-term heart rhythmdisturbances.

NERVOUS SYSTEM

- Brain size and weight reduces mainly from a decrease in volume of the cerebral cortex.
- Many brain neurons accumulate abnormal intracellular deposits.
- Blood flow decreases.
- These structural changes are linked to less efficient neural processing, harder access to memory, less sensitivity of the special senses and reduced precision of movement.
- The total number of olfactory neurons and taste buds reduces with age and remaining receptors are less sensitive, so elderly people can have difficulty detecting smell and taste.

EYES AND VISION

- Lens opacities form with increasing age, creating cataracts, which reduce vision.
- Reduced elasticity of the lens leads to presbyopia, a form of longsightedness.

EARS AND HEARING

- The tympanic membrane becomes less flexible, the joints between the ossicles stiffen and accumulated damage from loud noise and injury reduces the number of hair cells and hence hearing perception is reduced.

INTEGUMENTARY SYSTEM

- Epidermis thins, leading to injury and infection.
- Reduced vitamin D production causes muscle weakness and reduced bone density.
- Reduced melanin production produces paler and more light-sensitive skin, which is more susceptible to sunburn (see above).
- Hair follicles stop functioning – hair thins and goes grey/white.
- Dermis thins, and the elastic fibres reduce causing sagging and wrinkling which is most prominent in sun-exposed areas.
- Skin heals more slowly.

BODY FACT

The secrets of long life

- Among older people, the food most closely associated with a long life is … beans! Every 20g (0.8oz) increase in average daily intake is linked with an eight per cent lower risk of death from a medical cause at any age.
- Researchers following 21,000 twins for over 22 years found that those who slept for between seven and eight hours per night lived longer than those who habitually slept for shorter or longer periods.
- Regular exercise reduces the risk of death at any age, from any medical cause, by almost a quarter – even if the exercise is not started until middle age.
- Flossing your teeth daily adds over six years to your life, as people with inflamed gums have a mortality rate that is between 23 per cent and 46 per cent greater than for those with healthy mouths (bacteria entering the circulation may hasten arterial damage).
- People who reach the age of 100 tend to have high circulating levels of protective antioxidants such as vitamin E and selenium.

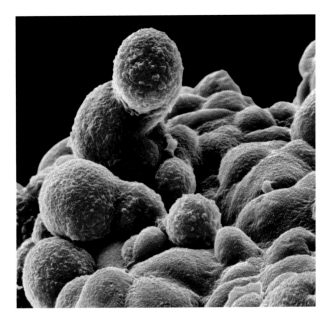

IMMUNE SYSTEM

- T-cells become less responsive to antigens, B-cells are less active so infection becomes harder for the body combat.
- Immune surveillance of abnormal cells declines so cancer cells, such as those causing prostate cancer (see above), are able to grow unchecked.

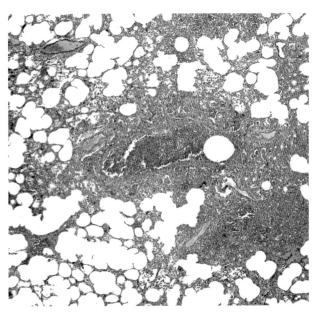

RESPIRATORY SYSTEM

- Elastic tissue deteriorates with age, which reduces lung capacity.
- Chest movements may be reduced, increasing the susceptibility to fluid build-up and chest infections such as pneumonia (see light micrograph, above).

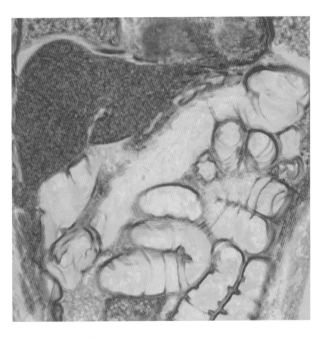

DIGESTIVE SYSTEM

- Epithelial stem cells lining the gut divide less rapidly with age so damage from acid, abrasion and enzymes is more likely.
- Action of smooth muscle decreases so motility is less leading to constipation (see CT scan of impacted bowels, above), and heartburn.

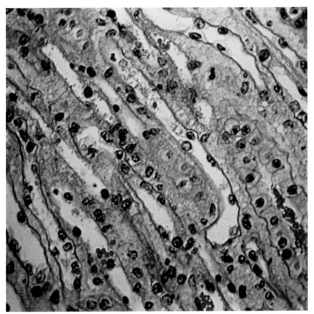

URINARY SYSTEM

- Reduction in the number of functioning healthy nephrons (kidney filtration units), slows kidney function (see above).
- Sphincter muscles lose tone leading to leakage and incontinence of urine.
- The prostate gland enlarges in men compressing the urethra and restricting flow of urine.

Theories of ageing

Ageing is a progressive process in which our body's cells and tissues degenerate. As you might expect, theories abound as to why we age.

The Hayflick Limit Theory suggests that body cells can divide only a certain number of times. The Telomerase Theory of ageing proposes that this depends on the length of your telomeres – the repetitive lengths of DNA (on the end of chromosomes TTAGGG, see page 22) that shorten with each cell division. Once the telomere reaches a critical length, cell division stops. If you inherit long telomeres, your cells can replicate more times and you may live longer as a result.

The Free Radical Theory of ageing, on the other hand, is based on the fact that cell structures, including DNA, are damaged by exposure to free radicals. These harmful molecular fragments are generated by normal metabolism and by exposure to ultraviolet light and pollutants such as cigarette smoke. Free radicals damage DNA and increase the build-up of abnormal proteins (such as amyloids) and glycosolated proteins (such as sorbitol), inside cells, which reduce cell function. Dietary antioxidants found in fruit and vegetables offer some protection against free radicals. In addition, scientists are seeking microbial enzymes that can break down and remove damaged proteins within ageing cells.

The Neuroendocrine Theory links ageing with the reduced production of hormones such as DHEA (dehydroepiandrostenedione). This may result from elevated levels of the stress hormone, cortisol, and age-related changes within the hypothalamus.

The Membrane Theory of ageing suggests that cell function deteriorates because their membranes become less fluid and more solid. This may be caused by an accumulation of lipofuscin – fatty residues that are produced during the recycling of cell components.

Lastly, the Mitochondrial Decline Theory proposes that ageing mitochondria – the energy-producing organelles (sub-units) within body cells – are less able to generate energy-rich molecules (ATP, adenosine triphosphate). As a result, certain cells – especially heart muscle cells – 'fatigue' and function less well. Mitochondria are the main source of free-radical generation within cells and lack antioxidant protection.

As well as inheriting genes associated with longevity, your diet and lifestyle are vitally important. People who eat a healthy diet, avoid becoming overweight, exercise regularly, do not smoke and drink alcohol sensibly are most likely to live a long and healthy life.

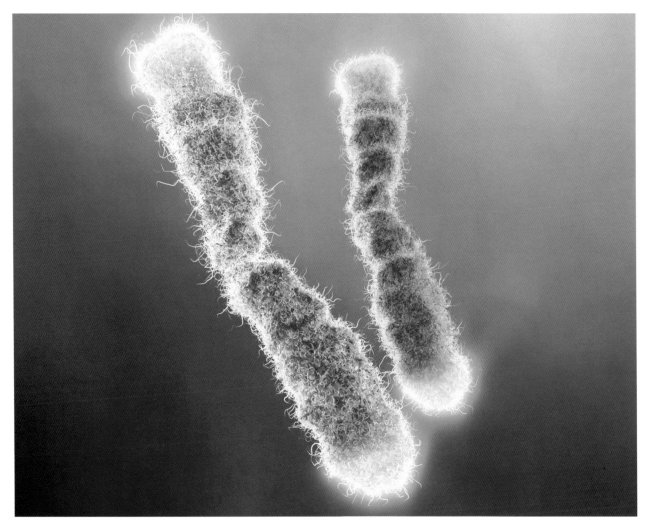

TELOMERES The telomeres within chromosomes are looped and consist of short, repeated sequences of DNA and proteins. The Telomerase Theory holds that telomeres play an important role in cellular ageing.

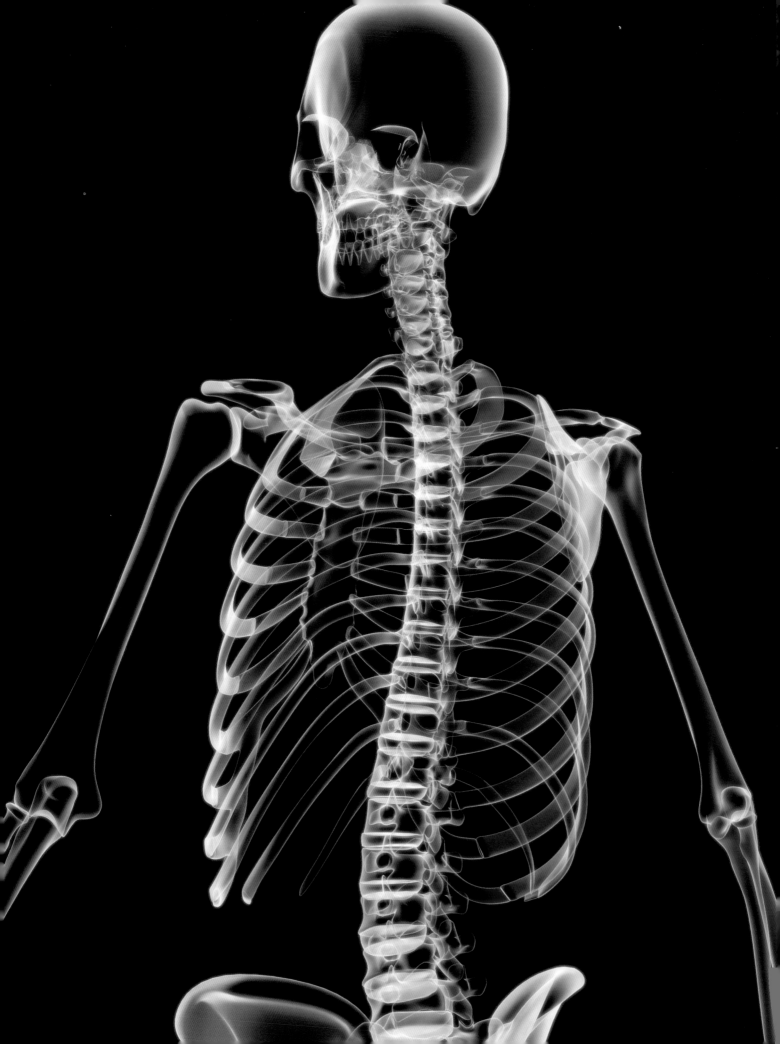

GLOSSARY

ADRENAL GLAND

An endocrine gland found above the kidney on each side of the body. The two adrenal glands, which are also known as the suprarenal glands, secrete hormones that regulate the body's stress response and salt and water balance.

ANTIBODY

An immune protein found in the blood and other body fluids. Antibodies (also known as immunoglobulins) are produced by immune cells to help identify and neutralize foreign substances such as bacteria and viruses.

APPENDICULAR SKELETON

The part of the skeleton that allows the body to move. It consists of the 126 bones, which form the upper and lower limbs, plus the shoulder and pelvic girdles that attach them to the axial skeleton (see right).

ARTERY

A type of blood vessel that carries blood away from the heart. All arteries, except for the pulmonary arteries (and the umbilical artery during pregnancy), carry oxygenated blood.

ATRIUM

One of two chambers found within the heart, above the ventricles. The left atrium receives oxygenated blood from the lungs via the left and right pulmonary veins. The right atrium receives de-oxygenated blood from the body via the superior vena cava, inferior vena cava and coronary sinus.

AXIAL SKELETON

The central part of the skeleton which forms the head and trunk of the body. It is made up of the 80 bones that form the skull, vertebral column and ribcage.

BILE

A yellow-green fluid secreted by liver cells (hepatocytes). Bile is stored in the gallbladder and is squirted into the duodenum during digestion to aid the digestion of dietary fats.

BLASTOCYST

A hollow ball of cells, with a fluid-filled cavity, that forms from the morula by the time a fertilized egg is ready to implant in the womb. The blastocyst forms around five days after fertilization has occurred.

BRAIN STEM

The lower part of the brain. Most of the nerve fibres supplying movement and sensation to the body pass through the brain stem to reach the spinal cord.

BRONCHIOLE

One of numerous small airways within the lungs. The bronchioles are smaller than one millimeter in diameter and allow gases to pass to and from the larger airways (bronchi) and the air sacs (alveoli).

CANCELLOUS BONE

A type of tissue found on the inside of bones. Also known as trabecular or spongy bone, it contains numerous small holes which helps to keep bones light yet strong.

CELL

The basic structural and functional unit of life. The human body contains an estimated 100 trillion cells, which are typically less than 10 microns (micrometers) in diameter.

CENTRAL NERVOUS SYSTEM

The part of the nervous system that co-ordinates the movement and function of the body. It is made up of the brain and spinal cord.

CEREBELLUM

The part of the brain that helps to co-ordinate the perception of sensations and the control of movement to maintain balance and posture.

CEREBRAL CORTEX

The part of the brain involved in higher functions such as awareness, thought, memory, language, consciousness, personality, interpretation of sensations and the initiation of voluntary movements. It forms a thin layer of highly folded 'grey matter', 2mm to 4mm thick, over the surface of the left and right cerebral hemispheres.

CEREBRUM

The part of the brain made up of the cerebral cortex, basal ganglia and olfactory bulbs. It lies on top, and in front, of the brain stem.

CEREBRAL HEMISPHERE

One of the two halves of the brain, which is divided into left and right cerebral hemispheres.

CHEMORECEPTOR

A sensory receptor that detects the presence of a particular chemical. For example, olfactory receptors in the nose detect the presence of certain volatile chemicals, to produce a nerve signal that travels to the brain and is interpreted as a smell.

CHROMOSOME

A single piece of highly-coiled genetic material (DNA) that contains numerous genes. Each human body cell contains 46 chromosomes. Each egg and sperm, however, contains only 23 chromosomes; when combined at fertilization, they result in a fertilized egg cell containing 46 chromosomes.

CILIA

Hair-like projections on the surface of some cells, for example in the lining of the respiratory tract. Some cilia produce wave-like movements that help to waft along fluids, mucus or sperm. Some cilia do not move and act as sensory receptors – for example, cilia in the inner ear are involved in detecting body movements.

CIRCULATION

A name for the circulatory system which transports blood cells, nutrients, oxygen, carbon dioxide, hormones and other substances around the body. The circulation of blood through the blood vessels is maintained by the pumping action of the heart.

COMPLEMENT PROTEIN

A series of over 20 proteins which are made by certain cells and released into the circulation. When activated by the presence of foreign particles, such as bacteria or viruses, complement proteins work together to help the immune system neutralize the threat.

DERMATOME

An area of skin supplied by a single spinal nerve, which carries sensations from that area back to the brain. The surface of the body on each side can be divided into dermatomes supplied by the eight cervical, twelve thoracic, five lumbar and five sacral nerves.

DIAPHRAGM

A sheet of muscle extending across the base of the ribcage to separate the thoracic and abdominal cavities. Movement of the diaphragm is an important part of respiration (breathing).

DNA

Deoxyribonucleic acid is a chemical found in the nucleus of almost all body cells except mature red blood cells. DNA contains all the genetic information needed for the development, growth and functioning of each individual.

EMBRYO

A stage of early human development that lasts from conception through until the eighth week of development. It is the stage during which all the tiny organs are laid down. Once all structures are in place, the embryo is known as a fetus.

ENDOCRINE CELL

A gland that secretes hormones directly into the bloodstream. Examples include the adrenal glands, thyroid gland and ovaries.

EXTRINSIC MUSCLE

A muscle that has at least one attachment inside the body part on which it acts, and at least one attachment point outside. Examples include the extrinsic muscles that move the eye, and the extrinsic muscles that move the wrist.

FERTILIZATION

The fusion of an egg (ovum) and a sperm (spermatozoon), at the time of conception, to produce a new organism.

GAMETE

A sex cell that fuses with another sex cell during fertilization. In human males, the gametes are called sperm (spermatozoa) and in human females they are known as eggs (ova).

GASTROINTESTINAL TRACT

The digestive tract, or alimentary canal, starts at the mouth and ends at the anus. The gastrointestinal tract is responsible for breaking down (digesting) food, absorbing water and nutrients, and excreting unwanted waste substances from the body.

GENE

The unit of genetic material that forms the basis of heredity. Each gene contains the information needed for the body to make a particular protein. Around 41,000 genes provide all the information needed to define each individual human being.

GLAND

An organ within the body that releases a substance such as a hormone or fluid. Examples include the salivary glands, which produce saliva; the mammary glands, which produce breast milk; and the pancreas, which produces body hormones (for example, insulin) and pancreatic juices involved in digestion.

HEPATOCYTE

A liver cell. Hepatocytes are involved in the production of proteins, carbohydrates, fats, cholesterol and bile. They are also involved in breaking down and detoxifying ingested drugs and poisons.

HOMEOSTASIS

The regulation that keeps the internal environment of the body as constant as possible. Homeostasis maintains a stable temperature, salt and fluid balance, and helps to keep the level of oxygen, glucose and other substances within the blood within their normal ranges.

HOMUNCULUS

A representation of a human being. The relative sizes of the parts of the cerebral cortex involved in moving particular parts of the body can, for example, be used to draw a picture of a man (homunculus) in which the size of the illustrated parts suggests the relative amount of brain used to control them.

HORMONE

A chemical messenger that, when released into the circulation by cells in one part of the body, has an effect on cells in another part of the body.

INTERFERON

Proteins produced by immune cells in response to viral infections. Interferons inhibit the replication of viruses within body cells. They also stimulate other immune cells, such as macrophages, to help fight the infection.

INTRINSIC MUSCLE

A small muscle that lies inside the body part on which it acts. Examples include the intrinsic muscles of the hand that both originate and insert beyond the wrist.

LACRIMAL GLAND

A gland that produces tears. It is found in the upper, outer part of each eye socket (orbit).

LEUCOCYTE

A white blood cell, which forms part of the immune system. Leucocytes are found through the body and travel in the circulation and lymphatic system. They help identify and fight foreign particles such as bacteria or viruses.

LIGAMENT

A strong, fibrous band of tissue that connects bones together within joints. Folds within the membrane lining the abdominal and pelvic cavities are also referred to as ligaments, for example, the broad ligament that supports the uterus.

LYMPH NODE

A small structure that forms part of the lymphatic system. Lymph nodes are found throughout the body and act like filters to trap foreign particles such as bacteria. They contain immune cells (leucocytes) that help to identify and fight infections. Lymph nodes become enlarged when they are actively fighting an infection or other disease.

LYMPH VESSEL

A thin-walled tube within the lymphatic system through which lymph fluid flows.

LYMPHOCYTE

A type of white blood cell (leucocyte). There are three main types: B-lymphocytes, which produce antibodies; T-lymphocytes, which regulate the activity of other immune cells and NK (natural killer) cells (see page 216).

MACROPHAGE

A type of white blood cell that is found within body tissues. It is derived from another type of white blood cell, a monocyte, which travels within the circulation. Once a monocyte leaves the bloodstream, it undergoes a series of changes to become a macrophage. Both macrophages and monocytes can absorb and destroy unwanted debris and foreign particles.

MEMBRANE

A natural barrier layer that separates one part of the body from another. Cell membranes separate the inside of a cell from the outside. Larger membranes separate larger body parts from each other, for example, the pleural membranes separate the lungs from the chest wall and heart.

MEMBRANE POTENTIAL

The electrical voltage difference between the inside and the outside of a cell membrane. The membrane potential allows nerve cells to conduct electrical messages.

MEIOSIS

The process in which a cell divides to form daughter cells that contain half the number of chromosomes found in the parent cell. This process produces the sex cells, or gametes, during sexual reproduction.

MITOCHONDRIA

Structures found within body cells that 'burn' glucose and fatty acids to generate chemical energy and heat and which regulate cell metabolism. Mitochondria possess their own circular strand of genetic material (DNA). They are believed to have evolved from primitive bacteria forming a symbiotic relationship with single-celled organisms around two billion years ago.

MITOSIS

The process in which a cell divides to form identical daughter cells, each of which contains the same number of chromosomes as the parent cell. This process is vital for growth and repair of tissues.

MORULA

A solid ball of cells formed when a fertilized egg divides. When the ball of cells starts to develop a fluid-filled cavity it becomes known as a blastocyst (see page 213).

MUSCLE

Lean, contractile tissue that allows parts of the body to move. Cardiac and smooth muscle (such as that within blood vessels and the intestines) contract without conscious thought. Voluntary (striated) muscle can be contracted consciously to move the skeleton, eyes and tongue, for example.

MYELIN

A fatty material made of neuroglia cells wrapped around nerve fibres to form an insulating sheath. Myelin provides electrical insulation so that nerve fibres running together do not short-circuit each other.

NATURAL KILLER (NK) CELL

A type of lymphocyte which can attack abnormal cells – for example, those that are either infected with viruses or which form part of a cancer.

NEUROGLIA

Cells found within the nervous system that provide support for nerve cells (neurons). Some neuroglia supply nerve cells with oxygen and nutrients; some act like scaffolding to hold neurons in place; some form the myelin sheath around individual nerve fibres, and some identify and destroy foreign particles.

NEURON

A specialized cell within the nervous system that can generate and transmit electrical impulses.

ORGAN

A group of tissues that come together to form a specific structure, with one or more specific functions, within the body.

OSTEON

The basic unit that forms the building blocks found within hard (compact bone).

OVULATION

The release of an egg (ovum) from an ovary. In women of fertile age, ovulation occurs, on average, once every 28 days.

OVA (PLEURAL) OVUM (SINGULAR)

The female sex cells or gametes.

PARTURITION

The process of childbirth or labour, during which a woman delivers a baby at the end of pregnancy.

PERIPHERAL NERVOUS SYSTEM

The part of the nervous system found outside the brain and spinal cord (which together form the central nervous system). The peripheral nervous system connects the central nervous system to the limbs and organs of the body.

PERISTALSIS

The rhythmic contraction of smooth muscles within the intestinal tract, which propels the contents through from the mouth to the anus.

PERITONEUM

A sheet of tissue (peritoneal membrane) that lines the inner surface of the abdominal and pelvic cavities and the outer surface of the abdominal and pelvic organs.

PHEROMONE

A non-odorous chemical which, when released from one individual, is detected in the nose of another individual, to modify his or her natural behaviour. Pheromones are believed to play a role in sexual attraction and in bonding between mother and child.

PITUITARY GLAND

An endocrine gland within the brain that secretes hormones involved in the regulation of body processes (homeostasis). Often referred to as the 'master' gland.

PLEURAL SAC

A sheet of tissue (pleural membrane) that lines the inner surface of the chest cavity and the outer surface of the lungs to form a sac. The two layers of the sac glide over one another during breathing, separated by a thin film of fluid.

PROTEIN

A type of chemical made up of amino acid building blocks. The sequence of amino acids is determined by the sequence of information contained within a gene.

PULMONARY SYSTEM

Another name for the respiratory system.

REFLEX

A rapid, automatic and involuntary nervous response to a particular stimulus, such as pain or bright light.

RESPIRATORY TRACT

The organs involved in the process or respiration or breathing.

SEBACEOUS GLAND

A type of gland within the skin that secretes an oily substance (sebum) to lubricate and protect the skin and hair.

SEPTUM

An anatomical division that separates two cavities. Examples include the nasal septum, separating the nostrils and the cardiac septum, which separates the right and left sides of the heart.

SPERMATAZOA (PLEURAL)SPERMATOZOON (SINGULAR)

The male sex cells or gametes.

SYNAPSE

The gap connection between two nerve cells. Communication across this gap may occur with the release of chemicals (chemical synapse) or by the electrical message jumping across (electrical synapse).

SYNAPTIC DELAY

The delay of around 0.5 milliseconds that occurs when an electrical message passes from one nerve cell to another across a chemical synapse. The transmission of a signal through a nerve pathway becomes slower as more and more chemical synapses are involved.

TENDON

The strong band of connective tissue that attaches a muscle to a bone.

THORAX

The part of the body between the neck and the abdomen that is bordered by the sternum, thoracic vertebrae, ribs and diaphragm. Also known as the chest.

THYROID GLAND

An endocrine gland found at the base of the neck, in the front.

TISSUE

A group of specialized cells with similar properties that come together to carry out a specific function. There are four main types of tissue in the body: muscle tissue, epithelial tissue, connective tissue and nervous tissue.

TRIMESTER

A period of three months, commonly used to describe the duration of pregnancy, which lasts around nine months.The first trimester describes months one to three, the second trimester refers to months four to six, while the third trimester describes months seven to nine.

UMAMI

A newly identified taste sensation which is 'meaty' and 'savoury'.

VEIN

A type of blood vessel that carries blood towards the heart. All veins, except for the pulmonary veins (and the umbilical vein during pregnancy), carry de-oxygenated blood.

VENTRICLE

One of two chambers found within the heart, below the atria. The right ventricle pumps de-oxygenated blood to the lungs. The left ventricle pumps oxygenated blood out to the rest of the body via the aorta.

VERTEBRA (SINGULAR) VERTEBRAE (PLEURAL)

The individual bones that form the flexible vertebral column.

ZYGOTE

A newly fertilized egg.

INDEX

Acknowledgements

ILLUSTRATION CREDITS

All anatomical artworks in this book © Primal Pictures Limited, London

Illustration p127 Amanda Williams

PHOTOGRAPHIC CREDITS

ALL IMAGES ARE FROM SCIENCE PHOTO LIBRARY, EXCEPT WHERE STATED:

p2, p13 Digital Vision / Getty; p14 Medical RF.Com; p16 BSIP, Jacopin; p18 Medimage; p20 CNRI; p22 David Mack, (Thomas Deerinck, NCMIR; p23 Leonard Lessin / FBPA; p24 (top, upper middle) Steve Gschmeissner, (lower middle) Biophoto Associates; p25 (bottom) Innerspace Imaging, (top); p26 Steve Gschmeissner; p45 Medical RF.com; p53 R Bick, B Poindexter, UT Medical School; p56 (top left) Eye of Science, (bottom left) Steve Gschmeissner, (bottom right) Asa Thoresen; p67 Riccardo Cassiani-Ingoni; p67 (bottom) Steve Gschmeissner, (top) Professor P Motta & D Palermo; p73 (top) BSIP, Jacopin, (bottom) Jean-Claude Revy, ISM; p82 Wellcome Dept. of Cognitive Neurology; p83 BSIP, VEM; p86 Medimage; p87 Steve Gschmeissner; p88 Eye of Science; p95 Manfred Kage; p96 Gunilla Elam; p98 Susumu Nishinaga; p99 (main) Medical RF.Com, (bottom) Steve Gschmeissner; p101 (top, middle, bottom) Anatomical Travelogue; p104 CNRI; p106 Susumu Nishinaga; p109 Professor P Motta & G Franchitto, University "La Sapienza", Rome; p111 Zephyr; p113 (top) Science VU, Visuals Unlimited; (bottom) Zephyr; p114 (top) Roger Harris, (bottom) Steve Gschmeissner; p115 (top) BSIP, VEM, (middle) ISM, (bottom) Steve Gschmeissner; p117 Photo Insolite Realite; p119 BSIP, PIR; p122 (top) Professor P Motta & Macchiarelli, University "La Sapienza", Rome, (bottom) CMEABG / UCBL1, ISM; p128 National Cancer Institute; p129 Dee Breger & Andrew Leonard; p131 Manfred Kage, Peter Arnold Inc.; p134 (left) Stem Jems, (right) Eye of Science; p136 Tim Vernon; p138 (bottom) Russell Kightley; p138 (bottom) Dr Tim Evans; p139 Dr Mark J Winter; p140 Steve Gschmeissner; p141 K Somerville, Custom Medical Stock Photo; p143 JW Shuler; p145 Steve Gschmeissner, (bottom) Professors P Motta, S Makabe & T Naguro; p147 Medical RF.Com; p149 (top) 3D4Medical.com, (bottom) Steve Gschmeissner; p151 Anatomical Travelogue; p152 Medimage; p153 Steve Gschmeissner; p155 Stephanie Schuller; p156 David Musher; p157 Image Source / Getty; p159 (top) Steve Gschmeissner, (bottom) Medical RF.Com; p169 CNRI; p170 Professors P Motta, T Fujita & M Muto; p174 (bottom) Marshall Sklar, (top) John Daugherty; p177 Pasieka; p183 Dr Yorgos Nikas; p188 Alain Pol, ISM; p191 Professor P Motta & Familiari, University "La Sapienza", Rome; p192 Dr Yorgos Nikas; p193 (top left) Professor P Motta et al, (top right) Biophoto Associates; p194 (top) David Gifford, (bottom left) Pascal Goetgheluck, (bottom right) Dr Yorgos Nikas' p195 Dr Gopal Murti; p196 Richard Lowenberg; P197 (top right) Professor P Motta & F Barberini, University "La Sapienza", Rome, (middle), Professor Stuart Campbell, Create Health, London, (bottom right) John Bavosi; p198 Dr MA Aansary; p199 Medical RF.Com; p200 Anatomical Travelogue; p201 Neil Bromhall; p202 Du Cane Medical Imaging Ltd; p203 Mehau Kulyk; p204 Medi-Mation; p206 (top) Alexander Tsiaras, (bottom) Pasieka; p207 © Rubberball/Rubberball/Corbis; p209 (right) Andrew Syred, (left) Athenais, ISM; p210 (top left) David McCarthy, (top right) Dr Keith Wheeler, (middle left) BSIP, Gondelon, (middle right) CNRI;p211 Hybrid Medical Animation; p212 Medical RF.com.

METRO BOOKS
New York

An Imprint of Sterling Publishing
387 Park Avenue South
New York, NY 10016

Text © 2009 by Dr. Sarah Brewer MA MB BChir
Design and layout © 2011 by Quercus

This 2011 edition published by Metro Books
by arrangement with Quercus Publishing plc.

ISBN: 978-1-4351-3243-6

Printed and bound in China

1 3 5 7 9 10 8 6 4 2